BENT
COPPERS

BENT COPPERS

THE INSIDE STORY OF SCOTLAND YARD'S BATTLE AGAINST POLICE CORRUPTION

GRAEME McLAGAN

WEIDENFELD & NICOLSON

Weidenfeld & Nicolson
The Orion Publishing Group Ltd
Orion House
5 Upper Saint Martin's Lane
London WC2H 9EA

British Library Cataloguing-in-Publication Data
A catalogue record for this book is available from the British Library

ISBN 0-297-83093-7

Printed and bound in Great Britain by Clays Ltd, St Ives plc

CONTENTS

THE PROBLEM

I do have a minority of officers who are corrupt, dishonest and unethical. We believe, sadly, that they commit crimes, they neutralise evidence in important cases and they betray police operations and techniques to criminals.

These bad officers sap the morale of their honest colleagues and they do immense damage to public confidence. Because of their training they are aware of the tactics we use to try and catch them. They are cunning, they are experienced, they are surveillance conscious.

Sir Paul Condon, Metropolitan Police Commissioner, in 1997

It was to be a perfect sting. It had been worked on for weeks by a secret team of detectives dubbed 'the ghost squad'. An undercover officer using a false name had rented a first-floor flat in a run-down area of east London. Police technical experts then moved in, installing tiny video cameras and microphones. An observation point was set up outside with another camera pointing at the ground-floor entrance. Then police planted 80 kilograms of cannabis in the flat. The plan was to lure a major criminal to the premises to steal the drugs, worth at least £250,000 at street prices. But this was not a straightforward entrapment operation. The squad was not targeting normal underworld figures. In their sights was a recently retired Flying Squad detective, a man with a long corrupt past. A bent cop.

Over on the other side of London, at Scotland Yard, the Metropolitan Police Commissioner, Sir Paul Condon, was in his eighth-floor office putting the finishing touches to an important statement. Much anticipated, it was on police corruption and the serious difficulties associated with catching bent officers. Sir Paul had already said that corruption was an increasing problem for the Met. But now he was going to lay it on the line when he appeared in Parliament, in front of the Home Affairs Select Committee.

The trap set at the east London flat was a totally new departure for Scotland Yard. Until then officers in CIB, the Complaints Investigation Branch, had always been reactive, only starting enquiries after a complaint of some police wrong-doing reached them. These retrospective investigations often ended in failure. It was difficult to get enough evidence that would stick in court, where juries were notorious for giving police officers in the dock the benefit of the doubt. In 1994 the ghost squad had been set up to gather intelligence on the extent of corruption secretly. The squad's findings led in 1997 to Scotland Yard deciding on a new strategy. Its aim was to get incontrovertible evidence against corrupt officers which would stand up in court. Bent cops were to be caught in the act, red handed. Then there was always the chance that the wayward detective would turn supergrass to save his skin. The hope was that he would 'roll over' when confronted with the evidence against him, and not only confess to his own previous crimes but also incriminate his colleagues.

The target of the east London sting was a very good detective who had served for several years with the élite Flying Squad. But he had turned corrupt and was suspected of having stolen many thousands of pounds. Intelligence reaching CIB suggested that he had told criminal associates that he wanted to move into drugs. But unknown to him he was under surveillance by the ghost squad, which had now been in operation for three years. It was decided at a high level to give him what he wanted. He was fed information that drugs were being stored in the flat by a dealer. The story was that they were there for the taking, and the former detective took the bait. The anti-corruption officers waiting to spring their trap had not been told that their ultimate boss, the Metropolitan Police Commissioner no less, was to appear in the House of Commons the very next day, 4 December.

With Sir Paul Condon in the committee room was his deputy, Brian Hayes, along with the officer in charge of anti-corruption measures, Deputy Assistant Commissioner Roy Clark. Facing them were Home Affairs Committee members, led by the chairman, the MP Chris Mullin, himself no stranger to police wrong-doing as he had led the campaign to free the Birmingham Six. The committee were looking at all aspects of police complaints and disciplinary procedures. Nervously, Sir Paul said he wanted to start by making a preliminary statement. This was prefaced with the brief customary words of comfort he used whenever talking about police malpractice. He said that he believed he commanded the most honourable large-city police service in the world, and that the overwhelming majority of the 27,000 men and women in the Met were honest, decent and brave. He then launched into the attack, delivering his message in stark terms:

> I do have a minority of officers who are corrupt, dishonest and unethical. We believe, sadly, that they commit crimes, they neutralise evidence in important cases and they betray police operations and techniques to criminals.
> These bad officers sap the morale of their honest colleagues and they do immense damage to public confidence. Because of their training they are aware of the tactics we use to try and catch them. They are cunning, they are experienced, they are surveillance conscious.

Sir Paul could have been talking about the subject of the east London trap. But this was not the case. Although he was aware of the problems facing anti-corruption officers, and knew that CIB was becoming proactive, seeking to obtain cast-iron evidence against suspect officers, he did not know the details. He had no idea of events about to unfold only a few miles away from the Palace of Westminster. It could have been a world away.

As the Commissioner was speaking to the Commons committee, the rogue ex-cop was preparing to visit the flat. He would not be alone. He had contacted two trusted colleagues who had served with him in the Flying Squad. The three men agreed to meet up that evening.

In Parliament Sir Paul was in full flow, expanding, under MPs' questioning, on the officers he was up against:

> The sort of people I am speculating about are experienced, cunning criminals who operate as police officers, who I think have been lost along the way. Experience suggests that they came into the service well motivated. They have operated as very good police officers, and at a superficial level they are still operating as very good police officers in some of the things they do. Sadly, they have given into the opportunity. They have been tempted by bribes or by the opportunity to make significant sums of money through their malpractice. It would be going into the realms of fiction to say that people will be prepared

to take the risk to join the police service in the hope that they would survive and prosper and eventually become criminals in the police service. It is just people who came in well motivated and have gone off the rails at some stage for a variety of reasons.

A few hours after the Commissioner and his entourage left Westminster, the trap was sprung in east London. The bent ex-cop and his mates met up and drove to the flat. The police team in the observation point saw them standing in a huddle on the pavement. They then broke into the flat using a jemmy. A camera inside caught them climbing the stairs to the first floor, one with what looked like a search warrant in his hand and another carrying a big wooden truncheon. A second camera hidden in a light fitting caught the main target searching the bathroom. He shouted to the others: 'Here you are. It's here!' He had found the drugs in a cabinet under the bathroom basin. The other two rushed to see the find, and then left the flat carrying the bags, heavy with drugs.

Dawn raids followed at their homes. When confronted with the video evidence, two of the three put their hands up and admitted that they had taken the drugs. This was itself a great success for the ghost squad, but there was better to come. The pair 'rolled over' and confessed to massive corruption. Over the next few months several of their former colleagues up to detective chief inspector level came under intense investigation. More than twenty Flying Squad officers were suspended from duty and nearly one hundred others were questioned about wrong-doing. Several convicted robbers were freed after it was accepted that they could have been fitted up with tainted evidence.

The country now had its first police supergrasses, and it appeared for some time that Scotland Yard's strategy was working very successfully. The big investment in the ghost squad had been justified because results were flowing in. Many more millions of pounds were spent in drafting in more than two hundred extra detectives to deal with investigations resulting from the sting, and from other arrests elsewhere in London. The tactics that had previously been employed against major criminals were now being used against suspect detectives. They were put under surveillance. Their homes were bugged. Telephones were tapped, their bank and building society accounts examined.

However, problems gradually started to surface. At first these amounted to little more than grumbles. But they were to grow in intensity as the numbers of officers suspended started to mount. There were setbacks in court cases, with anti-corruption officers – the Untouchables – admitting mistakes and to breaking the rules. The fear was not only that many of the suspect detectives were innocent of any wrong-doing, but that the extent of corruption had been much exaggerated in order for Scotland Yard and the Home Office to force through tough changes in police disciplinary procedures. These, it was argued, would also reduce the effectiveness of the mighty police trade union, the Police Federation.

In his long-prepared statement to the Home Affairs Select Committee, Sir Paul Condon did not specify how many corrupt officers there were in London.

But in the questioning that followed he responded to an enquiry that he and others high up in Scotland Yard later wished he had dodged. Asked how many 'rotten apples' there were in London, Sir Paul replied that there were up to 250. He continued: 'However tiny that is in percentage terms, the damage they can do to the reputation and the morale of the overwhelming majority of officers is enormous.' Putting a figure on the number of corrupt officers was a mistake that was to come back and haunt Sir Paul and his successor, Sir John Stevens. For there was little likelihood that even half that figure would ever be brought to justice. Giving an estimate of up to 250 provided suspect officers and their friends outside the force with a stick with which to hit back at their accusers.

What was also to become clear was that what had initially been portrayed as a fight between the good cops and the bad guys was not quite that simple. This was not a black-and-white issue, but a murky world full of shades of grey.

one

CORRUPTION THROUGH THE YEARS

They were failing to pick up the signs. They were failing to see there was corruption going on. There was a failure to supervise and a failure of leadership. It's not a scandal to have a corruption problem. It's a scandal not to recognise the problem . . . We had to break the cycle of corruption. It's like doses of antibiotics to deal with bacteria. Unless you take the full dose, the bacteria get stronger.

Deputy Assistant Commissioner Roy Clark

'We took our eye off the ball' was the refrain from senior Metropolitan Police officers attempting to explain why corruption was again posing a serious problem in the 1990s. Expanding on the thinking, they said that since the 1960s there had been periodic purges against corruption, which were only partly successful. On each occasion, some suspect officers had been rooted out, resulting for a time in fewer complaints about police wrong-doing. But later, the same corrupt practices returned. These ranged from criminals paying money to police for favours, such as obtaining bail or having the prosecution case against them watered down, through to the planting of evidence, 'fit-ups' and the straightforward stealing by detectives of cash or drugs, sometimes both. The anti-corruption officers of the 1990s would end their explanation of what had gone wrong with London police with the promise that there would never be such a wave of corruption again. This time they would not take their eye off the ball. Unlike previous campaigns against wrong-doing, this one would be properly resourced and would be never ending.

After the Second World War, there was widespread acknowledgement by senior police officers and criminals of serious, endemic corruption among CID squads, and occasionally among uniformed officers too, particularly in central London. But the official attitude, lasting into the

1990s, was wherever possible to deny the existence of corrupt activities, and where there was wounding publicity to mount damage limitation exercises. So it was in 1955, when the *Daily Mail* said that a detective superintendent had sent a report to the Commissioner revealing a vast amount of bribery and corruption among uniformed officers at the West End Central station. It involved, according to the superintendent, 'club proprietors, prostitutes, gaming house owners, brothel keepers and men living on immoral earnings', with some uniformed beat officers receiving up to £60 a week in bribes. The then Commissioner's reaction was not only to ignore the report's findings but to go personally to the West End station, jump on a table and tell the assorted officers that he did not believe a word of it.

It was not until the 1970s that the first big London-wide campaign was mounted to combat corruption. The event sparking the concern and subsequent investigations was a devastating piece on 29 November 1969 in *The Times*, then viewed as the newspaper at the heart of the establishment. It claimed to have proved that at least three detectives were taking bribes from criminals 'for dropping charges, for being lenient with evidence offered in court, for allowing a criminal to work unhindered'. *Times* reporters had taped the detectives' meetings with a criminal in which one of them had said: 'We've got more villains in our game than you've got in yours, you know.' The same officer went on to talk about corrupt officers in London being 'a firm within a firm'. He told the criminal: 'Always let me know straight away if you need anything because I know people everywhere. Because I'm in a little firm in a firm. Don't matter where, anywhere in London, I can get on the phone to someone I know I can trust, that talks the same as me. And if he's not the right person that can do it, he'll know the person that can.'

The man put in overall charge of the resulting inquiry was the much-respected Frank Williamson, one of the Inspectors of Constabulary, officials appointed by the Home Office to oversee the police. But under him and in operational charge of the inquiry was Bill Moody, who turned out to be one of the Yard's most corrupt senior officers. To what extent there were already suspicions about him when he was seconded to Williamson is not known. But it was certainly a strange appointment which was to be echoed during Scotland Yard's anti-corruption drive in the 1990s. Williamson himself divided Met officers into three types. First there were the corrupt ones, then there were those who were honest but knew of corruption and did nothing about it, and then there was the final group comprising those so stupid that they failed to realise there was any corruption at all. Williamson was to complain that his enquiries were frustrated by Met officers through 'a misguided loyalty to the CID, arising from a deep-rooted desire to avoid publicity from the prosecution of police officers'.

However, the three detectives were prosecuted and jailed, and there was to be further damaging publicity in 1972 leading to more prosecutions. This time it involved a specialist unit, the Drugs Squad, whose activities were exposed by the *Sunday Times*. Three officers were jailed for conspiring to pervert the course of justice, with the squad's head, Detective Chief Inspector Vic Kelaher, allowed to retire on medical grounds. Sentencing the officers, the judge, Melford Stevenson, said: 'You poisoned the wells of criminal justice and set about it deliberately. What is equally bad is that you have betrayed your comrades in the Metropolitan Police Force which enjoys the respect of the civilised world – what remains of it – and not the least grave aspect of what you have done is provide material for the crooks, cranks and do-gooders who unite to attack the police whenever the opportunity occurs.'

Once again it was newspaper publicity which led to the biggest police corruption scandal for many decades. The *Sunday People* printed a photograph of the head of the Flying Squad, Commander Ken Drury, on holiday in Cyprus with a major Soho pornographer, James Humphreys, at the criminal's expense. The newspaper alleged bribery and corruption involving payments to senior officers to persuade them to turn a blind eye to porn shops, and to tip off dealers when they were about to be visited with a periodic raid. In addition to Drury, among those arrested, and appearing with him at the Old Bailey in 'the Porn trials', were another very senior detective and ten others, including the head of the Obscene Publications Squad, Detective Chief Superintendent Bill Moody.

Shortly after the *Sunday People* story, the Met's then Deputy Commissioner took over the top job, determined to deal with the CID, which he viewed as dangerously out of control. Sir Robert Mark said he had come across wrong-doing in his thirty years' service in provincial forces, but recalled in his autobiography, *In the Office of Constable*, that when he took over as Commissioner, 'I had never experienced institutionalised wrong-doing, blindness, arrogance and prejudice on anything

9

like the scale accepted as routine at the Met.' He identified three kinds of police wrong-doing. The first was what he called institutional corruption 'of a comparatively minor kind' where detectives charged for bail and suppressed evidence, often using as cover what they claimed was the need to cultivate informants. The second involved more specialised or senior officers, those concerned with major crimes such as bank robbery, drugs and obscene publications. The third was quite different. Mark stated that there was a widespread acceptance that the system of justice was weighted so heavily in favour of the criminal and his defence lawyer that they felt justified in bending the rules, a practice later to be dubbed 'noble cause corruption'.

When Deputy Commissioner, Mark had set up the first unit dedicated to investigating complaints and corruption. Called A10, it later became CIB, the Complaints Investigation Branch, and its members were nicknamed 'rubber heels' because they were supposed to move stealthily and silently. To break the power of detectives to influence events, a uniformed commander was put in charge. After becoming Commissioner, Mark assembled representatives of the CID and was blunt: 'I told them that they represented what had long been the most routinely corrupt organisation in London, that nothing and no one would prevent me from putting an end to it and that, if necessary, I would put the whole of the CID back into uniform and make a fresh start.' Mark held the top job for five years, and during that time fifty officers were prosecuted and more than four hundred left the force after, or anticipating, disciplinary procedures.

Mark had dealt with the cancer of corruption in a refreshingly open way. Writing about that time, the then Assistant Commissioner, Gilbert Kelland, who led the Porn Squad inquiry, said: 'We strongly believed that, for the eventual benefit of the force, the crow of corruption had to be nailed to the barn door to convince and remind everyone of the need for positive action and eternal vigilance.' These were fine words, but it was back to the bad old ways a few years later when Yard bosses displayed their resentment when for the first time London police came under investigation from outsiders – officers from provincial forces.

Operation Countryman crept up on the Met, catching it unprepared. It started quietly without publicity after No. 5 Regional Crime Squad, based in Hertfordshire, reported that certain criminal supergrasses it was handling were talking about corruption surrounding three big robberies, two at national newspaper offices and one at a bank. What was being said was that the 'firm within a firm' still existed. Criminals were continuing to pay money to obtain information and bail and to have prosecutions watered down. The allegations meant that an investigation would have to be carried out. All three premises robbed were in the City of London, which has an entirely separate police force with its own detective squad, so it initially appeared that any investigation would not encroach on the Met, which had never before been subjected to an outside corruption inquiry. Some big provincial forces were offered the job of carrying out the investigation, but all declined, perhaps sensing that anything involving London detectives, whether Met or City of London, could turn into a huge and dangerous can of worms. And they were to be proved right.

The Chief Constable eventually agreeing to head the inquiry was Arthur Hambleton of Dorset, a county whose biggest and only city is staid Bournemouth, far removed from the murky world of big-time corruption. In operational charge was Dorset's Assistant Chief Constable, Leonard Burt. He was given no advice or guidance about how to proceed, so he turned to Frank Williamson, who had superintended the inquiry following *The Times* allegations. Williamson had retired an embittered man. He was disgusted by the obstruction he faced from the Met during his inquiry and his subsequent snubbing by the then Home Secretary, Reginald Maudling. Williamson had made a long and detailed report for the Conservative minister following his inquiry, and it contained a series of recommendations aimed at preventing more corruption. A mere twenty minutes after submitting it, Williamson received a message saying it had been 'noted'.

The Met offered Burt's team of twelve Dorset detectives accommodation in a Portakabin in the yard of a south London police station. But there was no security, especially at night, when the key was supposed to be left with the station's duty sergeant. Burt knew of the close links between Met and City detectives, and realised from an early stage that his inquiry into the City robberies would almost certainly lead on to Met detectives. He remembered Frank Williamson's advice that the first essential step in any corruption inquiry was to ensure that your office was secure. Burt asked the Met for alternative accommodation. When none was forthcoming, he and his team left London for secure premises in Godalming, Surrey. It was to be the first of a series of brushes with the Met.

Weeks into his inquiry, Burt received key evidence, tapes of a City of London detective chief inspector, Phil Cuthbert, talking about corruption going to the 'top of the tree'. Cuthbert had been secretly recorded by his new boss, Detective Superintendent John Simmonds. Both officers were freemasons, and when Simmonds asked Cuthbert to explain how CID worked to him, Cuthbert thought the conversation was 'on the square', i.e. confidential between fellow masons. In the recordings, Cuthbert said that after a robbery on the *Daily Express*, £20,000 had been handed over to police, a large share going to a senior officer, whom he named. He told Simmonds: 'You're new on the firm, but I know what X did. I know who got it for him. I know who took it to him and I know what he give them back . . . one of the sergeants only got £300. That was his share out of the twenty grand, and he got the fucking hump with it, thought it was a liberty . . . a lot of money changed hands, gov'nor. It's happened in the Met. It's happened in the City. It's happened for years and years . . .' Speaking to Simmonds in a pub, Cuthbert went on to say that, after a particular bank robbery, City detectives and those on the Met's Robbery Squad had all had 'a drink', a criminal term for a bribe. 'X was in a position of power and covered things,' said Cuthbert. 'All the blokes on the Robbery Squad had a drink out of it, going right up – Y and all the rest of them. It was a silly drink, not a big one.' Simmonds had been in the Met, and later in the conversation Cuthbert said the payments in the City were on a sliding scale, according to rank, 'as it used to be at the Yard, gov'nor. Don't pretend. I used to bung Z [a commander] and A [a detective superintendent] and it used to go up to the fucking top of the tree, used to go up to the Assistant Commissioners . . . mainly reward money, you know, insurance money.'

The tapes provided devastating evidence. Cuthbert was suspended and Burt started his inevitable look at the Met, expanding his team with detectives from other provincial forces, until the total was over a hundred. Burt rejected any officer who had served with the Met, City or Surrey. He laid down strict ground rules for his team to the effect that there should be no socialising with Met or City officers. When visiting police stations, they should park their cars well away. They should never accept a free drink, even a coffee, and in these days before mobile telephones they had to offer to pay for any phone calls they made.

There were also strict rules for dealing with criminals. Burt's team members were instructed to tell criminals that it was up to the Director of Public Prosecutions to decide whether they should be given immunity from prosecution for any corrupt payments they had made to police officers. This would not even be entertained if the criminal refused to make a witness statement. They were also warned that if they lied in any statement they could be prosecuted for wasting police time. If they admitted to other criminal offences during the taking of statements, they were to be cautioned and the information passed on to ordinary police to decide whether it required further investigation. Where someone who had helped the inquiry was on trial for other matters, Operation Countryman officers would also go to court to put in a good word for them. When asked why they were blowing the whistle on detectives out of whom they had done well, the criminals replied that the police had been getting too greedy.

As a home affairs reporter with the BBC, I started covering police corruption stories in the late 1970s and took a special interest in Countryman's fortunes and the allegations it was investigating. One of Countryman's main informants, Alf Sheppard, told me he had acted as a go-between, passing £80,000 from criminals to DCI Cuthbert of the City of London Police. David Shaw, a robber who passed money to police via Sheppard, said he and his associates could only function because they had bent detectives 'on side'.

The Met liked none of this, taking the view that Sir Robert Mark had purged the ranks of serious corruption, and that Countryman officers were behaving naively, going round prisons inviting corruption allegations from men with nothing to lose. Met detectives started circulating stories of malpractice by Countryman officers, and showed their contempt by branding them 'The Sweedey', a pun on the turnip variety and the Flying Squad nickname 'the Sweeney' (also the name of a TV series starring John Thaw).

During their first six months, the Countryman team had compiled a list of more than a hundred officers, the vast majority from the Met, against whom allegations had been made of corruption, perjury and conspiracy. But Burt's anti-corruption officers also started to encounter obstruction. Files they requested would disappear, or it would take weeks of constant pressure before they were handed over. Senior Met officers were suspected of tipping off subordinates that they were under investigation. Countryman was hampered further because the team had no special surveillance training and lacked technical support. They wanted to tap some officers' phones, but decided against it because those then in charge of the country's phone interception system belonged to the Met.

By 1980, after two years, Operation Countryman was in serious difficulty with complaints from the Met, City and Home Office that the team was out of control. It was argued that what had started out as an investigation into three City of London robberies had expanded unnecessarily to embrace the whole of the Met. Dorset's Chief Constable, Arthur Hambleton, retired, and in an exclusive BBC TV interview with me, complained publicly for the first time about the inquiry having been obstructed. 'Basically, you may say that we were stopped from cleaning up the Yard,' he said. It did not help. The Met's Commissioner, Sir David McNee, retorted that Hambleton had not complained to him, and if he had, something would have been done to remedy the situation. With Hambleton gone, Surrey's Chief Constable, Peter Matthews, took overall control of the inquiry. Burt, needed back in Dorset, was replaced by a Met Deputy Assistant Commissioner, Ron Steventon, and the rest of the original team started returning to their home forces.

The inquiry fizzled out. By its end, Countryman officers had taken 2,000 statements and pursued 200 separate corruption allegations. They had submitted 41 reports to the DPP, but only four prosecutions were sanctioned. Of these, only one trial resulted in convictions. Phil Cuthbert was jailed for three years and his willing assistant, Detective Sergeant John Golbourn, was sentenced to two years. No one ever told Burt how many officers faced disciplinary hearings as a result of the inquiry, and no one asked him to prepare a final report on what had been achieved or whether he had any recommendations for tackling corruption in the future. He wanted to compile a report. He believed Countryman had been a success, but had come in for a lot of criticism in newspapers, most of it unwarranted. Burt never wrote his report, fearing that if he did it would be a waste of time as it would be rejected by the authorities, just as Frank Williamson's had been a few years earlier. Len Burt retired from the police in 1984, determined not to become embittered by his experiences dealing with the Met, as had happened to Williamson, who had remained a good friend.

When preparing this book, I met Burt at his home on a Dorset clifftop overlooking the sea. As he recalled events of more than twenty years before, it was clear that he was still deeply affected by what had happened. He told me that during and after the inquiry he felt ostracised at meetings of ACPO, the Association of Chief Police Officers. 'People would try to avoid sitting next to me,' he said. 'The majority just couldn't comprehend what was going on. They were from provincial forces and they didn't believe there could be such a level of corruption, even in London. There was also a belief that the people we were dealing with were only criminals. I took the view that that may be the case, but they were people too, and should be treated fairly, within the law.' In a sideswipe at the Met and the authorities who turned against Countryman, he said: 'People get what they deserve. If they're not prepared to put in the effort to sort something out, then they deserve what they get.'

Scotland Yard was delighted to be back in control when Countryman was finally wound up in 1982. The Met's Deputy Commissioner, Pat Kavanagh, declared: 'Countryman has done great harm to our reputation. I will not have another one . . . Countryman is an argument against independent investigations rather than an argument for.' Kavanagh and the rest of the Yard hierarchy took the view that Countryman was badly run and the level of corruption inside the Met much exaggerated. He said the days of the 'firm within a firm' were long gone, with any remaining corruption confined to the loner, the rotten apple. And Scotland Yard was sufficiently on top of the situation to deal with it on its own, thank you very much.

That incorrect assessment and the complacent attitude were to remain until well into the 1990s. The reality was that corruption had not gone away. One positive effect of Countryman had been to make officers more wary of engaging in corrupt activities. But the inquiry's poor outcome also meant that criminals were less likely to blow the whistle on bent cops in the future. What was the point of speaking out if your complaint against Met detectives was to be investigated by Met detectives?

For many years, the only damaging publicity involving police wrongdoing causing any worry to Scotland Yard was over the use of supergrasses. A string of major criminals took the supergrass deal, accepting five-year prison sentences in return for what was supposed to be full confessions to all their crimes and the giving of evidence against former colleagues. But the supergrass system started falling into disrepute, with evidence emerging that both police and criminals were manipulating the procedures for their own ends. I exposed some of the system's failings in a BBC *Panorama* programme in November 1982, after an unsuccessful attempt at damage limitation by David 'Crazy Horse' Powis, head of the

Met's detectives. While acknowledging the growing unease over super-grasses in London, he argued that exposing their failures would have a knock-on effect in Northern Ireland, where the authorities were using supergrasses as their main weapon against terrorists. He wanted *Panorama* to water down its evidence, warning that failure to do so could damage the fight against terrorism, which represented a threat to every-one in the UK.

The programme broadcast a tape recording made of a phone call by Mickey 'Skinny' Gervaise, from the supergrass wing of a prison to a criminal associate outside. In the call, Gervaise explained that he had kept the criminal out of his supergrass confession and he now wanted payment for the favour. He demanded that money should be paid to his girlfriend, and if none was forthcoming he warned the criminal that he would 'drop him in it' by suddenly recalling for the police that he had been party to another crime involving the man telephoned. The pro-gramme also revealed that some supergrasses were getting away with murder, literally. They had admitted killing people during robberies, but Scotland Yard, worried about a public outcry if these vicious professional criminals were given only five-year sentences for serious crimes including murder, managed to get the charges reduced to manslaughter.

Panorama also detailed skulduggery over what was then the country's biggest robbery, the 1980 theft of silver bullion worth £3.5 million belonging, surprisingly, to then communist East Germany. The investi-gation into this daring robbery involved informants and the payment of rewards, both areas recognised by police everywhere as open to abuse. Informants were becoming increasingly important in the fight against crime, and detectives defended their close relationships with them, argu-ing that they were a necessary evil, and that without them information would dry up and crime increase. Commander Ken Drury, the head of the Flying Squad, had used the same argument during his Old Bailey trial when maintaining that he had gone on an all-expenses-paid holiday to Cyprus with a Soho pornographer so that he could groom him further as an informant. I was in court when a detective chief inspector was under cross-examination, having to justify why he had supported a bail application for a criminal charged with a major robbery. Freed, the criminal had then taken part in an even bigger robbery and had then disappeared, or gone 'on his toes'. There was no suggestion that the detective chief inspector was anything but honest, and he gave an honest reply to the defence counsel's question. He said he now regretted supporting the man's bail application, but 'he was my informant, and he was more use to me out on the street rather than in prison awaiting trial'.

The detective-informant relationship continues to be a very murky area. Evidence surfaces regularly of police turning a blind eye to informants' criminal activities, the justification being that the information coming in from the 'grass' far outweighs in value whatever crimes he or she is committing. In other words, the end justifies the means. In the 1980s Scotland Yard started to clamp down on police-informant relationships, introducing a series of rules and regulations to reduce abuse, particularly over the paying out of rewards, a linked area of wrong-doing.

For information, insurance companies usually offered rewards of 10 per cent of the value of stolen property, goods and money returned to owners. Sometimes very big money could be on offer, providing temptation to corrupt detectives and their grasses. It was right that genuine informants should receive all the reward money, but there was evidence that detectives were demanding their cut, sometimes dividing the money up round the corner from Scotland Yard, where the cash would have been officially handed over. Even more deviously, rewards could be paid out to people who had had nothing to do with the return of goods. This could happen when the police had been entirely responsible for the recovery of stolen goods. Rather than allowing big insurance companies to retain the reward, a detective could nominate an informant, falsely claiming that the key information had come from him. The pair would then divide the reward, the larger share often going to the corrupt officer. Deputy Assistant Commissioner David Powis tried to counter such corruption by appealing to the insurance companies to impose an upper limit of £5,000 on all rewards. The move came too late to stop the payment of a massive reward, then the country's biggest, in the silver bullion case.

A lorry carrying the silver ingots was hijacked in Essex after the driver was flagged down by Mickey Gervaise, dressed as a traffic policeman. The silver disappeared, but Gervaise, caught for other crimes, turned supergrass and eventually admitted being responsible for the robbery during questioning by one of Scotland Yard's greatest thief-takers, Detective Chief Inspector Tony Lundy. Gervaise was to claim later that he had only revealed who was holding the silver because he thought, mistakenly, that he would share in some of the reward then being offered for its return. He named the other robbers and said that one of them, Lennie Gibson, was looking after the silver. Lundy knew Gibson socially. I had obtained a photograph of them together at a charity function at the Dorchester Hotel. Lundy was subsequently to claim that he had no idea that Gibson was a major criminal. After receiving the information from Gervaise, the other robbers were arrested and Lundy questioned his friend Gibson about the silver's location. Gibson told him it was in a lock-up garage. Although he and another of the robbers both had keys to the lock-up on them when arrested, curiously the police who went to the garage smashed down the door to gain entry. When the stash was counted by police, twelve bars, worth nearly £100,000, were found to be missing.

The capture of the robbers and recovery of nearly all the silver was hailed as a great success, and DCI Lundy recommended that the reward offered by the insurance company should be paid to his long-time informant, Roy Garner, who was a friend not only of Gibson but also of Lundy himself. Garner also appeared in the photo of the Dorchester function. Lundy's boss, DAC David Powis, refused to authorise the payment. He did not believe that anyone deserved any reward. It had been Gervaise who had told Lundy that Gibson had the money, and it had been Gibson who had revealed where it was hidden. That pair had been responsible for the silver's recovery, but under the rules relating to reward payments they could not benefit from any pay-out as they had been the actual robbers. Why should anyone else be entitled to a reward? Eventually, after protracted wrangling and threats of legal action, loss adjusters for the company insuring the silver paid out no less than £180,000 to Garner with another £20,000 or so going to another criminal whose information had led to Gervaise's arrest.

Lundy's relationship with Garner came under further scrutiny after the *Panorama* programme was broadcast. An inquiry was launched by the Yard's A10 section, the forerunner of the Complaints Investigation Branch, CIB. But it was Customs which caught up with Garner. Apart from making money informing on other criminals, he had been running a business importing gold Krugerrands from the Channel Islands and reselling them in London. Charged by Customs with evasion of payment of VAT on the sales, he was sentenced to four years' imprisonment. On his release, Garner went into the increasingly lucrative drugs business, but was caught by Customs smuggling nearly 400 kilograms of cocaine into the country. DCI Tony Lundy spoke up for Garner later at the Old Bailey, along with Detective Chief Superintendent Roy Ramm, who went on to head Scotland Yard's Organised Crime Group, which included the Flying Squad. Garner was sentenced to twenty-two years' imprisonment, reduced to sixteen after an appeal. Angry at his treatment, he threatened the authorities that he would tell all to me, but he never did. Tony Lundy, meanwhile, retired on grounds of ill health. In Martin Short's book *Lundy – The Destruction of Scotland Yard's Finest Detective*, the former officer blamed his downfall on criminals, freemasonry and gullible journalists.

In 1990 Customs investigators were also responsible for exposing what was described as the worst example of organised police corruption in London since the days of Operation Countryman ten years before. Customs had been investigating a huge conspiracy in north London involving the non-payment of VAT on fruit machines in commercial premises. But when they launched raids, they frequently found that owners had been tipped off, and evidence moved. Customs' suspicions fell on the police, the only other agency to know of the investigation. Further enquiries revealed rumours that detectives at Stoke Newington police station were recycling drugs. Customs passed the information on police wrong-doing to Scotland Yard, and a team from what had by then become the Complaints Investigation Branch (CIB) was set up. Operation Jackpot was born, its name derived from fruit-machine pay-outs.

Under Detective Superintendent Ian Russell, Jackpot investigated allegations that police were involved in drug dealing, theft and conspiracy to pervert the course of justice. This could have been a proactive investigation, with CIB detectives carrying out surveillance operations against the suspect officers and arresting them once sufficient evidence had been gathered to mount prosecutions. It is not surprising that no one even seems to have thought of such an approach. At that time, CIB was simply not geared up to mount anything other than reactive investigations. Some of its officers had little detective experience, and one of those on the Jackpot inquiry was widely regarded as a buffoon. Barry Toombs's career as a detective had been on the slide after he had been refused entry to the Flying Squad because of serious character deficiencies. Like others with flaws, he ended up with CIB. Some years later he was charged with corruption.

One of Jackpot's main informants was a drugs dealer, Pearl Cameron, who ran a crack house, selling 'rocks' of crack cocaine at £25 a time to up to eighty people a day from the back window of her council house. She told Russell that she had only dealt to such an extent because of a police officer, Detective Constable Roy Lewandowski of Stoke Newington. She explained that she had been arrested for cocaine possession in 1989 and Lewandowski had persuaded her to sell crack for him, with him providing some protection. She said she had often paid the officer £1,000 a week, and on one occasion nearly £2,000. Cameron was jailed for four years in 1992, the judge telling her that the relatively light sentence was because her dealing stemmed from the advances of a corrupt police officer. Lewandowski was given an eighteen-month sentence, not for drugs dealing, but for stealing £3,000 worth of valuables from a murder victim whose killing he was investigating.

Other dealers and some of those convicted for drugs offences came forward with information about other Stoke Newington officers, alleging that they had planted drugs on suspects and stolen their money. They displayed the same arrogance as corrupt officers who had gone before them, believing that their wrong-doing was very unlikely to be uncovered. And if dealers did complain, who was going to believe those with criminal records? As the Jackpot investigation progressed, the local MP, Brian Sedgemore, instituted a House of Commons early day motion condemning 'those nasty, vile and corrupt police officers at Stoke Newington Police Station who have been engaged in drug trafficking and perverting the course of justice . . .' The MP's attack appalled the officer in charge at the station, Chief Superintendent Roy Clark, who was faced with a collapse of morale. By this stage, two officers had been suspended, one had committed suicide, and eight had been moved to other police stations. Clark stressed that those suspended or moved should be presumed innocent pending the outcome of the Jackpot inquiry. Years later one of those suspended, Ronald Palumbo, received a ten-year prison sentence for smuggling cannabis, and another officer was later charged separately with serious corruption.

Chief Superintendent Roy Clark was to play a leading role in Scotland Yard's fight against corruption. At Stoke Newington, he was shocked by what had been found. Although he publicly supported his officers, and was critical of the motives of some of those attacking them, privately he knew that corruption among Drugs Squad officers ran deep.

He had experienced corruption years before, early in his career, as a temporary detective constable. He recalled that he had made what he thought was a perfect arrest; the criminal was held in the police station cells with a considerable amount of evidence stacked against him. A sergeant then told Clark that he had released the man without charge. Clark was amazed, but as a young man wanting to make it as a detective he did not question the senior man's decision. A few weeks later he became a full detective and his inspector told him to shadow 'the best detective in the world'. After being out on a couple of jobs with this respected officer, Clark was told by him that the inspector was 'the best in the world', and if he ever got 'a drink' (money from a criminal), he should give some to the inspector, who would always look after him. Clark knew what was being suggested, but remained silent. He wanted advice about what had happened to him over these few short weeks at the police station, but did not know anyone he could turn to or trust. His dilemma was solved a few weeks later when he was suddenly told he was being transferred to another station. It was a most unusual move as he had been doing well, having an above-average tally of arrests and crimes solved. He took it that they had got rid of him because he had not fallen in with their corrupt ways.

Clark told me that he thought corruption had died away until he went to Stoke Newington. What he found there was more than the odd rotten apple. It was much more worrying. What had developed was a cell of organised corruption involving constables and some sergeants. He carried out his own unofficial inquiry to establish how it had started, and concluded that the corruption had festered under a sergeant who had by then moved on to another part of London.

When Clark went to Scotland Yard in 1993, he encountered worries among other high-ranking officers that corrupt detectives were once again presenting a problem. They were in several different parts of London, in what were to be termed 'pockets of corruption'. Clark had joined SO11, the Yard's Intelligence Branch, then headed by John Grieve, who later ran the Anti-terrorist Branch and then the Racial and Violent Crimes Unit. SO11 had its own informants and targeted big-time criminals with surveillance operations, tapping phones and using bugging devices to try to stay one step ahead of them by learning in advance what crimes they were about to commit. For example, a public house in east London used by one well-known criminal family was penetrated by the Met and useful information obtained, with undercover police officers posing as bar staff. The opportunity for the covert operation had come about when the brewery chain owning the pub had approached the police for help in dealing with the clientèle. The police moved in, installing bugs. Unfortunately, many of the recorded conversations were difficult, if not impossible, to follow, because they were drowned out by the noise from the pub juke-box. But from what was audible, and from similar intelligence from other sources, a disturbing picture emerged. Criminals in different parts of London were once again talking of having detectives 'on side', as in the old days of the 1960s and 1970s. These officers were said to be selling information about important police operations, willing to arrange for bail and prepared to sabotage prosecutions by watering down evidence or by other methods.

Clark and Grieve believed this was more than just talk, more than simply a criminal boasting to another about the favours he could obtain. There was separate evidence that some police operations or raids had 'blown out', with the targets apparently forewarned. Some important court cases had also failed, with suggestions of sabotage from within. Detectives would tell criminals about to stand trial that they and their lawyers should concentrate on particular areas of the prosecution case vulnerable to attack. The more Clark and Grieve researched the position, the more their concerns grew. Eventually, they raised them with the Commissioner.

Clark sent a report to the Commissioner, stamped 'SECRET' in big red letters. Warning of the growing corruption problem, it said: 'The police service has with justification long been proud of the low level of corruption within its ranks. The purges of the 1970s and early 1980s did much to eradicate corruption amongst CID officers. However, there is evidence that there remains among detectives well placed to monitor top level operations, a number of officers, probably very few, who are of immense value to professional criminals and who do great harm to police target operations . . .'

The report went on to say that officers were involved in recycling drugs, had penetrated intelligence and were selling valuable information to criminals.

The greater use of intelligence and surveillance presents a real threat to the liberty of professional criminals and in consequence will be matched by a greater determination to counter police intelligence. Criminals have vast sums of money available and will not hesitate to use it to corrupt police personnel or systems. This threat to policing must be matched by a far greater awareness of the danger of corruption and a radical strategy which takes advantage of the fact that corrupt officers and criminals are blind to senior officers' awareness of the problem . . .

Clark was to say later that lack of leadership and of control had prevented the force from rooting out corruption. There had been 'wilful blindness' among managers and supervisors. 'They were failing to pick up the signs,' he said. 'They were failing to see there was corruption going on. There was a failure to supervise and a failure of leadership. It's not a scandal to have a corruption problem. It's a scandal not to recognise the problem . . . We had to break the cycle of corruption. It's like doses of antibiotics to deal with bacteria. Unless you take the full dose, the bacteria get stronger.'

The radical strategy Roy Clark favoured was the creation of a secret unit which would work in two phases. First, it would assess the level of corruption in the Met and then it would move on to devise a plan for dealing with it. Clark knew of the limitations of the existing CIB and the difficulties associated with investigating corruption. He believed CIB was 'a leaky ship', its officers generally naive, largely untrained as detectives and swamped by so many relatively mundane complaints that it was incapable of tackling big-time corruption. He recalled, for example, passing on to CIB intelligence that a corrupt officer was to meet a criminal who was to pay him cash for information. Clark later told CIB that the venue for the transaction was not known as the pair had spoken only of meeting 'at the usual place'. On learning that the information was imprecise, CIB officers lost whatever interest they had in the case, managing to both infuriate and depress Clark. Any worthwhile investigative unit would have pursued the case by at least asking Clark for more information or intelligence, but no such request was ever made.

Clark wanted the new unit to be what he called the ultimate secret squad. He argued that it would be no good drafting in the best detectives from the London boroughs to serve on it because their disappearance would be noted. Word would leak out about what they were doing, alerting the corrupt officers they were supposed to be targeting. Instead,

Clark wanted the new unit to comprise recently retired officers and serving officers with particular skills, and also those known to have made a personal stand against corruption. Clark's report ended with a warning that if the Met did not put its own house in order, then others would move in and do it for them. Waiting in the wings was the security service MI5, which after a downturn in violence in Northern Ireland was looking at areas it could add to its empire. It had told the Home Office that it had the know-how to tackle major organised international crime, but it was unwilling to share its secrets with police officers. Not only had the police not been properly vetted, but there was also the fear that secrets could leak through corruption. MI5 was suggesting that it could root out the corrupt officers.

Clark's report was received sympathetically by the new Commissioner, Sir Paul Condon, who had taken over from Sir Peter Imbert. One of the last things Condon wanted so early in his tenure was interference from another state agency. As he and other senior officers pondered what to do, Scotland Yard was hit by another corruption scandal. This was much more serious than the Stoke Newington affair, which had been treated by many news organisations as a local story, unworthy of national coverage. Scotland Yard was to react to this new unwelcome publicity with a combination of denial and damage limitation, as it had done so often in the past.

Early in 1993, BBC's *Panorama* programme had been approached by Kevin Cressey, a criminal awaiting trial for large-scale dealing in cannabis. Cressey told the BBC that he had paid £18,000 for bail to John Donald, a detective constable with the élite South East Regional Crime Squad, known by its acronym SERCS. The pair's corrupt relationship was continuing, with Cressey paying for the sabotage of the prosecution case against him; he was also acting as a middleman between other criminals and Donald and his colleagues. The programme tape-recorded conversations between the pair. It was clear that Donald was prepared to sell very secret information about police operations against even major criminals, such as Kenny Noye. Noye had killed a police officer investigating him for the country's biggest robbery, the £26 million raid on the Brink's-Mat warehouse near Heathrow Airport. He was acquitted of murder, but was later jailed for handling some of the robbery proceeds. On his release, he was suspected of involvement in a massive conspiracy to smuggle cocaine from the United States. The US authorities had learned of the plan and had started a joint operation against Noye's gang with Scotland Yard and Customs. Donald told Cressey of the international operation and asked him to warn Noye. Cressey obliged and paid the corrupt detective £500, saying it had come from Noye. On one of the tapes, Donald asks Cressey for £10,000 from Noye for more information about the operation. He also indicates that there are other police officers involved:

'We've got to support two people here, me and someone else,' says the bent detective.

'Go on, say what you want, and I'll tell him,' Cressey responds.

'Say about ten large ones to him.'

'Ten grand?'

'Yeah.'

'All right, then.'

In another tape, Donald offers to sell Cressey the original SERCS observation logs which showed him dealing with another criminal, David Fraser, one of 'Mad' Frankie Fraser's sons. The original logs would be of immense help to Cressey, because without them in court his prosecution would almost certainly fail. On the tapes, Donald tells Cressey that he and his sergeant, Alec Leighton, are prepared to burgle the police station where the logs are held. But Cressey is unhappy about the price being asked – £30,000 – and tries to bargain with Donald, who says he is now acting as middleman with DS Leighton.

'I've been thinking about it,' says Cressey to Donald. 'And for that one, I find it a lot of fucking money, John, to be honest with you ... thirty large, you know.'

'That's what I told him [Leighton] yesterday', replies Donald. 'I'll tell him that, and see what he says.'

'If he wants to come back to me with a different price, then I'll talk to him,' says Cressey.

'What if he says, "Well, what do you want"?'

'Well, I see it about ten large, John. That's the way I see it.'

In another taped conversation, Donald tells Cressey that he is able to obtain sensitive information from the ultra-secret and hugely important NCIS, the National Criminal Intelligence Service, an organisation set up the year before with five hundred staff and an annual budget of £25 million. Its job was to gather intelligence on serious, organised criminals and also to co-ordinate the work of Customs and police, agencies often at each other's throats. Customs believed many detectives were prepared to bend the rules and that some were straightforwardly corrupt, while the police nickname for Customs officers, 'Choirboys', reflected what they believed to be their naive innocence. Anyone working at NCIS had access to reports from Interpol, and there was also some input from MI5. Donald's NCIS contact was DS Tom Bradley, an officer, Donald tells Cressey, who can offer an almost regular information service.

Cressey asks: 'Would it be within his means to check without any comebacks?'

'Oh, yeah,' replies Donald. 'He does hundreds of them every day. He's got his own people he does them for, hasn't he . . . He just slips one in.'

About two weeks before the planned *Panorama* broadcast, Scotland Yard learned of the programme's contents and was furious with the BBC, arguing that if *Panorama* had informed police of Cressey's approach a joint investigation could have been mounted. Evidence would have been gathered acceptable to the courts, and all the wrong-doers put behind bars. But such a strategy would have been doomed to failure from the start. First, Cressey would never have agreed to co-operate with the police, and second, Scotland Yard knew from the likes of Roy Clark that it did not have the ability to mount the kind of big proactive investigation necessary to entrap Donald and other suspect officers. And the Yard knew that its position was even more potentially embarrassing.

Unknown to *Panorama* at the time, CIB had mounted an expensive entrapment operation earlier in the year against Donald and some of his colleagues, who were allegedly demanding £5,000 from a Bournemouth restaurant owner. But the operation ended in failure, after a leak to the corrupt officers from within police ranks. That was embarrassing enough on its own, but it also became clear later that the CIB investigators' failure was even more serious. They had been investigating Donald's wrong-doing but had failed to discover some of the detective's other corrupt dealings at the time of the Bournemouth blackmail, his clandestine meetings with his registered informant, Cressey, or the latter's dealings with the BBC.

Although Scotland Yard did not know that *Panorama* was unaware of the Bournemouth operation, the programme was clearly going to cause major waves. Prior to the broadcast, a very senior officer, Detective Chief Superintendent Ian Blair, was put in overall charge of what was to become a huge investigation into SERCS and NCIS corruption. A dilemma arose. If officers had been arrested quickly, legal restrictions would have meant the scrapping of the programme, scheduled for Monday, 27 September 1993. There was an unofficial agreement between Blair and the BBC that arrests would be delayed until that evening, with no charges until after the programme was broadcast. But others at the Yard objected. Instead of keeping to the arrangement, the police changed their plans. The arrests were to be brought forward. All the SERCS officers at Donald's base in Surbiton were to be asked to go into the office on the Friday, when some were to be taken aside and arrested. This would almost certainly have scuppered what would have been an embarrassing *Panorama*. When Blair learned of the change, I understand he threatened to resign. Whatever happened behind the scenes, it resulted in the Friday meeting at Surbiton being called off and rescheduled for the Monday of the *Panorama* broadcast.

But there were further leaks of information during that Monday, causing the Met more embarrassment. News had spread internally of what was afoot, and word reached the corrupt John Donald by the Monday morning, when he went to the office for the rescheduled meeting. He received at least two calls warning that he was in serious trouble. One of them came from his NCIS contact, DS Tom Bradley, who, when told that Donald was out of the office, left a message: 'There's something on the telly tonight and John Donald's on it. He's dropped me in the shit.' But Donald had already disappeared. He had received a pager message, telling him to go to a public telephone box away from the police station, where he could have a conversation without it being overheard or intercepted. The corrupt officer then did as many criminals would have done. He 'did a runner'. He went 'on his toes'. Although experienced surveillance officers had been following him from the day before, he managed to elude them completely, not giving himself up until two days later. Where he was in that time, and whether he was destroying incriminating evidence, is still unknown.

The programme had a devastating effect when broadcast. All the national newspapers followed up the story of corruption within the élite SERCS and in NCIS too. Donald's disappearance added extra spice. Publicly, Scotland Yard attacked the BBC, but privately it galvanised the force into taking action. The programme sparked what was to be until then the biggest single investigation into police corruption ever mounted in London. But, more importantly, it also resulted in a series of further high-level meetings with those calling for changes in CIB tactics eventually triumphing over the traditionalists, those who had continued to argue that corruption was not a major problem, and that throwing money and resources at it would be wasteful.

Within months of the programme – a short time in terms of Met bureaucracy – a momentous decision would be taken. A new squad was to be created. It would assess the level of corruption and then recommend new strategies for stamping it out. To avoid leaks, the squad's work was to be kept secret, totally divorced from mainstream detective work. Its costs were to be hidden in Scotland Yard's accounts. Even its name and very existence were to be kept secret.

two

FORMING THE GHOST SQUAD

So seriously was the threat of damaging leaks taken that not only was the unit's actual existence known only to a small handful of very senior officers, but its code-name was also kept secret and out of police documents . . .

'Deep legends' were created for undercover officers brought in from outside forces in order to get close to a suspect corrupt officer. DHSS and Inland Revenue records were changed or created, as were Land Registry records and electoral rolls, so they would show that someone had lived in a particular property for a number of years.

Detective Chief Superintendent Roger Gaspar was to become the head of the new ground-breaking squad in 1994. He is a career detective, a big, avuncular man, whose main form of relaxation is sailing. To remind him of life outside the Met, several large photographs of lighthouses decorate his office walls. He readily admits to their symbolism. These are lighthouses not standing securely on dry land, cliff-tops or promontories. These are lonely, solitary edifices perching on rocks, surrounded by stormy seas. One of the photos shows a lighthouse being hit by a wave so huge that it is a wonder how the structure, or the keepers inside, could possibly withstand such a battering.

Gaspar knew that to a large extent he would be navigating difficult waters alone when he joined CIB, the Complaints Investigation Branch, but he was still surprised at how turbulent and stressful the posting turned out to be. In 1993, he had been on a senior command course at the police college at Bramshill, along with another detective chief super-intendent, Ian Blair, who was put in charge of the CIB investigation into *Panorama*'s revelations about the corrupt South East Regional Crime Squad detective John Donald. At the end of the year, Blair was about to leave the Met for the Thames Valley force, and suggested to Gaspar that he put in for his job. Gaspar was in two minds. At that stage he was on the Met's Central Staff but not finding the bureaucratic work very interesting. Against that, CIB had a poor reputation and it would be a sideways move for him. But as the Met at that time was not promoting chief superintendents, and as he had heard that CIB was to be shaken up, he believed it would represent a challenge. He went for the job and got it.

At that time CIB was divided into two sections. CIB1 dealt with the administration of disciplinary procedures and CIB2 investigated complaints. Gaspar took over as head of CIB2, and was shocked at what he found. Tired investigators, nearing the end of their careers, waiting to retire, were no surprise to him. But the methods and systems used, or rather the lack of them, were a shambles. 'I was horrified at the quality of some of the non-corruption investigations,' he told me. 'I'm not criticising death-in-custody inquiries, but what could be termed normal complaints. There were speedier ways of doing the job, and penetrating the issues of the case. It's like the first twenty-four hours of a murder investigation being the most important. The more time it takes to get an investigation under way, the more chance there is of losing evidence.'

He also found that some people who telephoned with information, including police officers, were simply not listened to. 'Cops would ring up with concerns about possible corruption,' he said. 'For example, they'd say that someone was doing something in a strange way or a particular job had been a bit "iffy". I asked CIB what we did with such intelligence and I was told that we had never had such calls before. I don't know whether this was true or not. It appeared to me that anyone who had got such a call would say that CIB only dealt with complaints, and if there was no official complaint they could not handle it. Such intelligence calls weren't for CIB. There was no one to deal with them, so I set up a system.'

Then there were leaks. Some were inadvertent. This could happen, for example, when a CIB investigator was having a drink with old detective colleagues and would let slip some information about an inquiry he was working on. Word could then get back to the suspect officers, and that sometimes meant the end of an investigation. Two theories had been put forward as to how the corrupt John Donald of SERCS had learned of the CIB entrapment operation against him in Bournemouth. In both cases the leaks may have been inadvertent, but they demonstrate the difficulties facing CIB at that time due to a lack of foresight and resources. Unfortunately, whoever had booked the hotel for the CIB officers in the seaside resort chose one regularly used for police masonic functions. Tom Bradley, Donald's NCIS contact, was at one of these and recognised one of the CIB investigators. The tip-off may also have occurred because CIB did not have its own technical experts. Instead, it had to call on Scotland Yard's central technical unit to install recording equipment for the Bournemouth operation. It was discovered after the leak that one of the technical experts was a very good friend of one of Donald's colleagues. CIB detectives spent months trying to find the source of the leaks without success.

Some leaks were deliberate. Gaspar said that shortly after taking over as head of CIB2 he received information from a very senior and trusted officer, Commander Roy Penrose, to the effect that Customs were claiming that two SERCS detectives had been sharing in the rewards being given to an informant they were handling. Gaspar realised the importance of this, as Customs had been critical of some of the Met's detective work for many years. He asked whether there was anyone in CIB who could investigate the information, but was told there was no one available who could be trusted to do it properly. Gaspar decided to do the job himself, and assembled a small team. But without technical equipment, he had to borrow from the Yard's central unit. He realised that this made the operation more vulnerable to a leak, but he had no alternative.

> We covered a meet and I had to brief the team in great detail about what they were expected to do. I had to tell them things that they should already have known. What a lash-up! We had to use hire cars which, of course, had no police radios, and the equipment we got from SO11 [the Intelligence Branch] was the last they had, the bottom of the barrel. There were no proper aerials. So there we were using bright new shiny hire cars with two cops in suits sitting inside, trying to monitor meetings. Nothing happened on the first meet, and before the second could take place, the job was blown out. It was a disaster.

The suspect detectives had been warned that they were under investigation. The case caused embarrassment to the Met because it soured relations with Customs even further. Customs ('Choirboys' or 'Lilywhites' as they were known by the police) had given the original information in good faith, expecting a full and fair investigation. When it was reported back that there had been a leak, it simply confirmed Customs' belief that corruption in the Met ran deep and that great care should be taken before the capital's police were entrusted with confidential information in the future. But the episode was also to have a positive effect. It helped get the secret intelligence cell off the ground.

Gaspar and Commander Penrose conducted an inquiry into the source of the leak and eventually a senior officer admitted to having talked to a SERCS detective inspector, who had passed the information on to the two suspect detectives handling the informant. Gaspar was very concerned about the attitudes displayed, as none of the four officers involved believed they had behaved corruptly. The two detectives had 'ramped up' the reward for the informant. They had obtained more reward money for him than his information was worth, so they believed they were entitled to a share of it. The officers who had tipped the pair off not only sympathised with this view – they had another reason for their actions. They wanted the investigation to stop so it would go no farther than the two lowly detectives. It was a case of damage limitation. There was a worry that if the CIB inquiry continued it would open a bigger can of worms.

Gaspar discussed what had happened and his concerns about the entrenched views of corruption he was up against with senior Met officers. The overall head of CIB, Commander Peter Winship, suggested that they go and see the Commissioner, Sir Paul Condon, who was known to be concerned about corruption too. Gaspar agreed. But not wanting to be accused of exaggerating the problem, he asked for help from colleagues – senior detectives who had talked of encountering corruption in recent years.

The ten senior officers who agreed to help him gathered together one Sunday morning in April 1994 for a strange and highly confidential meeting. Gaspar asked them to list all the detectives they suspected of corruption, stressing that he wanted them to provide more than just anecdotes. Sitting separately, these senior officers came up with eighty-three names, giving pen portraits of what they knew of the history of each. These were passed to an analyst in another room, who drew up charts, linking the suspects, underlining names appearing more than once. Most of them were attached to the élite South East Regional Crime Squad. Gaspar now had a much clearer picture of the extent of corruption. It was serious and had to be dealt with. He knew how it should be done.

The following month, Gaspar gave a presentation to the Commissioner, Sir Paul Condon, the Deputy Commissioner, and the heads of detective operations, intelligence and CIB. Using an overhead projector and slides, he outlined his assessment of the problem and then went on to explain how it should be tackled. There were alternatives, he said, but most of them had drawbacks. They had either been tried before or represented only partial solutions. One way forward was to transfer suspect officers from detective squads to 'safer' duties, and amend regulations so that those who disobeyed or breached them could be sacked more easily. External investigators could also be brought in, as had happened with Operation Countryman over a decade before. But Gaspar said that Countryman had to a large extent failed, and looking to an outside force or MI5 for help would be an admission that the Met was incapable of handling its own difficulties. The problem was cultural, he argued, and you had to be inside the organisation to understand and fight it. It woud help to give extra resources to CIB2, so it could carry out covert operations with trained investigators and make use of surveillance teams with good equipment. But he favoured a more radical approach, dealing with the problem in a way never attempted before.

He recommended the setting up of a major covert operation, an intelligence-gathering unit that would function in total secrecy and whose existence would be known to only a handful of very senior, trusted officers. Its aims would be to examine the nature of the different types of corruption at play; to identify those responsible and then deliver hard evidence against them so they could be prosecuted or rooted out. The secret unit would operate under the cover of a commercial company on the outskirts of London, away from other police premises. Its staff would be hand picked and vetted and would have to live double lives, pretending they were executives and ordinary office workers while, in effect, spying on former colleagues. They would be fully trained in surveillance techniques and have the most up-to-date equipment available. The total cost of setting up and running such a secret operation would be £14 million, spread over three years. It was a very large sum, but Gaspar's argument was that if it was not spent the insidious corruption would increase, tarnishing the Met's reputation still further and making the eventual cost of clearing up the resulting mess much higher. Within days of the meeting, Gaspar was given the go-ahead.

The task facing him and the secret ghost squad he was about to form was much more difficult than that confronted during the last big purge of corrupt officers under Commissioner Sir Robert Mark. Criminals' payments to officers then were sometimes made on a regular basis. Police corruption in the 1990s was more opportunistic, and the officers involved, trained detectives, were cunning and skilled in covering their tracks. Sir Paul Condon's deputy, Brian Hayes, compared the two eras: 'A lot of the corruption and dishonesty then was extremely arrogant and blatant because people thought they could get away with it; money in brown envelopes passing in offices, the head of the Flying Squad going on holiday with a known criminal. It is now far more behind the scenes, clever, sophisticated, and is that much more difficult to deal with . . .'

Another leading anti-corruption officer told me:

> There are pitfalls on corruption inquiries. Robert Mark realised the difficulties involved with them and took a pragmatic view, pursuing corruption through discipline and forced retirement, rather than by prosecutions. He and Operation Countryman didn't solve the problem. It was just driven underground, becoming more sophisticated, more sinister and difficult to combat. The 1990s thinking was that people should not be allowed to retire with things hanging over them. They should be punished.

The corrupt activities of the suspect officers spanned the criminal under-world and sometimes mirrored its activities. There was opportunistic corruption, such as skimming off drugs and money during raids on drug dealers, thieves and robbers. Then there were the other types of corruption, which could start simply with the giving of a favour. Detectives could tip off journalist contacts about operations they were involved in, ensuring that the job and they themselves received the publicity they believed they deserved. But that could lead to payments for information and to damaging leaks which could destroy months of careful work. Similar consequences could result from a call to a detective by a former colleague working in a lawyer's office or in the private security sector, asking for someone to be checked out on the Police National Computer. That could lead to regular payments for information on the part of the ex-colleague, who could be passing on the information to criminals. Then there was sophisticated, well-planned corruption. One of those high up on the list of suspect detectives was thought to be extracting money only from major criminals, those known to have large amounts of cash available. But he went one step farther than the corrupt DC John Donald, exposed by *Panorama*. Not only would he tip criminals off about operations being mounted against them; it was believed he would also feed information to those awaiting trial that would result in them being found not guilty. Almost every prosecution case has its weak points, but often these are known only to the police involved in the original investigation. Tipping off criminals that their lawyers should concentrate on these flaws could lead to the collapse of a trial before the defence side is heard, or to the abandonment of a case before it has even reached court.

Chief Superintendent Roger Gaspar put a lot of thought and planning into setting up the ghost squad. Recruiting suitable staff and finding premises were major initial problems, but more important than both these, and an issue that was to cause increasing difficulty, was the continuing need for secrecy. There had been leaks from CIB before. If the existence of this new ultra-secret inquiry was ever disclosed, even partially, it would spell disaster for the whole strategy. The intelligence-gathering first stage of the inquiry depended on operational secrecy. If it had been a normal CIB2 inquiry, regulations would have required that the suspect detectives be told that they were under investigation and given details of the complaint or allegations against them. Abiding by these regulations had been a contributory factor in the failure of many anti-corruption inquiries. Warned that they were under investigation, the suspect officers could cover up their corrupt activities by taking any one of a number of steps to frustrate CIB enquiries. These could range from losing paperwork showing where they were at a particular time to the straightforward threatening of witnesses. Under this new inquiry, there would be no such official warnings. The ghost squad would gather intelligence on an individual target or detective squad in total secrecy.

So seriously was the threat of damaging leaks taken that not only was the unit's actual existence known only to a small handful of very senior officers, but its code-name was also kept secret and out of police documents. It was called Operation Athona, named after an old Roman fort in Essex. I believe this to be the first time its name has appeared in print. I also discovered another secret about Operation Athona while writing this book. The assumption had been that its work was merged with CIB's after Sir Paul Condon went public in late 1997 about the extent of the corruption problem and how the Met was tackling it. But this is not the case. The unit still exists today as a separate entity and its secret intelligence work continues.

Forming the ghost squad in 1994 took up nearly all of Roger Gaspar's time, and it was not to be fully operational until well into the following year. First, Gaspar had to concoct a cover story to explain why he was away from his normal duties on the seventh floor of Tintagel House, CIB's headquarters overlooking the Thames, close to the MI6 building in Vauxhall. He solved that problem by announcing that he had agreed to supervise a secret inquiry into allegations of serious corruption involving a provincial force some distance from London. He said he would be working from another office behind heavily secured doors on the eighth floor. This effectively meant that no one knew what he was doing when he was not engaged in straightforward CIB work – supervising ordinary investigations into allegations of police wrong-doing, ranging from the relatively minor to deaths in custody and corruption.

Finding suitable premises for the new unit was the next task, and it proved far from easy. The operation was much more complex than establishing the kind of 'safe house' used by MI5 for informants or debriefings. Gaspar needed premises for a fake company that claimed to be a fully commercial organisation. A building was needed as far away from other police operations as possible, as none of those who would be working there wanted accidentally to bump into former colleagues. Estate agents were trawled for property on the outskirts of London, but very secure premises were needed, and when this question was raised potential landlords sometimes became suspicious. On at least one occasion a property company believed the officer making rental enquiries was representing a criminal gang! 'It took months to get premises,' recalled Gaspar. 'No one trusted us. We had buried our funding money so well that landlords didn't trust us. They thought we had crooked money.'

What was needed was a convincing story, what's called 'a legend', backed up by solid references. The story decided on was that the outfit had been a small company which was now expanding and hoping to achieve multimillion-pound status. Scotland Yard's contacts in the banking world were happy to provide the necessary references for individual 'businessmen'. They had done the same before for officers investigating fraud who posed as businessmen, but on this special occasion they were not told that the business was to be much more than simply a short-term paper exercise. Armed with the references, surveyors and valuers were employed by the company to find premises. After a suitable building was found in west London, Roger Gaspar's next task was recruitment to the ghost squad.

The men and women he wanted were not exclusively detectives or even necessarily police officers, although most were. At least one had an MI5 background, another had worked in military intelligence, while others had financial skills, including one who used to be an accountant. More mature or experienced people were favoured. Lists of those joining the Met as normal police recruits were scoured for those with particular work experience who had decided on a change of career. At least one such man was approached just a few days before he was due to start a training course for new recruits at Hendon police college in north London. He joined the ghost squad, but faced serious problems later when he eventually left the team. By then he had years of highly specialised police intelligence-gathering experience, but he had been invisible in the service and still had no basic police training, making it virtually impossible for him to find a police job through his own efforts without disclosing his secret past. Strings were pulled, and he was eventually found a good job without his background becoming known.

Apart from those with specialised skills, others were hand picked from detective ranks, particularly those known to have made some kind of stand against corruption. All potential recruits had to be positively vetted before they were accepted. Secrecy was of paramount importance throughout the whole selection process and beyond. Just as with MI5, it was important that no one outside was aware of the kind of work being undertaken. Each new recruit had to come up with a story to explain their disappearance from normal police ranks to colleagues. Some said they were fed up with London and were transferring to a provincial force, while others said they were retiring or getting out of police work altogether. One inspector said he was leaving the police because he was suffering from cancer and wanted to enjoy the remainder of his life. His story was so convincing that colleagues had a whip-round and bought him an expensive set of golf clubs. When it emerged years later that he had been working for the ghost squad, these same officers were outraged by the deception, especially on learning that some of them had been the targets of his anti-corruption enquiries.

Other problems, some of them unexpected, resulted from the fact that the ghost squad company was trading as a legitimate business. Money for staff pay came from Metropolitan Police funds, but this could not be revealed because of the need for secrecy. Instead, the money was laundered, going through different hands before reaching individual bank accounts. A further problem related to tax. Each 'employee' had to pay tax from their earnings with the company, but the claiming of allowances was to cause difficulties. Normal detectives are able to claim mileage for the distance travelled between home and work as their vehicles are regarded as tools of trade. But the Inland Revenue, believing the company was legitimate, argued that its 'staff' were not entitled to the allowance as their cars were not essential to their work. Ironing out such financial problems took time and effort, and was not helped by the fact that Scotland Yard accounting was then under close scrutiny because of an entirely separate inquiry into a Met accountant's fraudulent activities.

The main aim of Athona was to build up a strategic picture of the extent of corruption. Who was corrupt and in which of several possible areas? These included recycling drugs, selling intelligence, and sharing in rewards. Using the list of names of suspect corrupt officers secretly compiled by Gaspar's colleagues at Scotland Yard, the ghost squad would carry out 'lifestyle surveillance' on each, determining how they spent their time, who they mixed with, who their informants were, and so on. If suspicions appeared justified, the surveillance work would move to a higher level, involving telephone tapping, the bugging of homes and offices, covert camerawork, and even recording devices in cars. Although the informants of corrupt officers were approached for information they were dealt with warily. Many had become too close to their detective handlers and could not be trusted not to pass information back to them. More likely to help were informants who were known to have fallen out with suspect detectives.

Obtaining sophisticated up-to-date surveillance equipment presented further problems. Much of police mobile surveillance work is done by officers on motorbikes, which offer greater ease of movement in traffic and, because the riders are helmeted, those under surveillance cannot recognise them. But the Met's surveillance teams tend to use the same make of motorbike, bought in bulk. There were dangers in the ghost squad using the same machines because they could be recognised by the trained detectives who were the targets, alerting them to the fact that they were under investigation. To avoid the risk, Roger Gaspar bought a different type of motorbike.

The same difficulties arose over obtaining bugging and other technical equipment. If Gaspar approached sellers in the UK, the worry was that word would leak to the specialist detective squads, which were buying the same kind of equipment. Among them was CIB itself, which was being kept in the dark about the creation of the new ultra-secret unit. Gaspar had to go to the United States to buy much of the equipment, using a false identity. He also had to go outside the Met for specialists to operate the technical equipment and train ghost squad staff in its use. At that stage, the Met had so few specialists of its own that approaching them for help could have blown the team's cover.

False identities were created for all staff, the number of which fluctuated around the twenty-five mark. These fake identities would be used, for example, if a flat was being rented to carry out surveillance, technical or otherwise, on an officer in a neighbouring property. Only police officers within the ghost squad were used for physical surveillance, because if challenged by another officer they knew the correct procedures and could produce a warrant card. This could help in various potentially dangerous situations, whether being stopped for speeding while tracking someone or entering a police station to plant a bug or gather other intelligence. The warrant card would be in a false name, but would stand up to scrutiny if a corrupt detective or anyone else started making enquiries. If phone numbers were given out by a ghost squad member posing, for example, as a company representative from the north of England, anyone telephoning would unknowingly be diverted to Athona headquarters in west London. 'Deep legends' were created for undercover officers brought in from outside forces in order to get close to a suspect corrupt officer. DHSS and Inland Revenue records were changed or created, as were Land Registry records and electoral rolls, so they would show that someone had lived in a particular property for a number of years.

The need for secrecy extended from top to bottom of the organisation. At times it verged on the paranoid. Gaspar himself regularly kept in touch with developments and exchanged information with the two other driving forces behind Operation Athona, John Grieve, who then headed the Yard's intelligence branch, and Deputy Assistant Commissioner Roy Clark, later to be put in overall charge of the Met's anti-corruption drive. The trio used to meet in the evenings at a hotel south of Lambeth Bridge, each getting their drivers to drop them off some distance away. This was to avoid the possibility of their drivers meeting up and gossiping about what their bosses were up to. The three avoided the hotel's bar. To have been overheard or even seen together in such circumstances would have raised eyebrows, leading to rumours that could have signed the squad's death warrant. Instead, on each occasion, a room was booked in a false name.

Detective Chief Superintendent Roger Gaspar had barely started on the long and complex job of forming the ghost squad when he received a startling phone call. It led to a secret meeting and a golden opportunity to penetrate the ranks of officers widely regarded as being seriously corrupt. Gaspar grasped the opportunity, gaining considerable evidence and an amazing insight into major corruption. But the episode turned sour, and was to haunt Gaspar and the Metropolitan Police's anti-corruption drive for years. Even in 2002 efforts were still being made to resolve the affair.

three

CORRUPTION IN ELITE DETECTIVE SQUADS

Brennan told them the £30,000 was in his car . . . 'It was in a green Marks and Spencer bag, and he opened it up and he went 'Lovely'. 'All right,' he said, 'I'll be in touch with yer.' And that's how I parted with the thirty grand . . . So they've had £50,000 in total out of the money. So they was done. They'd been paid for their work to cover the job.

Only a few weeks after being given the go-ahead to create the secret ghost squad, on 14 June 1994, DCS Roger Gaspar received a dramatic phone call requiring immediate action. It led to armed police protecting a man, moving him and his family from their home for their own safety. The caller was the head of the Flying Squad, Bill Griffiths. He said that a reliable Flying Squad officer, Detective Sergeant Chris Smith, had told him that an important police informant had been compromised. Confidential police documents detailing his activities had leaked to the major criminals on whom he was informing. His life was in danger.

The man's name was Geoffrey Brennan. He was a big, excitable man given to lies, boast and bluster, with an unfortunate involuntary facial twitch when under pressure. As well as being a fairly small-time criminal he had been an informant for years, especially since the early 1990s, when he had got to know high-calibre criminals and various police officers. His best friend was Detective Constable Mark Norton. DC Norton had married Debbie Norris, widow of David Norris, murdered by contract killers in 1991. Norris had been a prolific informant for police and Customs officers. As a direct result of his information, up to fifty criminals had been jailed. But as happened with so many informants, he used his relationship with his handlers to cover his own criminal activities, which included deals with corrupt police. It was rumoured that the night before his death he had gone to meet a South East Regional Crime Squad detective in a pub, carrying £10,000. He was shot dead when he arrived home. Police called to the scene found no money on him. DC Norton had been on the murder investigation team, and there was widespread amazement when he married Debbie Norris. Norton was himself later to be accused of wrong-doing. He was dismissed for discreditable conduct – fighting in a pub car park.

DCS Gaspar knew nothing of these links when he met Brennan and DS Smith a couple of hours after the Flying Squad chief's call. However, one name that had cropped up in the phone conversation was of great interest to Gaspar. It was that of a SERCS officer, Detective Inspector John Redgrave, who had been involved with Brennan. Redgrave's name was on the list of suspect corrupt officers compiled by Gaspar's high-ranking colleagues only weeks before. An intrigued Gaspar hurried to the meeting on the banks of the Serpentine in Hyde Park. The story he was about to hear from Brennan that day and over the following weeks was an amazing one of intrigue, corruption, deception and double-dealing. Several senior anti-corruption detectives and lawyers have described it as the biggest can of worms they have ever encountered.

Brennan told Gaspar he had been informing on big-time criminals involved in large-scale drugs importation, gunrunning and money laundering. His handlers had been DI Redgrave of SERCS and a Flying Squad detective constable called Michael Charman. But he was now a frightened man, and had turned for help to another police contact, DS Chris Smith. Brennan said he had been told through a family friend that confidential police records of his activities were now in the hands of major violent criminals. The friend, a woman, had described how she had been at the home of one of them, who had links with criminals involved in Britain's biggest robbery, the theft in 1983 of Brink's-Mat gold bullion worth £26 million. She had seen the man wearing thin surgical gloves as he handled Brennan's papers, so as not to leave finger-prints. If Brennan's story was true – and Gaspar had no reason to disbelieve him, especially as it was corroborated by DS Smith – the consequences were immense. It meant there had been a serious leak of some of the most confidential information held by Scotland Yard. Corruption must be involved, as these potentially life-threatening documents were held very securely and not inadvertently mislaid. Brennan was presenting Gaspar with a great opportunity to penetrate a murky world. But first he had to be protected.

Gaspar told Brennan to return to his home in Kent with DS Smith, and armed officers would arrive to protect him. Gaspar recalled: 'As I walked out of Hyde Park, I believed there was a substantial threat to Brennan's life. I was satisfied there were sufficient concerns to press buttons immediately, and nothing changed my mind.' The main button pressed was to get Brennan taken into the Metropolitan Police's witness protection programme, and it had to be done quickly before anyone who wanted him silenced struck. Kent police were contacted to help with Brennan's immediate safety. By the same evening, six officers had taken up position in or around his home, all armed with a variety of weaponry. Brennan was moved to a safe house, and over the following months the Met helped him sell his home and buy a new one for his family. His name was changed and he was given a new passport and other papers in his new identity. The police even helped his parents find a new home outside London.

Gaspar was to have more than twenty meetings, interviews and phone conversations with Brennan over the next months. For his intelligence-gathering on the extent of police corruption, the detective chief superintendent wanted more from him about the leak of information, suspecting that DI Redgrave must somehow have been involved. He also believed that Brennan could tell him more about police corruption and hoped to use him as a witness. But Brennan made it difficult for him.

The first meeting after Brennan's move to a new home took place on 21 June at a Gatwick Airport hotel, in a room booked under a false name. Gaspar was there with another detective, and Brennan was with DS Chris Smith and the woman who had seen the criminal handling his informant files. She told Gaspar that she believed a contract to kill Brennan had been taken out. Gaspar had wanted to tape the meeting, but Brennan refused. However, he did allow Gaspar to make notes. Brennan's was a complex story, not helped by his habit of getting people's names slightly wrong. He persisted, for instance, in calling Redgrave 'Redgraves'. At the beginning of the next meeting, Gaspar told Brennan that he had had difficulty in following his story the week before and the notes he had made had not helped very much. He wanted to get the story and sequence of events down accurately, so would Brennan mind if he used a tape recorder? Voicing reluctance, Brennan agreed. Gaspar put the recorder on the hotel table between them and switched it on. Surprisingly, given his initial reluctance, Brennan launched into his story, soon going into overdrive, giving a free-flowing account of what had happened to him, alleging he had paid Redgrave and Charman £50,000.

From Brennan's account, and from what Gaspar learned from police sources, a clearer picture began to emerge. Brennan recounted how he had been a police informant while running a mobile-phone shop. During the previous summer, with the business in increasing financial difficulties, he had become an informant for Detective Constable Mick Charman, a Flying Squad officer based at the squad's Tower Bridge offices. He was giving him information about a robber who had moved into the drugs trade, importing cocaine from Venezuela. Brennan said that at the same time he had been contacted by a Texan wanting to buy mobile phones for use on offshore oil rigs. The Texan then introduced him to a Chinese-American, Sam Wang. Thousands of a particular type of Motorola mobile were wanted by Wang for resale in Hong Kong and mainland China, where they were unobtainable because of international licensing agreements. Brennan agreed to provide the phones, although he knew he would never be able to supply more than a handful. Wang flew to London to clinch the deal and met Brennan at an expensive London hotel. Wang was impressed by the presence of Brennan's good friend DC Mark Norton.

On tape, to Gaspar, Brennan related what he said the Texan had told him: 'He said, "You know, you are going to earn a lot of money out of this. We are all going to earn a lot of money out of this." And I thought, no, all I'm going to do is fucking relieve you of the money ... It's as simple as that.'

Brennan went on to describe how he had then met his police handler, DC Charman: 'I said to Mick, if this shapes up, I can relieve these people. It's an opportunity, and these things come up once in your life-time, without anyone getting hurt, if it can be done proper ... I said: "Look, Mick, I want to relieve them of all of it."'

Meanwhile money started arriving from Wang and his brother in the USA for the mobile phones that Brennan had no intention of supplying. The crooked businessman was to receive more than £400,000 in the coming weeks. He claimed that a plan was hatched with Charman so that police would provide him with cover as he pocketed the money. The police would pretend that Brennan was giving them information about a money-laundering operation being run from the US, and in return for the protection Brennan would pay over cash. Brennan alleged he gave a first payment of £10,000 to Charman, who told him he would introduce him to his old friend DI John Redgrave, who was now with SERCS, the South East Regional Crime Squad. The two detectives had worked together on the Brink's-Mat robbery.

'I give Mick £10,000 and at that time I was led to believe that five grand was going to Redgrave to start all this off,' said Brennan. 'We met John in the car park of the restaurant at South Mimms [a large service station at the junction of the A1 and M25] . . . He drove up in a metallic Cavalier. He come over and said, "Let's get back in the car." Then we took off like fucking . . . you don't know who you thought you had up your arse. He was going left, right, left, right, all round them round-abouts. Next thing, we're into the back of a hotel.'

According to Brennan's account, the three of them went to a room at the hotel which had been pre-booked by Redgrave. The DI then searched Brennan thoroughly, looking for a microphone or some kind of recording device. He had to take off his shoes and belt for examination, and said that Redgrave even went through his hair. As the search continued, Brennan said he remonstrated with Charman: 'I looked at Mick and Mick went, "Don't worry." I went: "No, Mick. What is all this?" Then Redgrave said, "I've got a pension to worry about, and I ain't being fucked. I ain't being fucked by you or anybody." I said: "Well, if you're worried about a set-up, you're a friend of Mick's and Mick's given me that you're OK." He said there was no problem. He's trying to defuse the situation, 'cos I'm now up in the air about it. Mick's going, "Calm down, calm down."'

Eventually the situation did calm down, said Brennan, with Redgrave apologising and then giving more details about the money-laundering cover story. Brennan would say he had been approached by some Americans who wanted him to launder money in the UK, and Redgrave would say he had authority for Brennan to act as a participating informant. After agreeing to the scam, Brennan said Redgrave asked him for £10,000, which Brennan got for him from Charman's car.

Brennan told Gaspar he had agreed to pay the pair a total of £50,000. With two amounts of £10,000 already handed over, he claimed the final payment of £30,000 was made a few days later in south-east London. Redgrave warned him that provided he stayed within Scotland Yard's informant-handling guidelines, telling the officers what he was doing, they could cover anything he wanted. Brennan told them the £30,000 was in his car. Charman went to get it. 'I said, "It's in there,"' said Brennan. 'And it was in a green Marks and Spencer bag, and he opened it up and he went "Lovely". "All right," he said, "I'll be in touch with yer." And that's how I parted with the thirty grand . . . So they've had £50,000 in total out of the money. So they was done. They'd been paid for their work to cover the job . . . everything was being covered as long as I stayed in with them guidelines, which I intended to do. I couldn't foresee a problem and nor could they.'

DI Redgrave had told Brennan that he had contacted the FBI, who said it was believed the Texans were into gunrunning and other crimes, including money laundering. Brennan's earlier information to DC Charman about British criminals involved in importing drugs was being acted on in an investigation code-named Operation Nightshade, and Redgrave now expanded this to include the Texans. With permission, Redgrave activated a special Scotland Yard account in the name of a fake company, Switch On Enterprises. This account had been set up in 1989 with the then Midland Bank for use in covert police operations. Whoever decided on its name must have been enjoying themselves. SO, the first two initial letters, stand for the Scotland Yard unit running the account, Specialist Operations. When the third letter, E, is added, it represents a throwback to the wartime Special Operations Executive. A fake contract was faxed to the US confirming that Switch On Enterprises were Motorola distributors and registered in the British Virgin Islands. The contract referred to SOE supplying six thousand of the special mobiles, and appeared to be aimed at calming any concerns Sam Wang may have had about the deal.

Brennan summed up the position at that stage for Gaspar:

> It was a case that we were going to earn a lot of money. At that time the Americans were talking about a further million or a million and a half. They were talking colossal amounts of money, and it was looking like money laundering. This is why the Switch On account was set up . . . It wasn't that we're going to relieve them of 470 odd grand [the cost of the mobile phone deal] and that's where it's going to stop. It was going to go on and on, and the payments were just going to go on and on . . . You must understand that I was doing it with the support of these two officers. I couldn't do nothing wrong . . . It was their aim to have what we've had, and to cover for me for what I was having, or

my part of it ... We definitely believed that the FBI had proved that these were crooks and this money was a money-laundering operation from America to turn bad money into good ... It was a total utter scam from start to finish.

Gaspar pointed out to Brennan that there would inevitably have come a time when Wang would have realised he had been defrauded. Brennan replied: 'It was a case of how long you could play it out for ... The fanny would go on till eventually Wang would go to Hong Kong and wait for the shipment to arrive and it was never going to fucking arrive. It was as simple as that.'

Once the £400,000 had arrived, Brennan took precautionary steps to avoid being found by the Chinese-American businessman. He quit his mobile-phone shop and moved house, turning up at his solicitor's with a suitcase containing £137,000 in cash to buy a new home. His plans seemed to be working. Wang did go to Hong Kong, but when the phones did not arrive he became increasingly concerned and flew to England to find out what had happened. Eventually, in October 1993, unable to trace Brennan, he reported what had happened to Kent police, in whose county Brennan's mobile-phone shop had been located.

Brennan told Gaspar that he expected help from Redgrave and Charman if he was ever questioned or arrested over the theft of Wang's money:

I done everything what they told me to do. They knew what the game was and what the plan was. You know, you can't relieve someone of four hundred odd thousand pounds and just walk away from it. I knew there was going to be problems and John [Redgrave] always said to me, 'Don't worry about it.' I said, 'Look, John, what happens when the curtain does come down? What's going to happen?' He said, 'Don't worry about it ... if the time comes that you are nicked or pulled in, or it's put to yer, just mention my name. I will get this docket [police file] and I will sit down with these people. If I've got to sit down with the CPS, don't worry. You've done everything by the guidelines. You've not got to worry about this.'

Brennan said he had continued to assist Redgrave in the police money-laundering investigation but he was arrested in November 1993. He told

Gaspar that he had asked for Redgrave, but he had been locked up overnight. 'I'm in the fucking shit here . . . I quite expected the door to open up and just be told, "OK, fair enough, you go." It never worked like that. It just turned into an absolute fucking nightmare.'

To what extent Brennan knew of the efforts Redgrave had made behind the scenes when talking to Gaspar is unclear. In fact, police records show that, when arrested, Brennan had asked for help from DS Chris Smith, his original handler and the officer who later introduced him to Gaspar. The records go on to reveal that the arresting Kent officers were later told by Redgrave that Brennan was an informant and that their enquiries were putting him and others at risk. Despite this intervention, the Kent police investigation into the alleged mobile fraud continued, however, and a report was sent to the CPS. Still working on the money-laundering investigation, Redgrave again stepped in, telling a CPS official of Brennan's informant status and of a bank account established by the police. The move appeared to have halted the CPS action, but a high-ranking SERCS officer, suspicious about events, instituted another investigation by a police financial specialist. This was still continuing when Gaspar first met Brennan in June 1994.

Brennan's story confronted the detective chief superintendent with a number of serious problems. After their initial meeting, he had two main aims. The first, shielding Brennan from harm, had been achieved by moving him to a safe house and giving him protection. The second was to pursue what the ghost squad had been set up for – namely to gather as much intelligence as possible about police corruption. Although Gaspar believed him, what Brennan had said amounted to no more than simple allegations of police wrong-doing. Such allegations had no chance of standing up in court without corroboration, even if Brennan agreed to appear as a witness, and he was refusing to do that. It would simply be Brennan's word, that of a criminal, against the word of two honest detectives with distinguished records. Another major problem stemmed from Brennan's admission that he had committed a serious theft, of £400,000. Gaspar should have cautioned him, warning him that anything he said could be used against him in court proceedings. But the officer believed that, if he had done so, Brennan would have stopped talking. There would have been no further disclosures about alleged police corruption, and Gaspar would have lost a valuable source of information.

He decided to continue his meetings with Brennan, hoping to get some solid evidence from him. Over the following months, there were up to twenty such meetings or phone conversations between the pair. Gaspar helped Brennan move from his police-supplied home to another. His then handler, Sergeant Chris Smith, was also asked to liaise with him. As for Brennan's theft of the £400,000, Gaspar knew it was under investigation by SERCS and decided to let this investigation take its course. The 'nightmare' described by Brennan was to become much worse, and Gaspar's fears that his dealings with the criminal informant would end in tears were to be more than justified seven years later. He was called to account during Brennan's eventual trial at the Old Bailey, admitting from the witness box that he had made various mistakes in his handling of the affair.

For their part, Redgrave and Charman strenuously denied all allegations of wrongdoing, and Brennan himself was to withdraw his claims against the two officers, as detailed in Chapters 12 and 15.

Meanwhile Gaspar did enjoy success thanks to an unexpected spin-off from the main investigation. He had taken two further steps to gather more information about Redgrave. A full investigation was launched into the detective inspector's financial affairs to determine whether there were any large, unexplained movements of money into his bank and building society accounts. This was to take time. But Gaspar had also instructed the ghost squad to monitor Redgrave's police telephone calls. By that stage, the DI had been moved from SERCS to a central London police station, Belgravia. A bug was planted in his office there and phone conversations were recorded. But other officers used the same office and the ghost squad also picked up their conversations, some of which were very interesting. Among the other voices picked up was that of another officer who had been in CIB2's sights.

Detective Sergeant Tom Bradley had been transferred to Belgravia after being caught up in the CIB investigation following the 1993 *Panorama* exposure of the corrupt SERCS detective constable John Donald. Bradley had been one of Donald's contacts in NCIS, the National Criminal Intelligence Service, which co-ordinates police, Customs and security service action against major criminals. He was suspended on suspicion of corruption, then reinstated and transferred from NCIS. But at Belgravia he and other officers started moonlighting, providing security and other services for Reg Grundy, the originator of the TV programme *Neighbours*. The idea had stemmed from Bradley having been called to Grundy's home following a burglary there.

Conversations about organising the moonlighting were picked up by chance through the ghost squad's monitoring. This meant changing the paperwork authorising the bug so that it included Bradley's name. The ghost squad alerted Roger Gaspar to what had been heard, and CIB then mounted a separate covert operation, managing to take photos of the corrupt officers on their protection duties. On one occasion the anti-corruption men dressed as joggers to observe the Grundy bodyguards in a central London park. When confronted with the evidence and suspended, Bradley and four others all went sick, some claiming that they were so unwell they could not appear before a police disciplinary panel. Under the rules then in force this meant that their disciplinary hearings could not take place. Bradley remained suspended, claiming illness the whole time. Eventually, Scotland Yard gave up and allowed him to retire on grounds of ill health. His 'illness' did not prevent him and another of those suspended from starting up their own security company.

The Bradley case caused great embarrassment to the Metropolitan Police, which was to claim that it was so bound by regulations that it had been unable to sack him and the others. Sir Paul Condon gave the Commons Home Affairs Committee details of what had happened and this led to the Home Office changing police disciplinary procedures, making dismissal easier. But this did not stop some others manipulating sickness rules and obtaining psychiatric reports saying they were too ill to stand trial or attend disciplinary boards.

four

THE GREAT FLYING SQUAD ROBBERY

*'Could arrangements be made with the Governor of HM
Prison, The Mount, to facilitate the release of Freeman ... in
order to assist the Flying Squad in the investigation of serious
crime ... Police will assume responsibility for conveying him
to and from The Mount.'*

A Flying Squad Detective writing to the Home Office

Geoffrey Brennan's allegations were serious and were to have important,
far-reaching implications, but they were minor compared to Detective
Chief Superintendent Gaspar's next major case. This began when landing on his desk came a tape recording made in prison by a violent armed
robber. It told an amazing story. Gaspar was staggered to hear the
prisoner describe how senior Metropolitan Police officers had managed
to get him out of jail to take part in a daring £1.5 million robbery on a
security van, and had then stolen about £250,000 of the proceeds. The
enquiries set in motion by Gaspar were to lead eventually to more than a
hundred officers with the élite Flying Squad coming under investigation.
This was to be Scotland Yard's most important and serious investigation
into bent cops. With all its intrigue, multi-layered deceit and strange
twists and turns, it is in a sense the story of the anti-corruption squad.

The security van robbery was itself spectacular, even though when it
occurred, on 20 January 1995, no one suspected the involvement of
Flying Squad detectives. Driving the van was Greg Hepburn, who just a
few weeks before had been attacked by robbers. However, that raid was
thwarted by police who were in the area by chance. Hepburn had worked
for the security company for only a few months and was consistently late
for work. On 20 January, however, he was on time. In the guard's seat in
the cab was a trusted employee, Mark Godfrey, who had been based for
two years at the company's depot, in a street off the Old Kent Road in
south-east London. On his way to work at 7.45 that morning, Godfrey
had noticed a man wearing a yellow fluorescent jacket sitting astride a

51

large, powerful motorbike outside the depot. He did not think anything more of it until later.

Godfrey got into the van and saw that Hepburn, in the driver's seat, seemed very quiet. He asked him if he was OK, and Hepburn replied that he was not feeling very well. Nevertheless, they moved off, driving the short distance to the Barclays Bank depot in Great Suffolk Street. Their van joined a queue of similar armoured security vehicles waiting to pick up cash to deliver to various premises in London. After half an hour, the loading of the bags of money started. There were sixty-seven bags containing £1.5 million in cash, mostly £20 notes. Godfrey sorted through them and then put them through a chute while Hepburn collected them inside the van. The driver waited until all the money was on board before telling his colleague what was worrying him. The bags should have been put into lockers and sealed, but when Godfrey climbed into the back of the van he saw them simply lying on the floor. He demanded of Hepburn, 'What's going on?' Shaking, and looking shocked, Hepburn replied: 'They've got my mum! They've got my mum!' He then blurted out that robbers were holding his mother hostage until they had robbed the security van of its cargo of money. He showed his colleague a photograph of his house and said he had been given it by the robbers as proof that they had his mother. Godfrey tried to calm him and said he would call the police, but Hepburn refused to allow him to do so, and, pulling up his jumper, said he had been wired with an explosive device. Taped to his chest was a box with wires and batteries attached. It looked like a bomb, and there was what appeared to be a microphone. The robbers could hear their conversation, said Hepburn, and had told him, 'One flick of a switch and you die.' If the alarm was raised he would be blown up and his mother harmed. Godfrey repeated that it would be best to get some help, but Hepburn was having none of it. To his partner, he looked terrified.

Hepburn got into the driver's seat with Godfrey beside him in the passenger seat. The security shutters at the Barclays depot went up, and the two men prepared to drive off. But Godfrey spotted another colleague, Chris Green, and beckoned him across. Believing the robbers were able to hear conversations through the microphone, and not wanting to alert them, Godfrey hit on an alternative idea. He scrawled on the back of a receipt book, 'Greg's mum is a hostage,' and held it up against the window, hoping that Green would raise the alarm. Green saw the message, realised what was happening, ran back to his van and tried to contact the security company's base by radio. But he could not get through, so he ran inside the Barclays building, shouting to a startled bank employee, 'Phone base – Greg's mum's been taken hostage.' The company was contacted. But it was too late to stop the robbery. The van had already left the bank premises.

Hepburn drove along Great Suffolk Street and a motorbike pulled up in front of the van. 'That's the bike I saw earlier,' exclaimed Godfrey, and Hepburn said: 'They are going to meet us here. I have just got to go on.' The van then followed the motorbike into the Old Kent Road. Godfrey looked at other photographs given to Hepburn. He was sickened to see that there were two pictures of his own home, and on one of them was a sticker with the names of his parents, Dennis and June, printed on it. He worried that they too were in danger. After a few minutes' driving along side streets, the van ended up in Pages Walk, on an industrial estate. A white Transit van with blacked-out windows then appeared, and the driver, wearing an asbestos mask and clear goggles, directed them inside a disused warehouse, the robbers' 'slaughter', the place where the van would be stripped of its contents. Godfrey started to climb out of the vehicle, but Hepburn said, 'No, don't get out! The man said don't get out.' One of the robbers outside then started banging on the side of the van and shouted, 'Come on. Come on. Let's have the bags.' Godfrey and Hepburn pushed the cash bags out of the van through the chute. The crash-helmeted figure instructed the two guards to 'wait five minutes. I don't want to hear you talking or using the radio.' After waiting several minutes, the two men raised the alarm.

The first police on the scene were three uniformed officers in a marked police car. PC Kevin Platt told later how the two security men were obviously in shock. 'We've been robbed!' said Hepburn. 'They threatened me with a gun outside my house and strapped this to me'. He lifted up the back of his shirt and Platt saw a plastic box strapped to the small of his back. There were wires running from it up his back and over his left shoulder. It looked like a bomb, and Platt called over his radio for specialist squads, and then cordoned off the area. An Anti-terrorist Branch officer then arrived and examined the device. Although it looked very realistic, designed to suggest it could be detonated from a distance by remote control, the officer concluded that it was harmless – a dummy bomb apparently aimed at frightening Hepburn into following the robbers' instructions.

Later that day, Hepburn gave a convincing and dramatic account to police of how he had been waylaid by the robbers while walking to work. He said he had passed a man wearing a hooded jacket, with the zip pulled up to his nose so that the lower part of his face was obscured. 'Having walked past the man, I then heard footsteps behind me,' said Hepburn. 'I heard them run right up behind me and I turned round. As I turned round, he grabbed my left arm, gripping me tight. He then thrust a gun into my left side. He said: "Don't make any noise, I've got your mum. Just do as I say."' Hepburn described being forced to lie down inside a van while the robber taped what he called a listening device to his chest. 'He then told me to roll over. I rolled half over and he screamed at me to roll right over. He continued to scream and then said: "I'm going to put this bomb on you so that not only will your mum get it, I'll blow your spine out." He told me it had a radius of one mile. He then strapped something round my waist. He taped wires and things to me. He pulled down my boxer shorts to do it.' Later, while being driven to the depot, Hepburn said he was told by one of the robbers to tell his co-driver on the security van 'not to be a hero'. He himself was reminded: 'Just remember, I've got your mum, and if you don't co-operate we'll write a letter to your family saying it's your fault that your mother is dead. You killed her.'

Hepburn's account was a lie – a charade to cover his own involvement in the robbery. He had not been threatened at all, but had co-operated with the robbers from the outset. There was, however, a far greater deception, and much of it was laid bare in the tape recording received by DCS Gaspar. The tape had been recorded in a prison cell two days after the robbery by a professional criminal, a devious and violent man. For legal reasons, his name has been changed (as have others). He will be called Bobby Freeman in this book. Freeman revealed that he had been the man on the motorbike, having been allowed out of prison by police to take part in the robbery. And he disclosed that Greg Hepburn, far from being an innocent victim, had been a willing participant. He was the 'inside man' at the security company. I have obtained a transcript of the tape recording and it suggests a level of police corruption, intrigue, mendacity, double-dealing and cover-up which is seriously disturbing, if not frightening.

Freeman explains on tape how he had been let out of prison temporarily by two detectives. He then describes the robbery in detail and alleges that some of his share of the proceeds was stolen and that officers took Hepburn's share, £200,000.

The detectives who had arranged for Freeman's release from prison the day before the robbery had obtained high-level Scotland Yard approval for their plan. The idea was that he would take part in a security van robbery as a 'participating informant' in order that Flying Squad detectives could catch red handed two major robbers they had been after for some time. Under strict police rules, anyone acting as a participating informant has to play only a minor role in a crime, taking no part in the planning, for example. Allowing someone out of prison to take part in such a big robbery appears to have been unprecedented. Certainly, several senior detectives all told me they had never heard of such a thing ever happening before or since. The plan was suspect from the start, ripe with potential disaster. What if someone was killed during the robbery? What if Freeman decided to do a runner, and take off with his share of the proceeds, disappearing back to his native West Indies? Even a cursory look at his background makes him a very unlikely choice for the role of participating informant. The question of why so much trust was invested in such a lying, violent man remains to this day a mystery.

Bobby Freeman had been a professional criminal from an early age, with convictions for dishonesty, assault, kidnap, possession of firearms and armed robbery. His first major crime involved kidnapping a woman with a loaded pump-action shotgun, for which he was sentenced to six years' imprisonment in 1985. Released three years later, he embarked on a series of robberies, including raids on security vans and a jeweller's. Incredibly, during this time he managed to get a job with a big security company, which appears not to have checked whether he had any previous convictions. In April 1989 he took part in a £700,000 robbery on a Group 4 security van. In addition to his share, he stole £30,000 of the £100,000 set aside for the inside man at the company. Although he was later to claim that he spent £20,000 bribing detectives to lose evidence against him, he was charged with the robbery. While on remand and in custody, he tried to bribe two other police officers who were looking after him at a preliminary court appearance. In the court's lavatories he offered to pay the officers several thousand pounds if they simply turned their backs and allowed him to escape through a window. The officers refused and the incident was reported, the fact that Freeman 'was not to be trusted' in any dealings with the police being noted. Eventually, for conspiracy to rob, Freeman was given a fifteen-year sentence in 1991, reduced on appeal to twelve.

The investigation was code-named Operation Earl, and the officer in charge was from the Flying Squad, the élite group tackling many of the country's major robbers, the 'pavement men' who attacked security personnel delivering or collecting cash from banks and other business premises. Some of the officers in this group were also corrupt. But they were able to operate, despite complaints from a number of criminals that police had 'fitted them up'. These claims ranged from the planting of guns or other weapons to 'verbals', incriminating admissions which detectives swore had been made to them by the villains. Sometimes there were claims that money had been stolen, but these were more rare, the criminals realising that they were doomed to failure, as were most of their allegations. Who would believe their word against that of honest, upright police officers?

Most Flying Squad officers are big, heavy, tough-looking men, but Freeman's detective did not fit that picture. Of only average height, and a neat dresser, he was quietly spoken and and was well educated. Operation Earl took him to St Lucia in the West Indies, where he found £20,000 that Freeman had secreted in a bank. A certain amount of mutual respect was established between the two men, who were both very good at the their jobs. Also thirty-one years old, Freeman was a big man, combining physical strength with an intelligence that was much more than simple criminal cunning. Many were surprised when he offered shortly after his conviction to become an informant, but the vastly experienced Detective Chief Inspector Albert Patrick decided to put him on the informants' register with the pseudonym Marshall Cook.

From prison, Freeman provided a stream of information about armed robbers and drugs dealing. He was allowed to use a prison office to leave phone messages for his Flying Squad handler, an inspector, who then called him back, and sometimes visited him. Information about robberies was passed to the Flying Squad, and anything he said about drugs went to the area crime squad. A second officer, a detective constable, became his co-handler. To what extent Freeman was a reliable informant has not been officially disclosed, but some of his information must have been good, because he was receiving regular payments from police funds. He also clearly believed that he could manipulate his role to his own advantage.

In January 1994, Freeman was transferred to The Mount prison, near Hemel Hempstead. This was closer to his wife and three children, who lived in Luton, Bedfordshire. The visits from his handlers continued. They made it clear that they wanted information on the activities of two major robbers, both known to Freeman. For legal reasons they will have to be referred to in this book as Don Willis and Ray Smith. The police arranged for Freeman to be allowed out of prison, so he could visit Willis, who was then nearing the end of a sentence at Maidstone prison. With a girlfriend called Lorraine Francis posing as Mrs Willis, and Freeman using the name Byron Marshall, the visit went well for the robber prisoner. He told Willis that he had a friend who knew a security company driver who 'wanted his van robbed'. Sums in excess of £1 million were regularly carried, and Willis expressed interest. Later on, Freeman's contacts with police and criminals became easier as he was being released from prison during the day to do community work at the nearby Woodfield special needs school. He was looking forward, with police support, to release on full parole in mid-1995.

He did not tell his handlers of the proposed robbery. 'I wanted the job to come off,' he said later, 'so I could make some serious money.' Instead, he told the two officers that Willis and Smith planned to rob a post office van. In November, his inspector handler went with the information and a plan to another detective chief inspector, the officer's new line manager. Suspicious, the DCI queried why Freeman was keen to help the police, and was told that he was due for parole and wanted police assistance. Satisfied with the explanation, the DCI then started to set the plan in motion. The operation was code-named Achillea. High-level Scotland Yard authority was sought and obtained for Freeman's participation in what police thought was to be a post office van robbery.

Meanwhile, however, the devious Freeman was also touting the security van robbery to other criminals, with a friend, who will be called James Moore in this book, acting as intermediary. Moore told a notorious gang of ruthless south London robbers that Greg Hepburn was willing to have his van robbed. So, at the end of 1994, Freeman was in a very unusual position. He was in prison and managing to fool the police. And he also had two separate criminal teams interested in carrying out a robbery on the same vehicle.

The south London robbers struck first, with Freeman expecting to get a substantial share of the proceeds as the person who had given the tip-off about the money being up for grabs. On 16 December 1994, they attacked Greg Hepburn's van in a busy street. But they failed. Police, on their way to an emergency call elsewhere, stumbled across the raid by chance and caught one of the gang, Dean Henry. He was later given a seven-year prison sentence. Although Henry kept quiet about the roles of Freeman, Moore and Hepburn, Freeman was worried that his plans were coming adrift.

Understandably, the other robbers, Willis and Smith, were angry that someone else had hit what they considered to be their van. Freeman pleaded ignorance, hoping to allay any suspicions they may have had about his role in the unsuccessful robbery. There was also the fear that following the robbery Hepburn could be suspended from the security company, and if that happened no further robbery could take place at all. Freeman had to move fast. He already had 'participating informant' status for the post office van robbery, which he had told police was to take place on 27 January 1995. But the new situation required a change of plans, so he told police that Willis and Smith planned a 'dry run', a rehearsal, the week before, on 20 January. His senior handler discussed the options with his detective chief inspector. They could have mounted a full surveillance operation on the robber pair, but that would have been expensive in terms of manpower and overtime payments, and it was also known that the pair were paranoid about police activity and were very surveillance conscious. Rather than blow this new operation, the two detectives decided that the best way of dealing with the situation was to get Freeman to take part in the dry run, so he could establish as far as possible what was to happen during the real robbery the following week. It was important for the police to know such things as which vehicles were to be involved, their routes and their destinations. This would allow a Flying Squad team to lie in wait and ambush the criminals when the real robbery took place. There was also another important factor behind their thinking. They trusted Bobby Freeman. They believed his story.

Freeman was expected to deliver up Willis and Smith. He was going to sacrifice them to the police, but he was also going to take a large share of the robbery proceeds himself, and make a further betrayal. Not only was the dry run to be the real thing, but Freeman was breaking all the police rules governing the use of participating informants. Far from playing a minor role, he was planning the robbery himself, and he knew guns were to be used. Cleverly, he had thought through every eventuality, aiming to stay one step ahead of the police. He reckoned, rightly, that if anything went wrong, the police would be so embarrassed about the latitude they had allowed him that they would try to cover the whole thing up.

At this stage the police had few doubts about the operation. Confirmation of some of what Freeman had told them came from what had been gleaned from tapping telephones used by Willis and Smith. It was clear from these 'intercepts' that the pair planned to meet up on 20 January, but exactly what they planned was not discussed. However, a big mistake was made by police early on the morning of the 20th. In 1995, the teams of people under NCIS, the National Criminal Intelligence Service, who listened into phone calls did not operate twenty-four hours a day. Their shifts ended at 11 pm, and they did not start the following day until 7 am. The authorities' view was that even major criminals had to sleep some time, and experience showed that little was picked up in the small hours needing immediate police action. Instead, any phone conversations were recorded on tape and were played back later in the morning. That policy was to change dramatically after what happened on 20 January. Round-the-clock coverage was introduced by the embarrassed authorities. If anyone had been listening to the pair at 4 am that morning they would have heard a conversation making it clear that what was planned that day was far from being just a dry run. Their mistake was not discovered until it was too late.

Freeman had been collected from prison by police at midday on Thursday, 19 January. The order for his temporary release now makes sad reading. It was written by the DCI on the 18th and sent to a police officer based in the Home Office. 'Could arrangements be made with Mr Webb, the Governor of HM Prison, The Mount, to facilitate the release of Freeman on Thursday 19th January am and returned pm on 20th January. Police will assume responsibility for conveying him to and from The Mount.' The note goes on to ask for Freeman to be released again a week later, when police had been told the real robbery was to take place. 'I would also ask that Freeman be released under the same conditions from Thursday 26th of January until Friday 27th January, in order to assist the Flying Squad in the investigation of serious crime.'

Freeman's two detective handlers picked him up and took him to

London, dropping him off so he could meet his co-robbers. He then went to the south London home of girlfriend Lorraine Francis, from where the two officers collected him that evening. He was keeping up the pretence of a dry run for the post office van robbery, and showed them the Eastern District HQ of the Post Office, where he said the van was based. He was then returned to Lorraine Francis's home, where he spent the night. The sequence of events that followed is taken largely from Freeman's own story to anti-corruption detectives and from the accounts of various police officers.

Freeman said he met Willis and Smith at 6.30 am outside an Underground station, and the trio drove in a white Transit van to pick up, as arranged, the guard Hepburn. The four men then went together to the 'slaughter', the warehouse in Pages Walk. The dummy bomb was then taped to Hepburn, the plan being for the guard to pretend that he had been picked up from his home and forced to carry out the robbery, claiming that his mother had been kidnapped. Freeman put on a motor-cycle suit and, riding a Yamaha 900, followed the van, which dropped Hepburn off a few streets away from the security company base.

Freeman then described how, after Hepburn's van had left the Barclays depot loaded with £1.5 million, he had cut in front of it on his motorbike, with the white Transit van containing Willis and Smith falling in behind the security vehicle. They drove in convoy to the 'slaughter', where, after loading the cash into the Transit, they headed for the 'divvy house', a flat on the Isle of Dogs. There the money was spread out on a carpet and divided up. After 'expenses' had been taken out, Freeman said he, Willis and Smith got £400,000 each, with £200,000 set aside for Hepburn. Willis was to give this money to the intermediary, James Moore, who had helped set up the robbery. Carrying his £400,000 in a black sports bag, Freeman then took a minicab to the home of another of his girlfriends, who lived in Leyton in east London. He hid £40,000 at the back of a wardrobe. Then, instead of going to his home in Luton, he went to his mother's, close to Latimer Road Underground station in west London, and hid the sports bag in a lock-up shed. By then, it was just after 1 pm. Freeman had decided to try to continue the pretence that he had been a genuine informant and had not known beforehand that the real robbery was to take place. From a phone box, using an agreed code-name, 'Selector', he paged his inspector handler: 'Believe double whammy. Am making my way back to Luton. Please contact me there ASAP. Selector.' From Luton he sent another pager message just before 3 pm: 'I am at home awaiting your call. Please call me ASAP. Selector.'

His handler and a team of Flying Squad officers arrived shortly afterwards. That morning, the officer had been on his way with his co-handler to pick up Freeman in London, to return him to prison after the supposed dry run. As the pair drove south, news of what police termed 'a tiger-kidnap robbery' started to come through on their radio. Information from Scotland Yard was being rebroadcast to Flying Squad offices and cars on Channel 7. Fearing the worst, that Freeman had double-crossed them, the DI then started a series of frantic phone calls. He tried to establish more details concerning the robbery and to contact Freeman at Lorraine Francis's. She answered the phone, but said the robber was not there, and she appeared evasive about his whereabouts. The DI later recalled his feelings at the time: 'I was in an emotional state and very angry. My whole heart and lungs were in my ankles. Everything we had worked on for years, my whole integrity was on the line. I was furious.' Then he received the first of Freeman's pager messages.

Meanwhile, the few people in the know at the Flying Squad office had put two and two together. 'Fucking stroll on!' exclaimed one senior officer. 'It's gone down!' They phoned their boss, the detective chief inspector in charge of the whole operation, who was on a day off, at home. He set off for the office, furious at what had happened and worried about what would emerge at the Scotland Yard inquest that would inevitably follow. At the office, he spoke on the phone to the DI, who was by then at Freeman's address in Luton. The DI explained that according to Freeman, Willis and Smith had only told him that morning that the dry run was off and that they were going to commit the actual robbery then and there. Freeman had added that he could not alert his handlers to the change of plan because he had been with the two robbers the whole time. The DI was instructed to recover Freeman's share. Interestingly, there appear to have been no real police moves that day against Freeman's co-robbers, although their identities were clearly known.

Freeman told the DI where he had put the money, so he and his Flying Squad colleagues set off with their prisoner for west London. Freeman did not disclose where the key to the shed was as he did not want it known that he had co-operated with the police to such an extent. The detectives were forced to try to break in. First, they used a wheel brace from the boot of one of their cars. Having failed with that, one officer was sent to the local police station to get a crowbar. But they failed with that too. Their antics had attracted the attention of neighbours, who were not too reassured by their protestations that they were police officers. As they pondered what to do, Freeman's brother appeared on the scene. Told to 'hand over the largee', the brother unlocked the shed door. The DI took the sports bag containing the money from the shed and put it into his car boot.

The police had been instructed to take the money and their prisoner to a north London police station. There the prisoner was booked in. By then it was Friday evening, and the station's custody officer was very worried about the security implications of having such a large amount of money on the premises, especially as it was uncounted. After he had voiced his concerns to the Flying Squad, the security company was called to collect its cash. Meanwhile, the atmosphere at the Flying Squad office was mixed after the initial shock of the robbery. As word spread of what had happened there were jokes and insulting remarks about the role played by Freeman's two handlers. 'The feeling was they'd been had over,' said one officer. 'Through them, we'd all been led a merry dance.' Some of the senior officers started to try to take control of what had been at the very least an almighty cock-up. But it was a difficult situation. One inspector who had not been involved in the operation said he tried to take 'the furthest back seat' during discussions about what had gone wrong and what they should do next. Another inspector was 'raving mad' on learning that no one manned the intercepts on Willis's and Smith's phones, or any other phones for that matter, for eight hours overnight. They had missed the 4 am call which would have made clear that the real robbery was about to take place. Although it is against the law to use intercept tapes during prosecutions in court cases, the information obtained from them can prove to be extremely useful during investigations. The Flying Squad officers claimed that if this particular 4 am conversation had been listened in to at the time, then the supposed dry run would have been monitored and the robbery prevented.

There were other major problems facing the senior officers that Friday evening, pulling them in different directions. They wanted to minimise embarrassment, and the best way of doing that was to keep as quiet as possible about their involvement. But they were also duty bound to pursue the robbers and recover the remaining estimated £1,200,000.

And they also had to protect their informant, Bobby Freeman, who was still sticking to his story that he had behaved honourably, maintaining that the robbery had been as much of a surprise to him as it had been to the Flying Squad. Protection of their grasses is of paramount importance to the police, who will sometimes drop a prosecution rather than risk revealing the source of key information. If the Flying Squad acted against Freeman's co-robbers too quickly, these violent men would realise who had 'grassed' them and take their vengeance. The officers could pretend that they did not know the identities of the other two robbers and hope to gather evidence against them over the next few days or weeks. But the pair were ruthless and clever, and it was thought they would leave little or no evidence to justify prosecution. If that turned out to be the case, the only evidence against them would be from Freeman, and it was very unlikely that he would ever stand up in court and publicly betray anyone. And what, anyway, should be done about Freeman? In arranging his release from prison, the Flying Squad had promised he would be back inside by early that Friday evening. Already the police had broken their agreement with the prison authorities, and the longer they kept him outside in their custody, the greater the danger he faced on his return, from fellow prisoners suspicious about his long unscheduled disappearance. In the longer term, if he were prosecuted on his own, he would be certain to maximise Flying Squad embarrassment.

Back at the Flying Squad office, Freeman's two handlers met the top brass. These officers were told of the circumstances of the robbery by the DI, who said he believed that Freeman had 'had them over'. The DCI said later that he had told the group that there was a straight choice to be made about Freeman. Either he could be charged or he would have to give evidence against his co-robbers. But the DI responded that, through fear, Freeman would never give evidence. The officer read through his 'incident report book', and the DCI agreed that it appeared to eliminate the option of charging Freeman with any offence. Later, the DCI had a further discussion with his three inspectors. At that stage, it looked as though the situation had been contained, and that there would be no further embarrassment. But loose ends needed to be tidied up. There would be an armed surveillance operation mounted the following day against Willis and Smith. Although it was thought little would be discovered that could be used against the pair, such an operation had to be undertaken, especially if the Flying Squad was to escape further criticism. The news was greeted with enthusiasm by the officers who would be taking part. Although it meant working on a Saturday, there were hours of lovely overtime to be earned. It was also decided that Freeman would be returned to prison without being charged.

On Saturday, 21 January, Freeman was returned to The Mount. Later he was to claim that he had been tricked into revealing the whereabouts of the £200,000 being held for the guard, and that it had been stolen – by police!

five

INVESTIGATING THE FLYING SQUAD

'Just a bit of friendly advice. Keep your nose out, then you have no problems.'

Unsigned message sent to the pager of a Hertfordshire detective

At first, Freeman was relieved to be back inside The Mount prison in Hertfordshire. The previous two days had been very trying, and, before them, there had been all the planning involved in the actual £1.5 million robbery of the security van. Acting as an informant, he had successfully deceived and manipulated his two police handlers into believing that the robbery was to be a week later. Although the police had seized the bulk of his share of the proceeds, he had still managed to squirrel away £40,000, which he would be able to retrieve later. But now with time on his hands to think, his worries began to grow.

It had not helped that, when he was checked back into the prison after being in police hands for more than forty-eight hours, he recognised another prisoner helping the 'screws' in the reception area. Would he face trouble from fellow prisoners, suspicious after his long absence that he was a grass? Then there were the police. He had made them look foolish. Would they get back at him somehow, maybe stopping his parole, or spreading word within the prison and outside that he was indeed an informer? Additionally, there were all the other criminals and their associates involved in the daring robbery. He knew that if his ruthless co-robbers learned of his betrayal they were capable of violence. How would Greg Hepburn, the inside man on the security van job, react if he learned that his share of the robbery, £200,000, had been retrieved after Freeman had revealed its location? There was also the south London gang that had tried to rob the same vehicle a few weeks before but had been caught in the act. He had offered the job to them. Would they now claim some of the proceeds of his successful robbery?

The day after arriving back at The Mount, Freeman decided to contact anti-corruption detectives at Scotland Yard's Complaints

Investigation Branch (CIB). He seconded as an intermediary a legal representative, Jeremy Newell. Using the built-in microphone on his ghetto-blaster, and an old music tape, he recorded an account of what had happened over the previous days. Much of it is a lying, self-serving version. For instance, he kept to his story that he had not known that the real robbery was to take place. But while minimising his own role in the crime, he attacked the police in the recording, and was clearly a worried man. 'I want this to be my assurance policy if anything should happen to me or my family or I again get arrested or charged with this robbery,' he said on the tape to Newell. 'I want CIB involved and I want this tape passed on to them.'

Jeremy Newell received the tape, listened to it, and then sent it on to CIB at Scotland Yard, where it eventually reached Detective Chief Superintendent Roger Gaspar. The head of CIB2 knew that he faced major problems in pursuing Freeman's allegations of very serious police corruption. First, and of prime importance, was the need to protect him as an informant – not only in terms of the robbery, but also because of what he was now telling CIB. That led on to a wider need for secrecy. However, there was a requirement under police disciplinary rules that the subject of any complaint should be informed that he or she was under investigation, by serving them with a Regulation 163 notice. The problem was that if the Flying Squad officers learned of Freeman's accusations of corruption they could not only take action against him but were very likely also to close ranks and frustrate any inquiry by losing or even destroying any potential evidence against themselves. The decision was taken that Freeman's allegations should not be made into an official complaint. It was thought that by dealing with them under the umbrella of an intelligence-gathering operation, there would be no need to inform any of the Flying Squad officers involved.

The strategy was put into effect immediately, and made retrospective, as became clear from the juggling and cleansing of paperwork early in 1995. Detective Sergeant John Gallagher had been 'early turn reserve officer' for CIB2 when Freeman's legal representative, Jeremy Newell, had telephoned. Gallagher summarised the long conversation in CIB2's records file as message no. 14, and later spoke to DCS Gaspar about what had been said. After talking to his boss, Gallagher removed the message from the file, substituting a short, anodyne replacement. He then sent the original longer message to Gaspar in an unregistered docket or file. This meant that the file would not circulate to others. No police officer apart from Gallagher and those on the secret squad knew of this early contact from Newell and Freeman.

For Gaspar, what was to present a much more difficult task than preserving the secrecy of the matter was the problem of checking out Freeman's allegations and then, if they appeared to stand up, gathering sufficient evidence to warrant charging and prosecuting the wrong-doers. The first step was to meet Freeman, listen to more of his story and establish some kind of rapport with him. What was to be called Operation Spy was under way, but it did not get off to an auspicious start. On 3 February, Gaspar's number two, Detective Superintendent David Bailey, and Detective Sergeant Judith Evans went to meet Freeman and Newell at Hemel Hempstead police station, near The Mount prison. Bailey went 'wired up', wearing under his clothing a small tape recorder, a Nagra 'body set'. The meeting itself went well, but the Nagra worked only intermittently. On numerous occasions, no discernible speech or other coherent sound was heard. Another conversation between Bailey and Freeman took place a few days later. This time it was on the telephone, and the officer recorded it successfully on a Gee-Marc machine.

There then followed a series of meetings, all taped. Rather than relying on Metropolitan Police technicians, the two CIB officers, Gaspar and Bailey, chose to use two technical support officers based at Hertfordshire police headquarters in Welwyn Garden City. Marc Warman and Andrew Cremins went to The Mount on the evening of 16 February. After liaising with one of the prison governors, they installed a Gee-Marc telephone recorder on extension 232. All they had been told was that it was for the use of a prisoner. On 3 March, Bailey was again wired up when he went with Gaspar to meet Freeman in Docklands at the City Airport, a favoured meeting place for the head of the secret squad. Later the same month, Warman went with Bailey to The Mount and fitted another Gee-Marc machine, this time on extension 333.

More extensive preparations were made to record an important meeting in April. At that stage the anti-corruption detectives were pursuing two Flying Squad officers, alleged by Freeman to have been among a group of officers who had stolen some of the robbery proceeds. CIB wanted to know what the pair would say to Freeman. The prisoner had got a message to the two officers to the effect that he wanted to see them to discuss a problem. They had agreed to visit him at The Mount at

10.30 am on the 4th. Two hours before the planned meeting, Superintendent Bailey and Cremins went to the prison and met Freeman. Rather than fit him with the body set recorder, which could be discovered if anyone patted him down thoroughly, it was decided to hide a covert radio microphone on his body. A receiver and tape machine were placed in the room below the meeting place. The two Flying Squad officers arrived at the prison and spent about fifteen minutes with Freeman. The recording went well, but the conversation between the three was inconclusive, not proving anything. Whether the two detectives were guarded in what they said because they were suspicious about Freeman's motives, or whether they had somehow been tipped off that they were under investigation, is not known.

Even more precautions were taken to record another meeting, this time outside the prison. Freeman was to go to an office for a discussion with some of those involved in stealing the robbery proceeds. It was known that these people would be very wary, suspecting that he would be carrying recording equipment or a transmitter. The secret squad believed the suspicions would be so strong that those looking for hidden machinery would do more than simply pat or rub him down. He faced being strip-searched, and if anything was found on him, not only would he himself be in great danger, but the whole secret investigation could be blown and come to an abrupt end. A clever solution was found. Freeman would pretend he had broken his arm and be wearing a plaster cast in which was embedded a tiny microphone and transmitter. If he was strip-searched, nothing would be found, and the ensuing conversation would be picked up in a covert vehicle parked near by, manned by anti-corruption officers. The first part of the plan worked well. Freeman was indeed strip-searched and nothing was discovered. But virtually nothing was recorded by the anti-corruption officers. Only fragments of speech were heard, and they were at such a low level that the conversation was unintelligible. Later, during an inquest into what had gone wrong, it was concluded that either the microphone or the transmitter had not been powerful enough to function properly under the plaster.

By the summer of 1995, the secret investigation into Bobby Freeman's allegations had made little progress. It was not so much the technical problems which were to blame, or that Freeman was not believed. The anti-corruption officers knew that he had glossed over the depth of his own involvement in the robbery, but they accepted his basic allegation that Flying Squad officers had stolen about £200,000 of the proceeds. The major problem facing the investigators at the beginning of their inquiry remained. How could they gather evidence against allegedly corrupt officers without the existence of the secret squad becoming known? Little had been obtained from the recordings of meetings and phone calls. The Flying Squad officers had closed ranks, and there was a growing suspicion that they knew they were under investigation. More positively, the CIB team had obtained some of the telephone records for the day of the robbery and that following. These provided some back-up for Freeman's account, but what would have helped immensely was sight of the records of phone calls to and from the Flying Squad office, and more importantly access to a record of the calls made by Freeman from the custody suite at the north London police station where he had been held. All these records were stored, but it was felt that if attempts were made to extract them, the Flying Squad detectives would soon know about them. The CIB officers' dilemma was to be unexpectedly resolved by Freeman.

A few weeks after the robbery, Freeman had been visited in prison by his friend James Moore, the intermediary who had helped set up the job and the previous robbery on Greg Hepburn's van by the south London gang. Moore told Freeman that the south Londoners were becoming heavy, threatening to harm him and Freeman if they did not hand over some of the money from the successful second robbery. Freeman's fear that his life was in danger became reality in the summer, prior to obtaining his much-desired release from prison on parole. While on home leave, he had a very lucky escape from death. His motorbike, parked in the garden, was covered by a tarpaulin which became stuck as Freeman tried to remove it. He went to the front of the machine and, bending down over the front wheel, was horrified at what he saw. There, wedged between the spokes of the wheel, was a lethal hand grenade. A length of wire was attached to the pin of the grenade. The other end was attached to the tarpaulin. Freeman's pulling at the tarpaulin had brought the pin about three-quarters of an inch out of its socket. If he had pulled only a little more, the grenade would have exploded. Bedfordshire Police were called and Bomb Squad officers confirmed that it was a live grenade. They made it safe.

Shortly after the grenade incident, there was another worrying scare. But this time it involved a warning to a police officer. The sequence of events started when another prisoner at The Mount, an informant, contacted his police handler, a Hertfordshire detective constable attached to SERCS at Harlow in Essex. The prisoner told him that another inmate, Bobby Freeman, had carried out a robbery in January which had been 'set up by the police'. Freeman was also claiming that he had another 'high-ranking' Flying Squad officer 'in his pocket'. The Hertfordshire detective told two senior officers of the allegations, one of them a Metropolitan Police officer working at Harlow. The Met officer was embarrassed as he was a good friend of one of the Flying Squad detectives involved in the affair. He advised the Hertfordshire officer to 'leave it alone'. One week later an unsigned message was sent to the pager of the Hertfordshire detective. It said: 'Just a bit of friendly advice. Keep your nose out, then you have no problems.'

Meanwhile, Freeman had reported the grenade episode to CIB, which then helped him to move to 'safe' accommodation elsewhere under their protected witness scheme. But he wanted to get away entirely, possibly to return to the West Indies. He had retrieved the £40,000 hidden in his girlfriend's wardrobe, but he wanted more. He asked CIB for money, but they refused to give him more financial help. Freeman saw a chance of obtaining more money when he read an advert. The security company was advertising a reward of £50,000 for the return of the cash still missing from the robbery, more than £1 million.

Using the name Rogers, Freeman contacted the company, which had been kept in the dark about the background to the robbery. The Flying Squad had returned more than £300,000 to the company, representing Freeman's share of the proceeds, but there was little contact after that. The company's national security manager, Mike O'Neill, himself an ex-detective chief superintendent, kept telephoning a Flying Squad detective chief inspector, trying to find out more about who had been involved in the robbery and how the investigation was progressing. The DCI did not tell him that a participating informant had been involved and would not even confirm that there had been an 'inside man' within the company. O'Neill, who had worked in the Flying Squad, had his own suspicions about the guard-driver, Greg Hepburn, especially as his van had been raided before. What puzzled the security chief was why Hepburn had waited until the money was on board the security van before telling his colleague, the guard, Mark Godfrey, that a raid was taking place. O'Neill had concluded that if Godfrey had been told before, the alarm could have been raised, and the robbery thwarted. O'Neill voiced his suspicions to the DCI, saying that if the police were going to do nothing he planned to employ a private detective to look into Hepburn's affairs. According to O'Neill, the DCI requested him not to do anything as it might jeopardise their continuing enquiries. The company was unable ever to prove anything against Hepburn. He had gone sick after the robbery and in the summer he was eventually sacked.

Months later, in November 1995, O'Neill received a series of phone calls from a man calling himself Rogers, wanting to give information about the robbery in return for the reward. 'Rogers' eventually arranged a meeting with O'Neill in the Kentucky Fried Chicken restaurant in the Old Kent Road, not far from the slaughter where the money had been grabbed from the security van. Rogers asked him not to say anything to the police for reasons he would understand when they met. But the security manager had already contacted the Flying Squad DCI because 'Rogers' clearly knew something about the robbery. He also had a West Indian accent, and one of the robbers had been described as being black. The DCI told O'Neill that he would arrange for a surveillance team to cover the meeting. Freeman went heavily disguised, according to O'Neill's gripping, cloak-and-dagger account of what happened inside the Kentucky Fried Chicken restaurant.

> I entered and immediately a man came in behind me and sat down with me. He was a West Indian, aged about thirty, wearing a blue bobble hat. He had dark glasses and, I think, a wig. He was well muffled up and was wearing a track-suit bottom, and he appeared to have injured his leg because he was walking with the aid of a stick. He asked me if I was Mr O'Neill and I replied, 'Yes.' He said he was Rogers and asked me if I had informed the police and I said that I hadn't. He asked me if the guy behind was with me and I said that he wasn't.

Apparently reassured, Freeman then recounted his role in the robbery. O'Neill listened with increasing amazement which was to turn to anger later when he realised how the police had concealed the truth from him. Freeman explained to him that after £200,000 had been set aside for Hepburn, the robbery proceeds had been split three ways. As a participating informant he had given his share of the money back to the police, apart from £40,000. O'Neill's account continues: 'Rogers went on to describe how the £200,000 being held for Hepburn had been taken by officers.' Freeman also told him of the grenade incident and claimed that a £10,000 'contract' had been taken out to kill him. 'He said he had been screwed by officers,' continued O'Neill. 'They were corrupt. He said the money was shared out among the police, and that was why he didn't want me to go to them.'

O'Neill was shocked by the allegations. The meeting lasted for about forty-five minutes, and afterwards O'Neill spoke to the DCI. 'I told him that Rogers was one of the robbery team,' he said. 'He was the man on the motorbike and he was making allegations about the money, but he had given no names. The DCI asked me to come to the office straight away and see him, but I said that would take time and I wanted to think about what had been said and I arranged to meet him at nine o'clock the next day. I did not keep this meeting but telephoned him to say I would be in touch. I have not spoken to him since.'

O'Neill's anger grew as he pondered what to do next. Freeman had told him that everything had been reported to CIB shortly after the robbery, and that he had been dealing with Detective Superintendent David Bailey. The robber offered to take O'Neill to CIB to meet Bailey, but the security man declined. Now, as he sat in his car near the restaurant, O'Neill realised that he should see Bailey by himself. Later the same day he went to the CIB offices at Tintagel House on the Thames Embankment and saw Bailey. The officer confirmed that the man known to O'Neill as Rogers had made allegations of police corruption and that he was investigating them. In an interview with me, O'Neill said that he had not been very impressed with Bailey, who had told him that he was due to retire shortly. He said that later that same day he received a telephone call from the head of the secret inquiry, Detective Chief Superintendent Roger Gaspar. He was asked whether he would be willing to wear a hidden tape recorder and go to a meeting with a Flying Squad officer. But O'Neill declined, reasoning that he was not telling the police anything that they did not already know. It also irked him that there had been a breakdown in the trust that he believed existed between senior security men and police officers. For nearly a year he had been told nothing, eventually learning something of the truth from the kind of person he despised – a violent robber.

Back at his office, O'Neill spoke to his company's chief executive, who was also shocked at the sequence of events. A letter was written to the Metropolitan Police Commissioner, Sir Paul Condon, demanding an explanation and a fresh investigation into what had happened to the robbery proceeds. By approaching the company seeking a reward, Freeman had brought the whole affair into the open and had inadvertently ended CIB's difficulties in trying to gather evidence secretly. What had until then been a covert inquiry was now to become an overt investigation. Sir Paul's deputy, Sir Brian Hayes, met the angry company representatives. What the company told him amounted to a substantial complaint against the Met, but there was also the threat of legal action over the missing money. The net result was that the Met was forced to open a new investigation, and it would have to be done officially, according to the rules. However, before changes were introduced, Freeman again pushed for action. He was still trying to obtain some of the reward money, but he also wanted to provide confirmation of his claims that police had stolen the driver's share of the robbery proceeds.

Without contacting CIB beforehand, Freeman turned up at its offices in Tintagel House with his friend James Moore in tow. Moore was to provide the anti-corruption officers with another missing piece of the jigsaw. He told Detective Superintendent Bailey and Sergeant Craig Denholm that he had been given the driver's share and had passed it on to another man for safe-keeping. Moore said the man had told him later that two men had arrived to take the cash. Detective Superintendent Bailey was surprised at what he had been told, but knew it was worthless as evidence without a formal interview under caution. Moore said he would only co-operate if he was given immunity from any kind of prosecution. Bailey refused and Moore then left the building, followed by Freeman.

Sir Brian Hayes appointed a no-nonsense Scot, Detective Superintendent Dave Niccol, to head the new inquiry. A stickler for detail and proper procedure, Niccol had worked on several major Scotland Yard inquiries before moving to CIB2 in 1995. He was the officer who had taken charge of the case against the five detectives involved in the 'moonlighting' episode, providing security for *Neighbours* creator Reg Grundy (see Chapter 3). Niccol reviewed what had been achieved by Gaspar and Bailey's intelligence-gathering operation. He decided that, as it was now an open inquiry, the officers allegedly involved in the robbery affair should be served with the Regulation 163 forms informing them that they were under investigation. The DI who had handled Freeman responded: 'I totally reject that I took any money.

The fact that this was a dry run was reported to SO8 [Flying Squad] management. I was not the operational head of this operation. I was just the informant handler who reported all information in accordance with force instructions.' Another officer responded: 'This is a totally malicious allegation made by a devious liar.'

It soon became clear to Detective Superintendent Niccol that CIB on its own simply did not have enough detectives to pursue the corruption allegations as well as investigate the other robbers and their associates. It was decided at a high level in Scotland Yard that he should have help from the very Flying Squad section under investigation. Although this decision to institute a form of joint investigation has since been described to me by a senior officer as 'farcical', at the time it did make a certain amount of sense, as some of the squad's officers had continued to investigate the robbery, looking particularly at Freeman's co-robbers, Willis and Smith. The information gathered would be used in the fresh inquiry, and the Flying Squad officers with their expertise, local knowledge and network of informants were ideally placed to pursue the villains, while CIB continued to investigate the alleged corruption.

By the end of the year, after the disciplinary notices had been served, the vast majority of Flying Squad officers were still untainted by the affair. Four were sent to CIB headquarters at Tintagel House. The idea was that the two teams would work separately, with Niccol liaising with the detective inspector he was told was to head the Flying Squad men. Senior Scotland Yard officers had vouched for his integrity. However, with hindsight, it turned out to be an unfortunate choice. He was himself later to face a very serious allegation of corruption.

However, by March 1996 enough had been learned to warrant raids on Freeman's co-robbers, Willis and Smith, and some of their relatives and friends. Most of the evidence gathered against them related to their financial dealings. Altogether, sixteen people were to be arrested. Reinforcements were needed to help make the arrests. Officers from the Yard's firearms unit were drafted in because it was known that some of the targets were violent and could be in possession of guns. On Tuesday, 23 April, more than fifty officers attended a 4 am briefing given by Superintendent Niccol on that day's raids. The most dramatic of these was at the home of the robber I have called 'Smith', in Loughton, Essex. Shortly after five o'clock, a ten-man firearms team took up position around the house. There were also back-up officers, an ambulance crew and two dog handlers, one of them with a dog called 'Justice'. The arrest operation started with PC Nigel Flint, wearing body armour and carrying a Glock pistol, trying to force the front door. As he did so, someone was seen moving at an upstairs window and one of the officers shouted, 'Armed police! Can you hear me? We are armed police.' From inside the house came the sounds of heavy footsteps accompanied by wild shouting and screaming. A naked Smith then hurled himself against the front door, trying to close it on the advancing police officers. PC Alkan Ali pushed his long shield against the door, to prevent it from shutting. Out of control, the violent robber continued shouting and screaming, trying to grab the gun Ali was carrying in his right hand. Using a baton, another officer, PC Philip Parker, hit one of Smith's arms and then his head. Still struggling, Parker struck him again, and then, with Flint's help, grappled him to the floor, where he was handcuffed. PC Ali then obtained clothing from Smith's wife and children and covered his naked body. There was blood on his forehead, and one of the ambulance crew gave him medical attention. Another officer then moved in and told the now subdued robber: 'You are under arrest for conspiracy to rob on 20 January 1995.' Later, at Ilford police station, he was arrested and cautioned for being in possession of a flare gun with two live rounds which had been found in a search of the house.

In east London, Willis's house was surrounded by another firearms team with a similar amount of back-up. At 5.05 am, two officers forced the front door and shouted 'Armed police' several times. Willis decided to go quietly. From the upstairs landing, he called out: 'I'm coming down'. On reaching the bottom of the stairs, he was flung over a settee and handcuffed. A gun was found in his house also, a black revolver with two rounds inside. Willis was taken outside where he was officially arrested.

Willis and Smith gave 'no comment' interviews to the police. But as well as the guns found at their addresses, a vast amount of other material was seized from them and the others raided. In a safe-deposit box, £40,000 in cash was found, divided into four bundles, each containing smaller bundles of £1,000. Other evidence tied Willis and Smith to the robbery. Mobile phones had been bought by their wives and accounts established with Mercury One-2-One. Print-outs were obtained of calls made on the morning of the robbery. No fewer than ten calls were made between the two mobiles in the space of three hours, starting at 6.39 am.

It all amounted, at the very least, to good circumstantial evidence against them, but there was much more. The robbery pair had also both bought new £20,000 Vauxhall Fronteras. One was ordered from a showroom only a few days after the robbery. Smith made cash deposits totalling £36,000 into five separate bank or building society accounts in the six months after the robbery. Over the same period his wife paid in nearly £20,000. Then there were property transactions, with Smith buying a house for £70,000. He paid cash, but the purchase was made in the name of a friend who then lived there. The friend had an extension built costing about £15,000, and Smith himself had plans drawn up and approved by his local council for a £30,000 extension to his own house.

It was all fairly damning evidence, as was pointed out in a letter to Scotland Yard from the security company's chief executive, Ian Whitmore.

> ... Several people have been arrested in connection with the robbery, and safe deposit boxes containing cash, newly purchased cars, a house and other property have been traced to their possession, and may reasonably be considered the proceeds of the robbery ... At this stage, pending the decision of the Crown Prosecution Service, we have to consider taking civil action to recover our losses. Will you please note our interest, and we wish to apply for restitution or compensation, whichever is appropriate in this case, and may in due course take civil action to recover these robbery proceeds. Will you please forward a copy of this letter to the Crown Prosecution Office dealing with this matter and advise us of any developments which may affect our interest.

This threat of separate civil action contributed to the eventual decision not to prosecute the robbery suspects. But there were also other more important factors. Incredibly, the report to the CPS was written by the Flying Squad detective inspector attached to CIB. It was largely negative, and one senior anti-corruption officer reviewing it a year later suggested that it had been prepared in such a way that it would receive exactly the response it received from the CPS – 'insufficient evidence' to proceed.

To be fair, there would have been problems in bringing to trial all sixteen of the robbers and those of their associates who had been arrested. Such a large number would have necessitated more than one trial, as not all the defendants could have been accommodated in one dock at the Old Bailey. Three trials, or even four, would have been required. These would all have taken time and would have been a drain on the public purse, because under the legal aid system each of the defendants would probably have had two barristers. And the chances of conviction were far from certain. Freeman would have been a devastating witness, but he claimed that he had been assured immediately after the robbery that he would not be charged, and would not have to give evidence because of his status as a participating informant. His absence from the proceedings would itself lead to questions about his role, and probably put his life in danger. Without him in the witness box because of the guarantees he had been given, the remaining evidence was largely circumstantial. Strong evidence had been obtained from tapping the robbers' phones, but it was against the law to use any of it in court as evidence.

A further major problem arose over 'disclosure', the process by which the Crown gives the defence any relevant information that could help their case. The feeling was that it would be difficult to pursue a prosecution without having to disclose Freeman's role as an informant. Then there was the additional problem of the investigation into the police officers. All the evidence gathered by CIB against the detectives would have to be disclosed, and this would inevitably be used by the defendants to muddy the waters, making not guilty verdicts more likely. In addition, the information likely to come out if a prosecution went ahead would not only be extremely embarrassing for Scotland Yard, it would also hamper what was said to be the continuing operation against those officers suspected of involvement in stealing some of the robbery proceeds. So, in the final analysis, it was decided not to proceed with any trials. It was also recognised that if the security company wanted to mount a civil case, suing the robbers for the return of the money, then the Met could benefit from any fresh evidence emerging in a civil court.

In April the following year, the threatened civil action was launched by the company's solicitors, Clyde and Co., who were frustrated by the lack of progress and the Crown Prosecution Service's decision not to prosecute any of the robbers. Although the company had been told of the allegations of police corruption surrounding the robbery, the 'statement of claim' was not against the Metropolitan Police but against

Bobby Freeman's two co-robbers. In a writ taken out against them, the pair are referred to in formal legalistic terminology as 'Defendants'. The plaintiff, the security company, claimed that their van was carrying a little more than £1.5 million when 'it was held up by the Defendants, who were armed, and subsequently all the said bags were stolen. Part of the stolen property, namely bank notes to the sum of £313,000, has since been recovered by the police. The Defendants have not returned the balance of the stolen property, namely the sum of £1,203,000, to the Plaintiff and wrongfully detain it from the Plaintiff.'

By 1997 it looked as though the Metropolitan Police had given up its investigation into Flying Squad corruption. Certainly, the CIB2 inquiry had largely fizzled out. The officer who had been in charge of it, Detective Superintendent Niccol, became involved in other inquiries. CIB2's 'failure' did not eventually matter. That April a new team of anti-corruption officers was being formed after an order from the Commissioner, Sir Paul Condon. These detectives were younger men, highly skilled at using a range of intelligence techniques and information. It was believed that they would be able to crack the Flying Squad robbery and all the other suspected corruption by using new tactics. They would become proactive and use sting operations. The hope was that when caught red handed and facing double-figure prison sentences, any bent cops would 'roll over', make full confessions and implicate others. The plan was to achieve dramatic and astonishing success later in the year.

six

PHASE TWO

'We recognise that a small number of officers either through bad behaviour or corruption can have a disproportionate impact on our reputation. We want them to be in constant fear of exposure.'

Sir Paul Condon, Metropolitan Police Commissioner (1996)

By the end of 1996, the secret ghost squad had been in existence for well over two years. As outlined in Chapter 2, it had taken time before its officers had been able to get down to their main task of trying to assess the extent of corruption, its nature and how to tackle it. Recruiting more than twenty officers for such sensitive work had taken far longer than expected. Many of them had to undergo special training in carrying out highly skilled surveillance work. Finding suitable premises for the unit away from police stations had been difficult, and there were continuing problems over their cover story – that they were working for a newly formed company in the communications business.

Other problems surfaced only when the squad was up and running, but centred on a simple question. How can you investigate when you don't exist? The ghost squad could not even carry out their own checks on the PNC, the Police National Computer. Instead, they had to channel such enquiries through Roger Gaspar or his number two at CIB. The need for secrecy meant that those carrying out physical surveillance, although well trained, were limited in what they could do. Normally Scotland Yard's surveillance officers, and those working undercover, could rely on a huge back-up operation to follow up their information, but this was not the case for ghost squad members, and it led to an inordinate amount of time being spent on researching relatively simple intelligence. Sometimes, follow-up checks were not made at all.

If, for instance, a suspect was followed into a bank where he carried out a transaction at the counter, the 'normal' surveillance officer could either make immediate enquiries with bank staff or arrange for it to be followed up later. But the ghost squad watcher could do neither. He did not exist, and the back-up machinery was virtually non-existent. Similar problems occurred at police stations. Ghost squad members could get inside a police building using their false police identities, pretending, for example, that they wanted to check with the station's collator of intelligence on a local criminal's associates. But how did they find out at which desk a suspect officer usually sat, so they could plant a bug there? How did they find out when the officer was next due on shift? Asking even simple questions could arouse suspicion and lead to a suspect finding out that he was under investigation.

Further problems arose over electronic surveillance. By law, police need the prior permission of the Home Secretary to intercept calls on telephones in private premises. Because the ghost squad wanted its operations kept secret, it rarely applied for permission to tap officers' home phones, preferring to monitor their calls in police stations, which did not require official outside authority. The ghost squad also had sophisticated technical equipment. They used very sensitive bugging equipment, favouring the 'probe', because this meant there was no need to gain physical entry to premises. Installing a probe involved silently drilling a tiny hole in a suspect's home, usually in a window frame or through the wall of an adjoining property, and the insertion of a microphone-transmitter so conversations in a room could be picked up and recorded near by. Where the difficulties for the ghost squad lay was in the huge amount of time needed to listen to and study all this recorded material. Police tapes of normal criminals' conversations would be sent to an outside agency for transcription, but the need for secrecy meant that this option was not available to the squad. Listening to and transcribing tapes was kept 'in house', and because both tasks were boring, very time consuming and often fruitless, they were approached in a disorganised manner, with some recordings remaining unplayed altogether.

Maintaining the unit's secrecy had taken precedence over all other work and there was a clear need for it. There was evidence that those the investigators termed the 'enemy', the corrupt officers, were trying to find out what was going on, so that they could stay one step ahead of any anti-corruption inquiry into their activities. The ghost squad's head, Detective Chief Superintendent Roger Gaspar, was playing two other roles. He was also in charge of CIB operations at Tintagel House, but as part of his cover story he had another secure office on the eighth floor of the building. From there, he was supposed to be in charge of a special unit carrying out a hush-hush inquiry into corruption in a provincial force, far away from London. This was a lie. There was no such inquiry. It had been invented, and word of it allowed to spread in order to provide cover for his secret work running the ghost squad.

Proof that the strategy was working came from listening to the telephone calls of one of the officers being targeted for corruption. He had been told of the 'provincial inquiry' that was taking up so much of the CIB chief's time, and he remarked: 'That's good to know. We've been trying to find out what's going on in that room.' He then went on to say something to the effect that if a provincial inquiry was all Gaspar was involved in, then he and other corrupt officers had nothing to worry about. In fact, the secret anti-corruption group trusted virtually no one, not even senior CIB officers at Tintagel House. Even they were fooled by the deception, because Gaspar heard he was being criticised by some of them for spending too much time away on the provincial investigation, neglecting his duties with the Metropolitan Police as head of CIB2.

Those working under Gaspar at the secret location in west London were all leading double lives, pretending to be employed by a commercial company while working for the ghost squad. This led, perhaps inevitably, to confusion and mix-ups. Gaspar had more than one identity. He used different names for different occasions and had separate credit cards and identification documents for them all. On occasions even he forgot who he was supposed to be, leading to embarrassing moments. Once, correctly using a credit card in his false name to pay for a hotel room, he signed the payment slip with his own name. Realising the mistake seconds later, he apologised and asked the hotel receptionist for the slip back. She said it did not matter, tore up the paperwork, threw it into a rubbish bin and made out a new form. Gaspar signed it with his false name, but he was worried that not retrieving the original slip, even though it had been torn up, could backfire in some way and expose his double identity. He again asked for the slip back, but once again the receptionist said it was unnecessary. Becoming irritated, he had to insist on it being returned to him before the woman eventually retrieved it, totally mystified by his performance.

Working for the ghost squad, away from former colleagues, led to other unforeseen problems. The strains involved in leading double lives away from colleagues and normal police work resulted in staff falling out with one another, and to arguments, with 'inappropriate' language being used. Luckily, the stresses caused were never serious enough to warrant major disciplinary action – a move to another mainstream police department or even dismissal. 'Imagine if we had had to sack someone from a unit so secret that it didn't exist,' Gaspar said to me.

Sorting out all these problems meant that much less had been achieved after two years than had been anticipated when the ghost squad had been formed. As head of CIB2, Gaspar had also been forced to spend a great deal of his time on two totally separate inquiries. One of these had been into leaks to newspapers of details of the police investigation into the mysterious death of the Conservative MP Stephen Milligan, found trussed up with ropes with an orange in his mouth. The second investigation was into allegations of a huge conspiracy involving corrupt police who were all freemasons. Gaspar and other senior officers, experts in corruption investigations, all play down the significance of any masonic influence, taking the view that the fact that some police officers are masons and get together at masonic functions does not mean that they are part of a large-scale corrupt conspiracy.

In terms of the ghost squad's performance, the intelligence-gathering side had gone fairly well, with further information obtained about corrupt detectives involved in all the areas originally targeted by the squad. These included Stoke Newington in north London, the south London bases of the South East Regional Crime Squad, and sections of the Flying Squad. But there had been difficulties in turning this intelligence into evidence strong enough to mount prosecutions or take disciplinary action. Part of the problem lay with CIB itself.

When Gaspar took over in 1994, he found a department in which most of the senior officers were nearing retirement, and unwilling to put themselves out or take risks. As an example of this tired attitude, he outlined a case where a prostitute had complained late one afternoon of having to pay protection money to an officer whose next visit was to be in the morning. The woman was happy to co-operate with CIB, agreeing to have her room bugged. The job was given to a senior CIB officer, who went home, declaring that it was too late to set up a surveillance operation. It was left to a more junior officer to try to sort something out. He managed to install recording equipment in time for the morning meeting and everything went smoothly. The corrupt sergeant arrived at the prostitute's premises and was recorded demanding £300 from her in protection money.

'With me looking after you, you're not going to get any hassle,' he said. 'The alternative is I can bust you, and you go down. Now, not only am I offering you protection, I'm also saying we ain't going to do you.'

Prostitute: 'So, well?

Sergeant: 'Three hundred. Not too steep.'

'Sorry?'

'Three hundred, not too steep?'

'No, that's not too steep at all.'

'Well, don't say that because I might raise it.'

'Don't do that, please.'

CIB officers monitoring the 'shake-down' conversation then burst into the room and told the startled officer: 'We're from CIB. You've been videoed. You are under arrest for corrupt practice.' Subsequently Sergeant Ian Vale was convicted and given an eight-year prison sentence for corruption and gross misconduct.

Other inquiries could have been handled better by CIB2, but there were limitations on what could be achieved with few staff, most of them inexperienced in proactive work and lacking up-to-date equipment. One early case Gaspar oversaw involved a Turkish woman who was a drug dealer and heroin addict, and had turned police informant. Given the pseudonym 'Gina Flowers', she made a series of complaints against one of her handlers, a SERCS detective sergeant. Her allegations ranged from him, along with other officers, stealing four kilograms of heroin to his sharing in her police reward money and pestering her for sex, which she claimed amounted to rape. A full-scale operation could have been mounted against the officer and his colleagues to prove corruption, but lacking the resources for this CIB chose to concentrate on the sex allegations. Evidence here would be easier to obtain because his demands for sex were continuing, and the woman agreed to co-operate with CIB2. A protected witness, Gina had been moved to a safe house in Essex, and this represented a problem for the anti-corruption officers. The plan was to put a bug in the woman's bedroom to record the conversation between her and the detective, while CIB officers waited outside the property, ready to move in and arrest him if he forced himself on the woman. The operation was potentially dangerous, as no one knew how the detective would react or whether he would be with anyone else. If the safe house had been in the Metropolitan Police area, there could have been back-up. Help could have been obtained from Essex, but there was concern that word of what was planned could leak out if an official request was made. CIB decided to go ahead on its own.

The observation team was exposed. If they encountered trouble, they had only old radios on which to call for help, and there was no certainty that they would function properly at all times outside London. There was also another unforeseen problem. Although the bug worked, and the suspect detective arrived at the flat, the waiting CIB officers could hear from the conversation between him and the woman that he was not interested in sex. He said he was 'feeling knackered'. Although the woman had been briefed to behave normally, she, in fact, was making all the running, asking the officer to go to bed. For the apparent benefit of those listening outside, she then gave a commentary on what was happening, referring to him 'penetrating' her. She then told him to stop, but he replied that he was not doing anything. If he was not physically aroused, it appeared that his suspicions were, because he asked why she was acting strangely. At that stage, the CIB officers burst in and arrested the detective.

A report went to the CPS, setting out what had happened in the bedroom and setting out evidence of other alleged wrong-doings. But eventually the CPS decided that a prosecution was impossible. There had been no rape and there was little or no evidence against the detective for any of the other alleged offences beyond the word of the woman herself, and she was likely to be viewed as unreliable in any court because she was a drug addict. Interestingly, both she and the detective had known that her heroin use would cause just such a problem. She had related a particular conversation with him when first interviewed by the CIB officers, prior to the sting operation. She told them that she had threatened the officer with exposure for rape: 'I said, "I'll have you. I'll go down to the police station, and have you done for rape." I said it many times. He said to me, "Who are they gonna believe? An ex-junkie with a boyfriend in prison, or me, a detective sergeant? I'll say you wanted it."'

Three years after he was arrested and suspended, disciplinary action was finally taken against the SERCS detective for interfering with a protected witness. The officer had been on full pay the whole time, and this continued as he frustrated the disciplinary process by declaring that he was sick. Eventually he was sacked, and it is believed that he retained his pension rights.

Gaspar likened a corruption inquiry to a murder investigation, where the first twenty-four hours after the crime are by far the most important for gathering evidence. 'I had to push all the time,' he told me. 'CIB just didn't understand that we had to win the mental battle. CIB argued that officers had to be properly interviewed and it would take time to prepare for such interviews. I said that was nonsense as it was known they were going to say nothing. Just get them and tell them they'd been caught doing so and so. They're not going to say anything.'

As well as 'dinosaur attitudes', there was another associated problem in trying to turn the ghost squad's intelligence into evidence, eventually recognised by Gaspar. 'You couldn't gather evidence and stay secret at the same time,' he told me. 'The idea that you could simply drop in our secret intelligence to operations wasn't always working. Questions would be asked about where the information came from. How did anyone know it was reliable? It was difficult to answer such questions without revealing our existence.'

However, a different complexion was put on the problem by another senior officer who later became involved in the anti-corruption drive. Critical of this area of Gaspar's operation, he said: 'Years ago, evidence for investigations would be gathered secretly, and then the executive arm would be called in and they'd work on the material and then make arrests. That way the baddies never knew where the stuff was coming from. Gaspar and company started doing the same, but they were five years behind the times. The rules and regulations had changed. They were floundering.'

In addition to CIB investigators' natural curiosity about the origin of the intelligence information given to them, major changes to the law meant that prosecution evidence in court cases had to be fully sourced in order to withstand defence challenges over its veracity. This meant, for instance, that it was no longer enough simply to produce a tape record-ing or a bank statement in evidence. The officers making the recording or obtaining the statement could be required to appear in court. Giving evidence in legal proceedings had been causing MI5 and the Special Branch problems in Irish terrorist trials. Most of the work of these agencies was done covertly, and the security service did not want to have secret techniques made public or made available to 'the enemy' through pre-trial disclosure. Undercover officers who had penetrated Irish groups and MI5 informants were at particular risk, unable to give evidence because their lives would be in danger. Even simple confirmation of the existence of a well-placed intelligence source could result in a flow of information being stemmed, and to secret operations being aborted.

The original idea had been that ghost squad intelligence would be drip-fed into CIB for further action. But CIB2 was still essentially a reactive organisation, geared up to act only in response to a complaint or a crime that had already taken place. Not only was it not up to the job of properly developing intelligence information, but any requirement that its evidence be sourced could lead to the secret squad's existence becoming known. The implications of this horrified Gaspar. It would have meant the end of the ghost squad.

The Scotland Yard hierarchy that had authorised the setting up of the secret operation faced stark choices. Millions of pounds had been spent on it over two years, but on the surface there was little to show for all the expenditure. Strong, useful intelligence had been gathered which showed that there could be two hundred corrupt detectives in the London area. But because so much time had been spent on forming the squad and maintaining its secrecy, it had not delivered on the second of its original important aims – an effective way of tackling the bent cops. It had made two big breakthroughs into a murky world, but both were unresolved. Investigations into Geoffrey Brennan's allegations that he had paid £50,000 to two officers, detailed in Chapter 3, had come to nothing. Speculation that he may have manipulated Gaspar's team for his own ends was to receive some confirmation early in 1997 when he withdrew his allegations and complained about CIB. The other example concerned investigations into Flying Squad wrong-doing. After nearly two years there appeared little prospect of anyone being charged over stealing some of the proceeds of the £1.5 million security van robbery. Corruption appeared to be flourishing.

Although Operation Countryman, the last big corruption inquiry, enjoyed only limited success in the early 1980s as far as prosecutions were concerned, publicity about it had at least caused enough of a stir to deter corrupt detectives for a time. But nothing similar had occurred as a result of the ghost squad's operation because the measures taken to preserve its secrecy had been totally successful. Only a handful of very senior officers outside the unit knew of its existence, let alone what it had been looking at. CIB officers were still viewed by corrupt detectives as sleepy and ineffective. Far from being deterred, some of those aware that they had been under investigation in 1993 were still 'at it' a couple of years later.

In 1993 the BBC's *Panorama* had exposed corrupt dealings by John Donald, a detective in the South East Regional Crime Squad. He took bribes totalling at least £20,000 from a drugs dealer for help in collapsing a prosecution against him and also for police information on other drugs investigations, including one into the notorious gangster Kenny Noye, now serving a life sentence for a road-rage murder. Donald himself was given an eleven-year sentence. It was this programme which helped kick-start the whole secret probe into Metropolitan Police corruption.

The *Panorama* programme also gave rise to another important corruption inquiry, the first major investigation into the workings of NCIS, the National Criminal Intelligence Service. As a measure of its seriousness and sensitivity, the then Chief Constable of Northumbria, John Stevens, was brought in to superintend it. Stevens at that stage was a rising police star, having conducted two investigations into claims that members of the Northern Ireland security forces provided loyalist paramilitaries with intelligence files. Stevens was called to London during John Donald's Old Bailey trial in 1995 after a serious breach of security. Transcripts of intercepts – phone taps – had been produced in court. This was not only against the law, which states that such material should not be used in evidence, but there had also been a clear breach of security at the sensitive NCIS headquarters, from where phone tapping is supervised. Direct verbatim transcripts of intercepts are not allowed out of the building. Detectives engaged in investigations involving the tapping of criminals' phones are allowed into NCIS headquarters at Spring Gardens in Vauxhall, south-west London, but they can only make notes from the transcripts in specially issued and logged notebooks. These notes must not themselves be copied, according to the strict rules applying at NCIS. They have to be handed back after a very short time period.

The Stevens investigation lasted a year, and the report he presented in January 1997 was devastating to NCIS's prestige. He found that nine hundred of the special notebooks had not been returned. Some were lost. Although many officers insisted that they had given them back, there were no records to support their claims. Other officers still had notebooks, and explained that they had not understood that they should have been returned. Stevens found procedures a shambles. He made ninety recommendations for change, all of which were accepted by NCIS. Later, after a spell as Her Majesty's Inspector of Constabulary, Stevens became the Met's Deputy Commissioner, which, among other things, put him in charge of corruption and disciplinary matters. In 2000 he became the country's top cop, taking over as Commissioner after Sir Paul Condon's retirement.

With corruption still rife at the end of 1996, Scotland Yard decided to launch the second part of its new anti-corruption strategy and to shake up CIB. Although to an extent disorganised, the ghost squad had largely completed the first part of its job in assessing and gathering intelligence on the level of corruption. Part two, tackling and rooting out the cancer, would now be got under way. Sir Paul Condon warned of what was to come in the summer of 1996. In 'London Beat', the Met's strategy for the new millennium, he said that undercover squads were being set up to target crooked officers, adding: 'We recognise that a small number of officers either through bad behaviour or corruption can have a disproportionate impact on our reputation. We want them to be in constant fear of exposure.' As part of the new crackdown, the Met later set up an internal confidential telephone system called Right Line which officers and civilian staff could call if they suspected any wrong-doing on the part of colleagues and were uncomfortable about telling senior officers. Somewhat disingenuously, the Deputy Commissioner, Sir Brian Hayes, said: 'This is not in response to any major problem we perceive in the Met of corruption, but there are always cases cropping up in a service as big as this. We need to make sure we are in there quickly, nipping them in the bud before they become a problem.'

The ghost squad's work would be incorporated into CIB and its intelligence information used to target suspect detectives. But instead of conducting retrospective investigations, they would now be proactive. Rather than using bugs, probes and intercepts to gather evidence on officers' past crimes, the same tools would be used to catch them in the act. If the suspects were too clever to be heard discussing anything of significance, then temptations would be put their way. If necessary, sting operations would be initiated against them, just as they were sometimes mounted against major criminals.

His job largely done, Detective Chief Superintendent Gaspar was told that he was to be transferred to one of two posts. He was either to take over as head of Scotland Yard intelligence or become commander in south-west London. Eventually he was told he would go to south-west London, as the boroughs wanted commanders with major crime experience rather than uniformed bureaucrats. Gaspar had wanted to stay working centrally, but admitted he was feeling burned out with the stresses and strains of leading a double life, and with handling such sensitive work. He had suffered in other ways too. Professionally he had been greatly respected, and that had been reflected in the number of Christmas cards sent to him by colleagues. He reckons that each year he used to receive about eighty cards. But after he had been heading CIB for a couple of years, the number sent to him had dropped to six, itself a reflection of the depths of ill feeling and resentment of what was viewed as CIB's unnecessary work. Gaspar says semi-seriously that those six Christmas cards were probably from people unaware of his move to CIB. This social shunning would have been even more severe if colleagues had known of his other role, heading the secret anti-corruption squad. Later in his career he returned to a key police role, becoming number two at NCIS.

seven

THE CANNABIS STING

'It was a groundbreaking sting – a defining moment. It proved to the police and to the outside world that we had big corruption. Together with the inquiry into the Stephen Lawrence murder, the whole course of policing was changed, not only in the Met, but throughout the country.'

The officer chosen to take over as overall head of CIB and transform the intelligence-gathering squad into a proactive operation was Commander Roy Clark, later to become Deputy Assistant Commissioner. He had been the man most directly responsible for persuading Sir Paul Condon to set up the secret squad in 1994. Clark then became head of the South East Regional Crime Squad in the aftermath of the John Donald corruption affair. He had kept in close contact with DCS Roger Gaspar, giving him information about suspect SERCS officers, much of which he obtained late at night, when, in relative safety, he scoured empty offices, looking through drawers and files. Through Gaspar, Clark kept abreast of developments and problems arising out of the secret inquiry. This meant that he already had answers when the then Deputy Commissioner, Sir Brian Hayes, handed him Gaspar's final report and strategic assessment and told him, 'You're in charge now. How are we going to tackle this?'

Like Gaspar, Roy Clark was a hard-working police officer, at his desk in Scotland Yard every morning by eight o'clock at the latest, staying until well into the evening. Dedicated to the job, he was not above telling the occasional white lie, especially when it meant preserving the secrecy of anti-corruption operations. While head of SERCS he wrote a memo to staff saying they should expect shocking publicity when John Donald came up for trial at the Old Bailey for corruption. However, his memo continued by saying that Donald was a 'one-off' and SERCS would recover. While the latter part of the statement may have been true, Clark knew that Donald was far from being a lone rotten apple in SERCS. Not only did Clark know at the time of writing that those closest to Donald at his Surbiton base were still under investigation and would remain so for some time, but he also knew there were suspect pockets of corruption at neighbouring SERCS bases. When asked later about this contradiction, Clark responded that circumstances forced him to write such a memo. If he had told the full truth he would have blown the secret inquiry and the already low morale within SERCS ranks would have sunk even further.

Clark began phase two of the anti-corruption strategy by starting the process of transferring the ghost squad's information to CIB headquarters at Tintagel House, close to the HQs of both the National Criminal Intelligence Service and the National Crime Squad. Later, another office was used at Jubilee House in Putney, also in south-west London. To act on the intelligence, a new secret proactive CIB unit was set up, the forerunner of a new department, known as CIB3. Experienced senior detectives were drafted in. All were known to be of the highest integrity, and all had either made some kind of stand against corruption in the past or had been directly involved in actual operations against bent cops. Despite those earlier experiences of this murky world, these officers were shocked on reading and being briefed about the extent of corruption uncovered by the secret squad. Some of them were to face personal problems. To their apparent surprise, they learned that some of their long-standing friends had been targeted as corrupt. For example, an officer who was godfather to one senior anti-corruption officer's child was later charged with corruption; similarly with the best friend of another officer. These new CIB detectives would have to minimise contact with these suspect officers, without their suspicions being raised. Questions were to be raised later about these relationships. How could these 'whiter than white' CIB officers have such close friends or colleagues without knowing what they had been up to?

The first of this new intake was Detective Superintendent Dave Wood, who took over as operational head in December 1996. He had not wanted the job. He knew of CIB2's reputation, and he had been very happy working for SERCS in south London, close to his family home. But the Deputy Commissioner told him he had no choice. Wood was joined early the following year by Detective Chief Inspectors Chris Jarratt and John Coles. All three were shocked on learning of CIB2's lack of resources and expertise. Wood, a bespectacled, avuncular man who had been a DCI under Roy Clark at SERCS, put it diplomatically in an interview with me. He said that CIB did not attract experienced, career detectives at that time:

> It attracted another type of police officer who may do their job very well, but these investigations into dishonest and corrupt police officers are the most complex and difficult investigations that can be done. The people employed there, generally speaking, didn't have the skills or experience to tackle such work. They did reactive investigations where you take statements and interview officers about what the statements allege. But that's what I would describe as the dorsal fin. There's a shark below the surface that hadn't been seen. There was a small number of corrupt officers and the extent of their criminality was quite astonishing.

Asked why officers became corrupt, he replied:

> It's a very difficult question to answer because there are all sorts of reasons. There's greed. There's exposure to large sums of money. Some of these officers are going into houses where there might be half a million pounds in cash, which has just come from a drugs deal. If the officer was to walk away with that half a million, the person is not going to complain. They'll be delighted because that's major evidence against them and it's going missing. These are the sort of temptations that Met police are faced with fairly regularly. Some officers will succumb to that temptation. Thankfully, ninety-nine per cent will not.

Those that did succumb, he continued, developed a certain arrogance.

> The very corrupt ones tended to be very experienced detectives who'd worked on regional crime squads or other squads like that. They were aware of the strategies the Met was using to investigate complaints. They were aware the people they were stealing from, or had corrupt relationships with, were not going to complain against police. And even when there was a complaint of any shape or form, the people who were going to interview them or try to investigate them had poor experience compared to the corrupt ones. So that gave them a confidence to go about their activity and, indeed, an arrogance about the way they went about it.

Wood was also to find that some of this arrogance came from corrupt officers' friendships and contacts with CIB2 officers. He suspected information was leaking from CIB, some of it deliberate. Wood had asked one CIB2 detective to make covert enquiries about a particular officer, but the detective had declined, offering the excuse that he was already overworked. The following evening, Wood's frustration with officers with little or no commitment to the job turned to fury when he attended a social occasion at a police sports club. As he parked his car, he saw the same CIB2 detective talking behind some bushes with the very same officer he had been asked to make enquiries about. The next day, Wood challenged the CIB2 detective. The officer said he had simply been having a social chat, but Wood was having none of that. Why were they talking in a secluded place in the car park? Wood called him corrupt and reported him. The officer was sent home on the police equivalent of civil service 'gardening leave'. He retired shortly afterwards.

The new men came under some pressure to produce results. Under Roy Clark's supervision, Wood set in motion what was to be the huge task of transferring the intelligence data compiled by the ghost squad to a newly created unit, the Complaints Investigation Branch Intelligence Cell, CIBIC for short. Much of this intelligence information had never been fully analysed. It included tape recordings from bugs and intercepts which had never been properly listened to, if ever actually played.

The secret squad had already cost several million pounds, and with some of London's best detectives being drafted in for its second phase in 1997, there were murmurings of dissent from the London boroughs and senior officers in the area specialist squads. They asked what was going on. Why were they being stripped of their best men? When told that the anti-corruption squad was being beefed up, they queried whether it was necessary, some disputing that corruption had reached a level that justified more money, resources and expertise being slung at it. Those high up in Scotland Yard knew from the ghost squad's intelligence that corruption had again taken hold and was increasing. But without revealing the secret squad's achievements, they had no immediate way of reassuring the doubters. The new-look CIB was asked to try to come up with a big case in which the evidence was so strong it would demonstrate that corruption was again at a very serious level.

Superintendent Dave Wood was in charge of new operations, with DCI Chris Jarratt heading CIBIC and looking after intelligence-gathering. The pair saw that the retrospective investigations had not progressed far, so they concentrated on trying to make use of some of the information gathered by the secret squad. They worked through the material collected over the previous two years, prioritising it, picking out what looked most promising. What were called 'intelligence packages' were produced and handed on to experienced operational detectives to develop. These 'packages' could consist of only two or three items. There might, for instance, be information about a suspect officer gleaned from tapping a telephone. This could be supported by surveillance on the officer which showed him meeting a criminal or another suspect officer, away from police premises. Sometimes the ghost squad had itself followed up such sparse material. But much of it was untouched. Either way, it was rare for any of it to have been used in prosecutions. It was up to the experienced detectives to develop it and obtain sufficient evidence to mount court cases.

According to one of the senior men drafted into CIB, much of this ghost squad material was flawed.

> I don't want to be too critical, because they had been doing their best, but quite frankly, some of the jobs the secret squad had worked on were in a mess. They had a lack of resources, so hadn't developed some of the intelligence material at all. These jobs had gone stale, so we were trying to play catch-up, which is always very difficult. And some of the jobs that they had worked on had been developed by them in the wrong way, making it impossible to get evidence which would stand up in court. If we had had the same raw intelligence, we would have pursued it in different ways.

The best way forward for the new team was seen to be the proactive targeting of the suspect officers judged most likely to be tempted by sting operations. Their vulnerabilities would be worked on, and if entrapment was successful, the aim would be to turn the corrupt officers into super-grasses, to provide evidence against their suspect colleagues. But the new team was not going to waste precious resources mounting sting opera-tions against individual suspect detectives thought to be acting on their own. They aimed to tackle squads in which corruption was believed to be endemic and systematic.

The measures taken, used routinely against major criminals, were unprecedented against police officers. The new men selected the Flying Squad for further targeting. Ironically a Home Office report at that time was applauding the Squad's use of proactive measures to catch robbers. The report, *Armed Robbery: Two Police Responses*, compared the Flying Squad's approach to that of the South Yorkshire force, which was largely reactive. It praised the Flying Squad and its ability to cultivate and handle informants, and urged other forces to set up databases similar to the Flying Squad's of all known and suspected robbers, with detailed offender profiles. 'The information held should include details on patterns and styles of offending, linked to trade marks of different offenders,' said the report. It was exactly this kind of information which had been produced by the secret ghost squad. It was now to be developed for use against the Flying Squad, and, in particular, against Detective Constable Kevin Garner.

The thirty-five-year-old Garner was one of the detectives allegedly involved in stealing up to £200,000 of the proceeds of the £1.5 million security van robbery in January 1995. But that was not the only reason why he became a suspect – there were other reports of his corrupt activities after this robbery. Garner came to CIB notice after making two checks on the Police National Computer. It turned out that these had been done on behalf of a criminal called Michael Taverner, who was under investigation for dealing in stolen cars, sending them abroad with false registration details. Taverner was also linked to the two robbers who had carried out the security van raid with Bobby Freeman. In fact, unknown to any anti-corruption detectives at the time, Garner's corrupt relationship with Taverner had started shortly after the robbery on the security vehicle, when he had bought counterfeit currency from him and switched it with real money seized by the police from criminals.

The team handling the stolen car inquiry visited Garner early in 1996 to ask why he had made the PNC checks. He explained that he was trying to develop Taverner as an informant, and to help that relationship had carried out what he claimed were 'harmless' checks for him on the ownership of two cars. Undeterred by the car squad's visit, in April 1996 Garner bought a stolen Mercedes from Taverner, registering it in the name of his partner, Jackie Coote, also known as Jackie Buisson. He believed his cover story had worked. Such was his confidence that he started discussions with Taverner over a plan for him and another detective to take part themselves in a robbery modelled on the security van 'tiger kidnap'.

What Garner was proposing was serious corruption – police officers were actually conspiring to commit an armed robbery with criminals. Garner developed his plan after being part of a team investigating another security van robbery earlier in the year. He had visited the robbed guard's home and found him a weak and vulnerable character who was short of money and required little persuasion before agreeing to co-operate in another robbery. Garner planned to fit him with a dummy bomb and microphone, copying what had been done to the security van driver-guard the year before. Taverner introduced another apparent criminal into the scheme, someone known to Garner only as Irish Mick. This mystery man was to play a key role in the Garner saga at a later stage. But in April 1996 the plan was that Irish Mick and Taverner would carry out the robbery while Garner and his trusted detective colleague would make sure that they were crewing the Flying Squad 'crime car' that day, ensuring that the robbers would make a clean getaway. However, unknown to the conspirators, they were under surveillance by anti-corruption officers, alerted to Garner by the stolen car squad officers.

The robbery plan left the CIB investigators in a quandary. Much of their information had come from phone taps which could not be used as evidence in court. So if they arrested the four men prior to the raid on the security vehicle they would have little usable evidence against them, and a prosecution would almost certainly fail. It would also have the effect of blowing open the whole covert investigation into alleged Flying Squad corruption. An alternative was to let the robbery go ahead and then make arrests. But such a strategy held greater potential risks. There would be a public outcry if some innocent person was shot, or even killed, as police moved in on the robbers, knowing beforehand that other police officers were involved. Anyway, the anti-corruption investigators simply did not have the resources, facilities or manpower to mount what would be a huge operation, monitoring and moving in on the robbers. Instead, it was decided to disrupt them, to frighten them into calling off the robbery. Such tactics were sometimes used for various reasons by other specialist police squads. It was known that if the Flying Squad, for instance, heard of plans to rob a bank but did not have resources that day to mount an ambush, they would deter the robbers by parking a marked police car close to the bank. A similar tactic was used to stop the Garner-Taverner robbery, but it was more subtle. The plan was that a surveillance team would deliberately 'show out' to Taverner, so he would realise that he was being watched and be forced to abandon the robbery. The ruse worked perfectly.

As Taverner changed a number plate on a car in the street outside his house, he heard the loud click of a camera shutter coming from bushes near by. Realising he was being watched, he stopped what he was doing, telephoned Garner and told him the job was off as the police were 'all over him'. Garner was worried too. If police were on to Taverner, it was for two possible reasons. Either they were continuing to investigate him for stolen car dealing or they knew something of the robbery plot. Garner decided to take no chances. He knew he already had a reputation among some of his colleagues for odd behaviour, which had started after he had left his wife. This had deepened when he spent time trying to penetrate a gang of hit-men who had carried out contract killings. He had also been attacked in a pub and hit over the head. Garner decided to go sick. Over that weekend he met a former colleague, Keith Green, who had moved on to the National Criminal Intelligence Service and retired on grounds of mental ill health following a shooting incident; he was mounting a civil claim against the Yard. Garner pumped him for information about how he had gone about making his claim. The following Monday, Garner went sick, never to return to the job. Later he was allowed to retire. But the intelligence operation against him continued. He was to become the key to providing evidence for use by anti-corruption officers investigating Flying Squad corruption.

DCI Chris Jarratt, in charge of intelligence operations, assessed what had been learned and made further enquiries into Garner. He took the view that Garner was weak and vulnerable and, if caught, would 'roll over' and confess. Jarratt himself had a reputation for being a hard man, dedicated to the job. He was given the nickname 'J. Rat' by his detractors, those he was hunting down. Unlike other senior detectives, he does not recall encountering corruption early in his career, probably, he says, because he had always taken a hard line over gifts and favours, believing that while an officer is on duty even a cup of tea should not be accepted without payment. Confirmation of this high-minded attitude comes from his vivid recall of an incident years before and his continued questioning of whether he had acted correctly over it. He had been on a day out in Brighton in a fish restaurant with his wife and children when some youths started causing trouble. Jarratt intervened and the youths disappeared. The restaurant owner was so grateful that he refused to accept payment for the family's meal. Jarratt persisted in trying to pay, but the owner was adamant and Jarratt finally gave up. He still wonders whether the owner guessed he was a police officer from his actions and was trying to curry favour, or whether his generosity was simply out of gratitude for a kind act. Jarratt's first encounter with real corruption was not until the late 1980s, when a shotgun seized during one of his operations went missing from a police station.

During the autumn of 1997, Jarratt and the other senior CIB officers assembled teams capable of surveillance work and intelligence-gathering and able to take part in complicated sting operations. The notion of strict 'sterile corridors' was introduced, so that each of the different units would not know what the other was doing. Everything was to be run on a 'need to know' basis. 'The corrupt officers we were targeting had great abilities, through what they had learned from their training and their various postings,' Jarratt told me. 'To work for us, we had to take in people who were totally untainted, so they couldn't be a mole to the other side, wittingly or otherwise. For example, if they had training as detectives, they could have been in contact with the quarry. We looked at people's postings, social meetings, etc. Clean people were needed, like the IRA needed for some of their operations here. They had to have integrity and ability, and, if necessary, an ability to be trained up to the job. That can be assessed in an interview, whether they're free thinkers, lateral thinkers.' For the sting operation to be mounted against Garner, Jarratt chose officers he knew who had worked with him in south London. He trusted them, and they were less likely to know Flying Squad colleagues of Garner.

Exact details of how the sting was set up are unclear. The officers involved are reluctant to give away the secrets of a successful operation because they may have occasion to use the same techniques again. Even Garner himself is unsure which of two criminals set him up, and he still does not know whether either of them was co-operating with anti-corruption police or whether what they did was done unwittingly. Garner was by then retired and working as a chauffeur and 'gofer' for a foreign embassy. But it was known from the intelligence operation against him that he was saying he wanted to get involved in the drugs trade, and he was still mixing with Michael Taverner and Irish Mick. CIB decided to give Garner what he wanted – drugs. Information that a large amount of cannabis was for the taking in an east London flat was fed to him. The information came from Taverner, who was then on bail for dealing in stolen cars, having been arrested and charged in April 1997. Did the police put him under pressure to betray Garner? There are clues as to what occurred in events following Taverner's prosecution. He had also been charged with possession of an automatic pistol and ammunition, but these charges were eventually dropped after he pleaded guilty to the theft and handling of a large number of stolen vehicles. Was the relatively low prison sentence he received because of a favour he had done for the police, or is the more likely candidate for setting the sting in motion the mysterious Irish Mick? The answer may be that it was both of them, with Irish Mick playing the more devious role. This Irishman's full identity remains a mystery. The police are determined to keep it that way.

Although it is only speculation, a version of events with an authentic ring of truth was given to me by a detective source. He told me that Irish Mick was an undercover officer, brought to London especially for work with CIB. The thinking was that if an undercover officer posing as a criminal was introduced to Garner as being from London or anywhere else in England, checks could have been made on his origins, with the risk that his pose would be seen through. But because he came from Northern Ireland, it would be impossible for any suspicious corrupt officer to penetrate his 'legend'. The detective said:

> Imagine what would happen if anyone with a London or English accent started making enquiries about a criminal from across the water, with all its terrorism and criminality. They'd get nowhere. It was the perfect cover. The police persuaded Taverner to introduce Irish Mick to Garner and to vouch for him. What did Taverner get out of it? He got a lighter prison sentence. Sure, nothing was said when he was being sent down. But these things can be fixed behind the scenes. Even his own lawyers don't have to know anything of the background. And where is Irish Mick now? Who is he? What's his full name? He's disappeared and probably still acting undercover now. My bet is that no one will ever find out what his real role was.

What is not in dispute in this intriguing story is that the flat chosen for the sting was 4A Albert Road, in Silvertown, east London, close to the old Royal Albert Dock and near the much newer City Airport. It had been rented by another undercover officer using fake documentation. He had spun a story to local estate agents to the effect that he wanted a flat for his brother and some mates who were coming to London from Australia for a visit. Having paid a deposit and a month's rent up front in cash, the undercover officer handed the keys over to other squad members for the sting's next phase. CIB's technical experts moved in to install tiny video cameras and microphones in the flat. One camera was hidden inside a dummy electric socket screwed to a wall close to the floor. It pointed down the stairs, to the front door, so that anyone coming in would be filmed. Another was hidden in a light fitting in the bathroom. Outside, police set up an observation point, an OP, in offices next to the Tate and Lyle sugar factory across the railway line running parallel to Albert Road. From the OP, the flat's front door could be seen, but it was too distant for accurate, clear video images, especially at night. So another small video camera was fitted at the top of a lamppost standing on railway land, across from 4A. It could swivel, remotely controlled by officers in the OP with monitor screens. The pictures obtained from all three cameras were sharp.

On 2 December 1997 80 kilograms of best Moroccan cannabis, taken from a Metropolitan Police warehouse packed with drugs seized in raids, were planted in the flat. The load was divided into bags and stuffed into a cabinet under a basin in the bathroom. The drugs had been specially marked. For evidential reasons, photos were taken of the stash in the bathroom cabinet the next day. With the trap set, it was then a question of the officers at the observation point waiting for the police thieves to arrive. CIB was so short of trusted staff that those chosen to man the OP had to work thirty-six hours at a time. Although the information about the drugs was aimed at Garner, it was not expected that he would pick them up alone. The information fed via Taverner and Irish Mick suggested that the flat was occupied, and the anti-corruption detectives believed that Garner would ask for help from his corrupt former Flying Squad colleagues, because they would be able to obtain a search warrant to make the raid on the flat look official. CIB was confident that someone would turn up to steal the drugs. The unknown factors were when that would be, and how many would be involved.

Chris Jarratt, the officer in charge recalled:

> The area was like Gotham City, dripping with atmosphere, especially at night. There were bursts of steam coming out of a big sugar factory

and noises from the trains going by. I've been involved in some stings before and the whole thing about this one was that it looked right. It wasn't one where the target would think, 'There's something's wrong here.' It was absolutely spot on. It was an area where you'd engage in criminality. The area and the flat were right for a level-two drugs dealer, someone likely to have a few sacks, and eighty kilos was the right amount to put in. If it had been twenty kilos, for instance, it wouldn't have been enough to make it attractive for Garner.

Told of the drugs stash by Taverner and Irish Mick, Garner prepared to steal the drugs from 4A Albert Road late at night on 4 December, and he would indeed not be alone. He had contacted two trusted colleagues who had been with him in the Flying Squad. Terry McGuinness, still a serving officer, had agreed to take part. Garner had tried to get another detective, another Squad officer, to join in to act as a 'heavy'. But the detective was on police duties elsewhere, so Garner enlisted another former Flying Squad officer, Keith Green, to act as lookout. The trio met up at a police station where McGuinness was on duty, on night shift. They drove in two cars and parked round the corner from Albert Road. Like common criminals, they were 'tooled up', ready for any eventuality.

The anti-corruption officers in the observation post watched developments from the monitor screens in front of them. The camera opposite the flat picked up the trio standing in a huddle on the pavement outside number 4A. As the tall and beefy Green kept watch, looking up and down the street, the other two broke in using a jemmy. Garner told Green to stay on the doorstep. The camera inside the flat at the top of the stairs then picked up McGuinness and Garner climbing up to the first floor, McGuinness carrying what looked like a search warrant. An ex-boxer, nicknamed 'Meathead', he looked tough and ready for business as he passed in front of the camera lens. Next up the stairs was Garner, and he was followed a little later by an equally tough-looking Keith Green, carrying a big wooden truncheon. They had come prepared to meet resistance. One of them shouted, 'Anyone in?' Having established that the flat was empty, they began to search for the drugs.

In the CIB observation post, there was a mixture of excitement and worry. There was relief that the intelligence had been right, and that all the resources put into the job and all the hours of waiting had not been in vain. People had turned up at the flat, and the fact that their faces could clearly be made out resolved another possible problem. It had been decided beforehand that if the thieves were masked then they would be arrested as they left the flat. That tactic was now unnecessary, as the thieves could easily be identified. But the trio were not recognised by the officers in the observation post. The operation had been mounted on a need-to-know basis, and it had been thought unnecessary to tell the CIB officers anything about Garner. This meant that they were virtually completely reliant on the video recording equipment working properly. Although the pictures on the screens were clear and sharp, if the recording equipment had broken down, later identification of the villains would have been very difficult, or even impossible. So there was worry about the equipment and worry that the trio in the flat would be unable to find the drugs. One of the detectives in the observation post told me: 'As we watched and heard them moving about the flat, we weren't saying to ourselves, "Go on, go into the bathroom – that's where the drugs are." We weren't exactly willing them to go there, but we were very relieved when one of them was seen by the second hidden camera going into the bathroom and bending down under the basin.' Garner was then heard shouting to the others: 'Here you are. It's here!' Just three minutes after breaking in, the trio emerged carrying the bags, heavy with drugs. They walked calmly to their cars, as though this was everyday work.

The secret watchers were jubilant that all their planning had worked. Jarratt was not there, so he was paged with the simple message 'Happy Birthday'. He knew what it meant and started telephoning, setting in motion the sting's next phase. The identities of the three were not positively established until the next day, when a group of anti-corruption detectives assembled to study the videos. Jarratt recognised Garner immediately. Others identified the other two. It had been decided beforehand that, whoever they were, no one should be arrested immediately, the thinking being that an experienced, well-trained detective could come up with a convincing story if arrested too quickly. Garner could say he had just been tipped off about the drugs being there and had taken them, seeking a reward. He could add that there had been no time to alert the police at that hour of the night, but he had fully intended to take the drugs to a police station at a later stage. The secret squad knew that any such false explanation would not hold water if the three failed to report what had happened within a reasonable length of time.

Further precautions had been taken to make sure the sting worked properly, but to the end it was a high-risk plan, with no certainty about what would happen to the drugs once they had been taken from 4A Albert Road. Sometimes, in operations against ordinary criminals, electronic tracking devices are hidden in the drugs so police or Customs can monitor their movements afterwards. But this was not done on this occasion because it was feared that Garner, a trained and experienced detective, would search the drugs for just such a device, and if he found one the sting operation would be blown. Instead, each kilo slab of the cannabis had been given a distinctive mark with a special pen which would only show up under fluorescent light. But would Garner do as he had been told by Taverner and Irish Mick, and take all the drugs to the designated lock-up garage, or would he skim some off, telling the pair that there had been less than expected in the flat? The CIB team had decided not to follow Garner as they did not want to run the risk of being seen. Given such a situation, Scotland Yard had accepted that some of the drugs could go missing. There was no honour among thieves, even if they were police officers. The possibility that drugs would be lost was to become a reality.

Garner took the haul to the lock-up, then met up with Taverner and Irish Mick and handed over the keys. At a second meeting the next day, the former officer was told by his fellow criminals that there was not as much cannabis as they had expected. They suggested that Garner had taken some of the drugs himself before putting them in the garage, but Garner denied it. He was promised £20,000 from the sale of the drugs, which he was supposed to share with McGuinness and Green. Taverner had meanwhile rented a house in Peterborough Road, Leyton, in east London, and he moved the drugs there. When police raided it several days later, they found only 54 kilos. About a third of the cannabis was missing. Who had taken it, and at what stage, remains a mystery.

There was a further hiccup when CIB went to arrest Garner, McGuinness and Green on 8 December. Their three homes were to be raided at the same time, 7 am, rather than the visits being staggered, so none of them could be alerted and disappear. Garner and Green were in, but there was a hitch over McGuinness. He was not at his family home. He had gone to a girlfriend's after work and was arrested there later. Garner's arrest was dramatic. Eight officers with a dog handler smashed their way into his house at Brentwood in Essex. They were led by DCI

Jarratt, who shouted, 'Police officers.' With his partner Jackie shouting, Garner was grabbed by one officer, and, when he resisted, Jarratt put an arm round his neck, wrestled him to the ground and shouted: 'You're under arrest.' Garner refused to put his hands behind his back for hand-cuffing, and continued struggling, so Jarratt put his foot on his head, pinning him to the floor while another officer managed to handcuff him. A search of his home revealed what looked like a sawn-off shotgun, and there was a crowbar in his car. Twelve bullets and a knife were found at McGuinness's home address. When arrested at his girlfriend's home, he went quietly, as did Keith Green, at whose home were found shotgun cartridges, a knuckleduster and a truncheon. Although he had retired from the National Criminal Intelligence Service, he had what looked like an NCIS identification card and also a police-style warrant card.

The sting had worked perfectly. CIB had got their main target, Garner. McGuinness and Green were unexpected bonuses. But there was apprehension about the next phase. Would the three confess, not only to their own corruption, but to other Flying Squad wrong-doing too? Garner was potentially a huge supergrass, and there were also rumours about McGuinness, who after leaving the Flying Squad had transferred to normal CID duties at a police station. Certainly he had been under inves-tigation by CIB for other wrong-doing. It had been alleged that he had accessed the Police National Computer for a national newspaper in order to get the home address and details of someone who had won the national lottery. He had also tipped off a newspaper about the whereabouts of an east London publican who had fled to Spain with £20,000 of money raised for victims of the Dunblane shooting massacre. Less was known about Keith Green, who had moved from the Flying Squad in 1993 after nearly being shot in the chest by McGuinness while arresting two robbers. Suffering from stress and other mental problems, he transferred to NCIS, and was allowed to retire on grounds of ill health in 1996.

The new CIB team had thought long and hard about attempting to turn officers into supergrasses. They recognised that the supergrass system had fallen into disrepute in the 1980s and since then had been used rarely. Wood and Jarratt looked at its failings and how criminals who had become supergrasses had been able to manipulate their status for their own benefit. The CIB officers decided on strict new safeguards to prevent abuse. Rather than using the harsh term 'supergrass', participants would be called 'resident informants'. They would be held separately from other colleagues who had also turned informant, and there would be a 'sterile corridors' policy for the police investigators too. One supergrass's debriefers would have no direct contact with another's questioners or with the teams of detectives who would be following up the information and leads coming from them.

The first task, however, was to find a means of turning arrested officers into supergrasses without offering them inducements that could be challenged in court. The prospect of a supergrass's evidence being thrown out at trial because he had been given promises or shown favours inducing him to talk was appalling. Such a scenario was unlikely to happen in this case, however, as the suspects were experienced detectives who knew the rules for informants. They did not have to be promised light prison sentences if they informed on their colleagues. They already knew that this would be their due. But CIB also had to cope with restrictions imposed by the Police and Criminal Evidence Act, PACE, which included the recording of any questioning about the offences committed by the arrested person. The anti-corruption officers got round this by introducing what they called 'intelligence interviews'. These would usually occur in the cells before or during questioning. The arrested officers would be told in general terms that there was a huge amount of evidence against them, but that they could help themselves by considering giving evidence against their colleagues. One tactic was to talk about 'meat-eaters' and 'grass-eaters', terms originating in the 1970s during corruption inquiries in New York. Officers described as 'meat-eaters' were vicious predators who instigated corruption while 'grass-eaters' were grazers who had simply gone along with their colleagues as part of the herd. CIB detectives could tell arrested men that they believed them to be simply grass-eaters, and that it was wrong that they should suffer while the meat-eaters escaped. Because these were 'intelligence interviews' the exact words used were not recorded, so a court would have no evidence on which to judge whether or not inducements had been offered, or whether there had been other malpractice.

The three former Flying Squad officers arrested for stealing the drugs were interviewed separately and the first indications were not encouraging. Green vehemently denied knowing that drugs were being stolen. He said he had been doing what he thought was a favour for his old friend Garner, who had told him he needed help in repossessing office equipment belonging to his then employer, the Argentine embassy. While

Green stuck to his story, the other two were totally uncooperative, answering 'no comment' to even innocuous questions from the anti-corruption officers. Superintendent Dave Wood started his interview with McGuinness gently, asking him whether it was correct that he'd been with the police for eighteen years.

McGuinness responded: 'No comment.'

Wood: 'During your eighteen years' service you've been posted to various police divisions, mainly as a detective, and spent five years on the Flying Squad. That's correct, isn't it?'

McGuinness: 'No comment.'

Wood: 'During your time, I understand you've had lots of dealings with drug cases. Is that correct?'

McGuinness: 'No comment'. . .

On and on the interview went in the same vein, until Wood eventually called a halt.

Detective Chief Inspector Jarratt was faring little better with Garner, but he felt he could break his silence and persuade him to talk with the help of his girlfriend Jackie Buisson. Garner said he wanted to talk the situation over with her. The pair met early the next morning, and Garner later told Jarratt that he was willing to assist. Before there was a chance for him to change his mind, Jarratt took him to an interview room, switched on the tape recorder, and three minutes later, after the formalities were over, asked Garner: 'Can you tell me in criminal terms how many people you think you can give evidence against?'

Garner: 'I've been thinking all night and things kept coming into me head. It's somewhere between twenty and thirty.'

Even Jarratt was taken aback by these numbers, and at first could only manage to respond with the words 'All right'. Then, to make sure that Garner was talking about bent cops, he asked him, 'Twenty to thirty police officers?'

Garner: 'Yeah.'

Jarratt: 'How many of those officers are serving now?'

Garner: 'Um, well, the majority of them . . . they're mostly SO8' (the Flying Squad) . . .

Garner had 'rolled over', and was to confess over the next few days to a series of corrupt acts in which he and many others in the élite squad had been involved. McGuinness followed him in turning supergrass, estimating that he could name between ten and twelve detectives as corrupt, including two chief inspectors, two inspectors, sergeants and constables. Between them, the pair were talking about massive corruption. Police had planned robberies, stolen huge amounts of money and fitted people up.

CIB's delight that the operation had worked and that Garner and McGuinness had turned supergrass was shared by the Metropolitan Police Commissioner, Sir Paul Condon, as events seemed to confirm and validate what he had told the House of Commons Home Affairs Committee on 4 December, the day of the sting operation. 'I do have a minority of officers who are corrupt, dishonest and unethical ... These bad officers sap the morale of their honest colleagues and they do immense damage to public confidence.'

Sir Paul had continued by attempting to get the problem in proportion:

> Clearly corruption is about human frailty and opportunity. The opportunity is at its greatest in the big city environment. That is where huge sums of money can be offered to suborn officers from the straight and narrow. It has to be accepted that the excesses of police malpractice are at their most pronounced in big city environments around the world because that is where the most serious criminals operate, that is where huge sums of money can be thrown at officers to suborn them. A small provincial force is not going to encounter the magnitude of the problem we have in London ...

Although the Garner case was shocking, the Commissioner and those close to him would use it to great effect in two ways, helping to silence their critics, at least for a time. First, they said it demonstrated how big a problem corruption represented, with the video film taken at 4A Albert Road providing apparently incontrovertible proof for those asking where the evidence was. Second, the Met was now seen to be starting to crack down on the problem, and would be justified in seeking further resources to tackle it even more effectively.

'It was a groundbreaking sting – a defining moment,' one senior officer told me. 'It proved to the police and to the outside world that we had big corruption. Together with the inquiry into the Stephen Lawrence murder, the whole course of policing was changed, not only in the Met, but throughout the country.'

eight

ROLLING OVER

*I certainly regret ever joining the Flying Squad, and that's not
because of being caught or anything like that. It's basically
ruined my life ... it's certainly ruined me and no doubt it's
ruined a lot of other policemen.*

Terry McGuinness, supergrass

Kevin Garner's questioning continued after his initial agreement to co-
operate with CIB by giving evidence against at least twenty bent detectives. His claim that he was able to finger possibly as many as thirty
colleagues had surprised Detective Chief Inspector Chris Jarratt, who
went on, gently, to probe for more basic information. Garner told him
he had been involved in at least ten episodes of corruption in which the
money stolen by officers ranged upwards from £10,000. His descent into
corrupt ways came after high honours in the army and police. But the
seed of what was to follow – a need to belong, a need to be accepted –
may have been sown long before with a tragic incident when he was a
teenager.

Garner came from what had been a close and supportive family, but
his father died in front of him when he was only fourteen. The pair had
been wrestling playfully in the front room of their home when his father
suffered a massive heart attack and died. The family blamed Garner and
never forgave him. Feeling rejected, he left school and home at sixteen,
signing up for the Grenadier Guards, which provided him with a new
home and direction. He was a top recruit, said to have shown courage
and dedication, becoming the army's youngest junior sergeant-major. He
was a lance-sergeant at nineteen, completing two tours of duty in
Northern Ireland, including dangerous undercover work during the
Troubles, before leaving the army as a full sergeant when twenty-one. He
then joined the police and was the top recruit in his year during training
at Hendon in north London. He became a detective, and in 1992 moved
to a Flying Squad section where, according to his lawyer, there was a

culture of corruption. 'It involved secrecy, camaraderie and dishonesty – a culture in which he became immersed . . . It reflected a code based on team membership and loyalty. You either fell in with it or your career came to an abrupt end.'

Garner described the set-up to his anti-corruption questioners. In charge at his base was a detective chief inspector with three teams under him, each headed by a detective inspector. But there was an 'inner echelon' of officers who were responsible for most of the work, and they were corrupt. These detectives' abilities had impressed him, and he was 'taken under their wing', running errands for them, and then, once trusted, taking part in their corruption. Before the end of 1992 he was a willing participant, sharing in the money stolen from criminals.

On 2 December 1992, Garner was one of a number of Flying Squad officers who followed a gang to Brighton, where a jeweller was robbed. The robbers were arrested, and it was later alleged that part of their proceeds were stolen by police officers. Garner described how one of the officers approached him afterwards: 'He slipped, I think it was, two hundred quid into me back pocket in fifty-pound notes and he said, "There, that's for you, a drink." I didn't question it. I didn't ask where it come from or how he got it. We had a debrief at the Brighton nick, and it happened there. I wasn't privy to it. I wasn't trusted or whatever at that point. I was given two hundred quid and we all had the opportunity of staying the night or coming home, and I opted to come home.' Garner said that some of the others stayed overnight in Brighton, 'drinking champagne', and one of them had difficulty getting a prostitute past the hotel concierge.

Although the money was not a very large amount, Garner knew that by accepting it he had become corrupt, and in a telling exchange about the cultural pressures he told his questioner, DCI Jarratt, that he was not making any excuses: 'No one forced my arm. No one made me do anything. I was getting accepted by what I considered to be fucking good detectives. I'm impressed by it all, I'm impressed by the work that they do. I'm suddenly getting brought into the fold.'

Jarratt queried his motivation: 'You know, when I was on the Flying Squad, if someone offered me £200, I think there'd probably be some extreme violence . . . What do you think would have happened if you hadn't taken the £200?'

Garner: 'Dunno, probably would have been . . . not outcast, but just one of the minions again. I wouldn't have been part of the good work. I'd have just been another bod in the back of a gunship [an unmarked police car carrying armed officers].'

Jarratt: 'It seems like you're saying to me, to be part of the good work on that team, you had to be corrupt?'

Garner: 'I would say that was a fair way of putting it.'

Jarratt: 'So you're saying you've never done anything criminal before . . . How did you feel travelling back from Brighton that night with bent money in your pocket for the first time?'

Garner: 'I didn't really feel anything.'

Jarratt: 'Did you feel it was wrong?'

Garner: 'Yeah, obviously I knew it was wrong, and I wondered more than anything what had happened for him to give me £200. What had I missed?'

Jarratt: 'Was it explained to you later?'

Garner: 'No, no. See, boss, the culture, you don't talk about it. You don't say to someone where d'ya get that from. You don't ask questions. It's just not something you do. There is no need.'

There were many interviews with Garner over the next few days during which he set out his and others' criminality. DCI Jarratt was content to let him do the talking, trying to get him to open up without challenging him too hard about the detail of any of his accounts. Much later in the debriefing sessions, crunch time came when Garner was confronted by another CIB officer, Detective Chief Inspector Martin Bridger. By that stage, February 1998, Garner was being held for security reasons in isolation outside London, in a police station cell with its own cooking facilities. Bridger had taken over the reactive side of the investigation from Jarratt, who was concentrating on wider intelligence aspects. It had been stressed to Garner before he was accepted as a 'resident informant' or supergrass that he had to tell the full truth, and if found to be holding back information or telling lies he could be thrown out of the scheme and find himself back in the normal prison system. On 26 February, DCI Bridger had a row with Garner, accusing him of not telling the full truth, and threatening to send him to prison without a good word being said to his sentencing judge about his valuable co-operation. Garner agreed to tell more.

His long confession to anti-corruption officers went into detail about other episodes, most of them unknown to CIB. He also described how he had worked with the criminal Michael Taverner, who he believed had helped set him up for the CIB cannabis sting. As described in Chapter 7, CIB had known previously that Garner had carried out PNC checks for Taverner and had planned to rob a security van with him. What was not known was that on two other occasions he and Taverner had helped switch counterfeit money for thousands of pounds of real money seized from apparent criminals. The first of these is described in Chapter 11 when I outline businessman Stan Goodman's fight for justice. The second swap and further corruption also involved Terry McGuinness, the other officer who turned supergrass after being caught with Garner in the cannabis sting.

McGuinness ('Meathead') was an ex-amateur boxer who had reputedly sparred with Frank Bruno, the former British heavyweight champion. Like Garner, McGuinness had given a 'no comment' interview to the anti-corruption officers after his arrest. Like Garner, he had been given an 'intelligence interview' and had then decided to roll over, accepting the deal being offered by CIB. Under the terms of this he was to be given 'resident informant' status with a good word being put in for him with the sentencing judge, provided he confessed to all he knew about corruption and gave evidence against corrupt officers.

McGuinness had joined the Met as a nineteen-year-old in 1979 and moved to the Flying Squad eleven years later. He claimed – again, just like Garner – that he had never been involved in corruption before then. This is how he explained what had happened to his interrogators, led by DCI Tim White, who went on to take over as head of the Flying Squad in 2001:

> Until joining the Flying Squad, I can honestly say I've never been involved in any criminal activity or malpractice or anything. When you go somewhere like the Flying Squad, and I should imagine it's like any other squad, the first thing you want is to be accepted. You want people to accept you. You want to get on well. You've got to keep your head down and you go into that sort of environment and it's going on all around you. There comes a time when you are tested, where they accept you're not going to, like, back off, or back down, or run away ... With it all going on around you, some of it does rub off, and, in short, you really lose the plot.

McGuinness went on to say that before joining the Flying Squad he had no idea that he should expect corruption. People he knew on the Squad had not said anything about malpractice: 'I went there, and it's like a gentle introduction to it, and then all of a sudden you're right in the middle of it. Of course, as your service progresses on the Flying Squad, you then tend to become more involved than on the outskirts.'

Asked how he felt now after talking about corrupt activities, McGuinness expressed contrition:

> I certainly regret ever joining the Flying Squad, and that's not because of being caught or anything like that. It's basically ruined my life. I was given a letter today from my mum. She regrets the day I joined the Flying Squad. She says she lost the son that she knew [who turned] into someone else. If you had asked me that question a week ago [before his arrest] I would have turned round and said, 'Yes, I enjoyed the Flying Squad.' I wouldn't have had a bad word said about it. But really, having had time to sit down and reflect – it's no excuse because I take full responsibility for my actions – it's certainly ruined me and no doubt it's ruined a lot of other policemen.

However, although McGuinness was claiming that the vast majority of officers at his base had engaged in some form of wrong-doing, he said others stood out, making it clear that they did not want to participate in corruption. On one occasion, according to McGuinness, when an officer refused to join in the stealing of money, a way was found round the problem, with the help of Kevin Garner. McGuinness said it happened when Flying Squad officers raided the home of a seasoned criminal and found £14,000 in cash under his bed. Hoping to avoid being arrested, the criminal offered the money to the officers. 'He denied the money was anything to do with him,' said McGuinness. 'He told the officers that Christmas had come early and he was inviting them to take it. Everybody there was willing to take that action apart from one officer. In view of that the money was brought back to the office and placed in the safe in the detective chief inspector's office.' Enquiries were to be made about the origins of the money, and if it could not be proved that it was the proceeds of crime, then it would be restored to the criminal. Annoyed that they had failed to get their hands on the cash, McGuinness, Garner and another officer then discussed how they could do just that. 'I joked that it was a shame that we didn't have any funny money to replace it with,' said McGuinness. 'Garner stated that he could obtain certain counterfeit currency. So it went from a joke to becoming basically a serious plan . . . Kevin Garner managed to obtain about £8,000 of funny money in £50 notes . . . at some stage the real money was taken out of the safe on the pretext of photographing the notes, and me and Kevin exchanged about £8,000 of the notes with counterfeit currency.'

McGuinness said the £8,000 was split three ways between himself, Garner and the other officer. Later, the money, more than half of which was by then counterfeit, was returned to the criminal from whom it had been seized. As the criminal was not to be charged with possessing the money in the first place, the three corrupt police officers counted on him not complaining about the switch, but they had worked out a cover story anyway. In case of a complaint, they were going to say that some of the money must have been counterfeit from the outset. They need not have worried. There was no complaint. Instead, according to McGuinness, there was a phone call from the criminal saying: 'I hope the boys had a good Christmas.'

Another colourful incident described by McGuinness involved a Flying Squad team going out in the dark looking for 'soggy money' left in a ditch. The cash was part of the proceeds of a robbery on a security van, said McGuinness, and had been left at the home of one of the robbers' girlfriends. When she heard of his arrest, she attempted to destroy fingerprints on the notes by washing them, and had then disposed of them before being visited by detectives, McGuinness among them. 'Because she'd been concerned about fingerprints on the money,' said McGuinness, 'she told us that she had tipped in lemon, orange juice, lemonade, and anything fluid she could find in her fridge, because she had seen on TV that fluids destroy fingerprints. Having soaked all the money in drinks of some sort or another, she split the money into two carrier bags and drove to a place, down a small road, which was dark, very dark, very unlit . . . We searched the ditch where she had thrown the bags. One of the bags was found and the search was called off.'

McGuinness said that the woman was not told they had found the bag, which contained more than £12,000. She was taken to the police station where the investigation into the security van robbery was centred and, according to McGuinness, the police involved in finding the bag went to the home of one of the team. 'As I walked in through the front door,' said McGuinness, 'I could see X drying out money ... It was hanging up, but it was damp, soggy money. You could actually see it. There were notes in the closed doors of wall cupboards, so that it was hanging down ... X made a comment: "I've been drying this fucking lot out for hours."' McGuinness and another detective constable were directed into the front room while money was counted out in the kitchen. The pair were then given white envelopes. McGuinness did not open his until he got home. Inside, he found £500 in £5 notes, most of them still damp.

There were almost comical moments in another theft confessed to by Garner and McGuinness. They claimed that this involved other officers, who between them stole an estimated £70,000. According to both men, it happened in 1993 when the Flying Squad was investigating the hijacking of a bullion lorry carrying £300,000 in ten-pence pieces from the Royal Mint in Wales to Barclays bank vaults. It appeared that security surrounding the container load was not as great as it would have been if one-pound coins had been carried, the thinking being that a lorry-load of ten-pence coins was less likely to be robbed because it would be more difficult to move. Physically, the coins were much heavier, with a total weight of around 20 tons. Then there was the problem of getting them back into circulation, as there was clearly a greater risk of attracting attention through, for example, spending £5 in ten-pence pieces rather than five one-pound coins. To what extent these considerations were weighed up by the criminals who stole the money is not known. According to McGuinness, the lorry driver was duped into leaving his cab and was then attacked, bundled into a van, and driven miles away to the outskirts of London, where he was tied to a tree. A man out walking his dog discovered him. The robbers had meanwhile driven the lorry containing the coins to Hackney. From there, they telephoned for assistance. Unknown to the robbers, police were mounting a long-term surveillance operation on the premises telephoned. The calls were being intercepted and there were also listening devices in the premises. These villains were known to mount big robberies every six months or so, and police were simply waiting for the next one to occur.

When the police listening in heard the call for help from the lorry hijackers, they made a mistake over the location. They thought the caller was saying the lorry was parked at 'Hackney Docks'. But there are no docks at Hackney. It was eventually worked out that what was being referred to was Hackney dogs, a greyhound racing track. But by the time Flying Squad officers swooped, it was too late. The lorry had just gone, leaving only a forty-foot space in a line of other heavy lorries parked there. Later, from the bugs and intercepts, police learned that the load of ten-pence coins had been divided into two, with both portions stored in lorries kept in separate yards. Rather than moving in immediately, the Flying Squad decided to wait, because precipitate action could have resulted in the robbers and their associates discovering that there was a long-term surveillance operation against them. Police wanted to keep the operation running, taking the view that the coin robbery was fairly small time. What they wanted was to catch the criminals taking part in a major robbery, a job that would be so big that very long prison sentences would be in order. The surveillance operation would not be blown if the police raided the vehicles when they had left their respective yards and were some distance from them. Such a tactic, it was believed, should also lead to the arrests of more criminals. A watch was kept on both yards.

Kevin Garner told CIB that he was put in charge of the operation on the lorry at the first yard. His team, augmented by surveillance officers from SO11, Scotland Yard's intelligence arm, swooped on the lorry. 'We hit 'em,' Garner related. 'It was only about half the load, about ten ton of coin. I jumped up in the cab to nick the driver, stuck the gun in his face ... He had the gun stuck in his face so all he done was look down the barrel rather than at my face, so I sort of ducked out the way and other police took over and that was that.'

One of those officers was McGuinness, who remembers that the weight of the coins was causing problems for the robbers: 'The weight was such that the wheels of the lorry had actually worn through the bed of the lorry. The suspension had come down so low the wheels had gone through.'

McGuinness said the lorry was driven to a police underground car park. It was a tempting load. Pallets were stacked five foot high with shiny new ten-pence pieces packed in handy bags each containing £100 worth of coins, and the corrupt McGuinness was appointed to look after it. 'The load on the lorry was secured by a padlock,' said McGuinness. 'I can't recall where we got it from, but it was one we had in the office. I was nominated to stay the night at the office. I cannot remember who by.' However, McGuinness does remember being with other officers when a senior officer going off duty handed him the office keys for safe-keeping overnight, and told Garner, 'Don't forget mine.' Garner recalled: 'I can't remember how it came to be, but it was decided to take some of the bags of coins, to nick 'em, nick some bags of coins ... We waited until everyone went home and then we took some bags.'

McGuinness described a Flying Squad feeding frenzy involving several officers:

> The padlock was opened, the back of the lorry was opened up and numerous £100 bags was removed ... Various vehicles were driven into the car park, bags were removed and placed into various people's boots. There was a total of £3,000 placed into the boot of my car. I know Kevin had £3,000, and I'm not sure, but I think it was only £2,000 taken for X which was taken by Kevin ... The total that came off that lorry I must put at around a minimum of £50,000 and anywhere up to £70,000. It was ages, it took ages and there were numerous, numerous bags ... there were eight or ten officers unloading ... I can remember one officer had an argument with another one outside, and that had something to do with them sort of not being allowed to take part in this theft. I don't know the reasons why, or how that came by, but there was certainly an argument outside.

Some of the haul was taken by officers to Garner's then home because he had offered to 'change up' the ten-pence coins into banknotes, charging his colleagues £300 commission per £1,000, a move that was to cause a certain amount of friction. McGuinness returned to his Flying Squad base, spending the rest of the night there. He handed over the keys to the senior officer in the morning as though nothing had happened. The lorry with the remaining coins on board was then driven under police supervision to vaults, where the money was counted and then held securely. But there was a virtual repeat of the theft two weeks later when the Flying Squad received information about the other half of the £300,000 load of coins.

From conversations picked up during the surveillance operation, officers learned that the second lorry was parked behind high walls in a yard at the rear of a pub. It was impossible to see the lorry from the road or the pub, so confirmation that a large lorry was indeed inside the yard came from a police helicopter, which flew above the premises. But this did not provide evidence that there were indeed coins on board, and it was certainly less than was needed for the Flying Squad to proceed with a daring plan to spread disarray among the criminals. A search warrant was obtained and a covert entry made to the yard by two officers in the middle of the night. Carpets were laid across the barbed wire on top of the high walls. The two officers then scrambled over and made their way to the lorry, which was covered by a large tarpaulin. Lifting it, the officers saw the coins packed in bags on pallets inside the vehicle. Because the criminals seemed to be happy to leave the lorry at the yard indefinitely, the police decided to move the vehicle themselves. But it would be done in such a way that the robbers would think it had been taken by other criminals, the hope being that this would cause the villains to fall out with one another.

Unfortunately for the Flying Squad, the night chosen for the entry coincided with a long after-hours drinking session at the pub, and, according to McGuinness, it was not until 4 am that things had quietened down sufficiently for the police to break into the yard. 'I cropped the padlock on the gates and the doors were opened,' he said. 'First off, a Traffic Department officer tried starting the lorry, but unfortunately the battery was flat. I think they had to break the steering lock, but it wouldn't start. Then they called up a Range Rover or a Land Rover traffic vehicle that came out. They tried towing the lorry out of the yard but apparently the air brakes locked on and it wouldn't move the lorry. They then decided to try and jump-start the lorry. It worked and a Traffic Department officer drove the lorry to the base. Again, the lorry was parked underneath.'

This time the Flying Squad officers were better organised in stealing coins from the lorry, although there was less on board than on the first vehicle. McGuinness said a senior officer was in command of the operation. He told his anti-corruption interrogators:

I'm not wanting to minimise my part, but he was instructing officers to remove bags, even to the amount each officer could take, and it was ten bags, £1,000 each ... There was a chain of officers, ten or twelve. If you appreciate the weight, you need a chain as you couldn't do it on your own. There were a couple in the back of the lorry, throwing down bags, and other people would be taking the bags and passing them to other people. An officer would be nominated to bring their car in, their boot would be loaded and they'd drive out, park up outside and

> another car would come in . . . As I was saying, Y was supervising the removal of these bags and there came a point where he instructed that's enough, and the vehicle was locked up.

McGuinness claimed that more than £12,000 was stolen on the second occasion. Some of the officers took an extra £1,000 each for colleagues who were not present, as had also been the case on the first occasion. Officer X did not take any, but gave it to Garner to 'change up' for him. When Garner did so, and he tried to charge his usual £300 commission, officer X objected. Garner commented to McGuinness: 'He wants every single penny in the fucking pound. Like he wants somebody to take on the hassle of getting rid of it and all the rest of it, with nothing in it for themselves.' McGuinness said he kept most of his share of the ten-pence coins in his workshop, taking about three or four years to get rid of them in 'dribs and drabs', paying small amounts into bank and building society accounts and passing the rest in pubs and shops. He said that virtually all his Flying Squad colleagues knew of the 'coins job'. Jokes were made about cars having broken down with the weight of money being carried, or even nearly overturning when going round corners. Asked what had happened to the second lorry, McGuinness said that it had stayed parked at the police car park for a long time and was still there when he last looked. No one had ever claimed it back.

Meanwhile, as planned by the Flying Squad, the criminals who had lost their load of coins were indeed thrown into confusion – and violence. One of the officers involved in the dramatic operation, while flatly denying receiving any of the coins, told me how he and his colleagues fell about with laughter when viewing and listening to covert recordings from equipment installed at the yard and the other premises. Although the police had made a great deal of noise getting the lorry started, its disappearance was not discovered until much later in the day. The video showed one of the criminals, a fat man, walking nonchalantly up to the yard gates. Hours before, when leaving, police had simply hung the chain through the two handles. The fat criminal appeared not to have noticed that the lock had been broken. He opened one of the gates, looked inside, and scratched his head in bewilderment. He closed the gate and then, as though he could not believe what he had seen, opened it again and took another look. Realising that it was not a dream, he turned and ran to the office, where another police bug was hidden. Clearly unused to the exertion, he arrived breathless and virtually speechless, but managed to convey to a second man that the lorry had gone. The second criminal then ran to the gates, and went through the same performance as the first.

The situation was to take a serious turn later. The criminals involved in stealing and looking after the lorry-load of coins held a conference at the pub to decide what to do. As the Flying Squad had hoped, the villains believed that another gang had stolen the coins. Prior to their meeting, they had already been asking questions about people spending or handling large numbers of ten-pence coins. In the conversation picked up by the police bug, the group discussed who could have been responsible. One man said he knew of someone spending a lot of ten-pence coins playing pool. It was decided that this man was either involved in the theft or knew who was. He was to be 'lifted' – kidnapped – and, if necessary, tortured into revealing the truth.

The criminals' plan once again presented the police with the same major problem as before. Should they jeopardise a good surveillance operation by taking action? On one hand, the covert recording devices were still in place. Good information was being gathered, and the Flying Squad were still waiting for the criminals to mount a big robbery. Against that, what would happen if the gang went ahead with their kidnapping and torture, and it leaked out that police had known of the plans all along? A sort of compromise was reached. But it was one fraught with danger. The Flying Squad would allow the kidnapping to take place, but they would tip off uniformed colleagues who could then move in, apparently by chance. By doing it this way – chance arrests without Flying Squad involvement – it was hoped the criminals would not realise that their every move was being monitored, and the successful surveillance operation would be able to continue.

The plan worked, but it came close to being a disaster. From the listening devices, the Flying Squad learned that the victim was to be kidnapped from a pub. They alerted uniformed colleagues, who closed in after the kidnappers left the pub with their victim in a van. The vehicle was halted in what appeared to be a routine stop, and those inside were arrested. It turned out that inside the pub the victim had been threatened with a gun held to his head. Luckily for the police, he did not resist. He agreed to get into the van. Freed by police, he declined to make a complaint against his abductors.

At the time of McGuinness's and Garner's arrests, their Flying Squad base was dramatically raided by CIB officers. Years' worth of work was seized. Vast amounts of paperwork, filing cabinets and exhibits were carted off for examination. The statements, interviews and debriefings of Garner and McGuinness were to lead directly to the arrests of several Flying Squad officers and to the suspensions of many more. Just over a month after that first round of questioning, on 27 January 1998, CIB3 officers made their first overt moves. They raided and searched the homes and offices of those alleged to have been involved in the corruption and served Regulation 163 orders on them. These were signed by a high-ranking CIB3 officer, Superintendent Brian Moore. The document alleged: 'Between 1992 and 1997, a group of police officers were engaged in committing a series of thefts, robberies, offences of dishonestly handling stolen property, and conspiracies to pervert the course of justice. You are one of those officers.'

What was to become the biggest anti-corruption operation ever mounted by the Metropolitan Police, dwarfing all previous such inquiries, was under way.

nine

FINDING EVIDENCE

*How can you help to convince us and everybody else that
what you're saying is the truth? Will there be documents, or do
you think people might have put money in accounts? Are there
people out there that can help us? We need to confirm your
story . . . Are you sure it's not a case of you spreading the muck
elsewhere?*

From the questioning of Terry McGuinness

By the end of 1997 there had been about forty-five detectives working
for CIB3, the new Complaints Investigation Branch squad responsible
for the cannabis sting and for proactively developing the intelligence
work undertaken by the ghost squad. After the turn of the year, once
Kevin Garner and Terry McGuinness had confessed, that number
increased dramatically. By the end of 1998 there were more than 250
officers actively engaged in investigating corruption, making it the
biggest single squad of detectives in the Metropolitan Police. Its operational head, Detective Superintendent David Wood, had been given
authority to recruit the best detectives in London. 'I honestly believe,' he
told me, 'that there will never be in this country a finer team of crime-
fighting detectives. They were the country's best detectives, people of
really great quality, dealing with the best of the country's corrupt
detectives.'

Although they probably were London's finest detectives, and of the
highest integrity, some were initially reluctant to join CIB, viewing it as a
posting for those nearing the end of their time with the police. At best
they thought it a sideways move in their careers. Others did not like the
idea of having to investigate former colleagues. But it was made clear to
all the doubters that the fight against corruption was now being given the
highest priority by the Commissioner; accompanying this was the
implied threat that if detectives wanted promotion they would have to
serve in CIB3.

The policy of 'sterile corridors' was formally introduced at the new CIB3 headquarters, Jubilee House, an anonymous-looking office block next to a cinema in Putney, south-west London. This meant that officers were not to talk to other CIB3 detectives about the particular inquiries on which they were engaged, even when they were part of the same overall investigation. So, strictly speaking, anyone following up Kevin Garner's allegations should not be talking to officers examining McGuinness's claims. The aim was to avoid contamination – the notion that an officer's view of how much credence should be given to one of the supergrass's claims could be influenced if he heard, for instance, that another officer had failed to come up with any evidence to back another of that same supergrass's claims. The sterile corridors policy would have been helped if separate CIB3 bases had been created. The original plan was to have three investigative centres, in addition to the ghost squad's secret base. Putney was to be the main office, with another in south London, in the Croydon area, while the third was to be sited in north London. If this plan had been carried through, it would also have cut down on the officers' travelling time to and from work. But it was not to be. Eventually, a southern office was created, not in Croydon, but at Camberley in Surrey, in a police station. No north London base was ever set up.

In the early part of 1998 many among the influx of extra CIB3 officers were working on aspects of the Flying Squad inquiry. Garner and McGuinness had offered a lot of evidence in their interviews, and it all had to be investigated. There was the security van robbery, the ten-pence coins job, switches of counterfeit currency for real money, and other incidents where money was stolen from criminals. Throughout the questioning of Garner and McGuinness, CIB officers attempted to elicit extra information from the pair which they could check to confirm or verify their claims, and which would also provide evidence against other officers they had named as corrupt.

The anti-corruption officers were aware of a possible credibility problem with the police supergrasses. If they were too young to remember the scandals surrounding the use of criminal supergrasses in the 1980s, then their bosses were not. Some of these criminals had manipulated the supergrass system so that they were even able to admit to killings and still get away with at most a five-year sentence, served in the relative comfort of a secure police station or in supergrass wings specially set up at a couple of prisons. In those days, in order to receive a

Sir Paul Condon (now Lord Condon) pictured with Detective Chief Superintendent Colin Smith (right), who is receiving a commendation for leading the investigation into John Donald

Commander Ian Blair (now Met Deputy Commissioner) who was in overall charge of the John Donald inquiry

DC John Donald, sentenced to eleven years for taking bribes in 1993

Dept. Assistant Commissioner Roy Clark, in overall charge of the anti-corruption strategy, now head of Crimestoppers

Det. Chief Supt Roger Gasper, who set up the 'ghost squad' to tackle corruption

Det. Chief Supt David Wood, first head of CIB3, the pro-active anti-corruption squad

John Coles, the DCI in charge of the first CIB3 operations under Wood. Headed the inquiry into Redgrave and Charman

Chris Jarratt, the DCI in charge of intelligence under Wood at CIB3

Redgrave (left) and Charman pictured together in the *Guardian*, March 2000
(Photograph by Sean Smith, the *Guardian)*

Geoffrey Brennan, convicted of stealing £400,000 from Chinese-American businessman
Sam Wang. Both are pictured at Brennan's mobile phone shop

The author outside the 'cannabis sting' flat in East London

Kevin Garner in Flying Squad days, having arrested Abraham Shakes, later freed on appeal and awarded £100,000 damages

Terry McGuinness, Flying Squad DC, who was caught in the cannabis sting

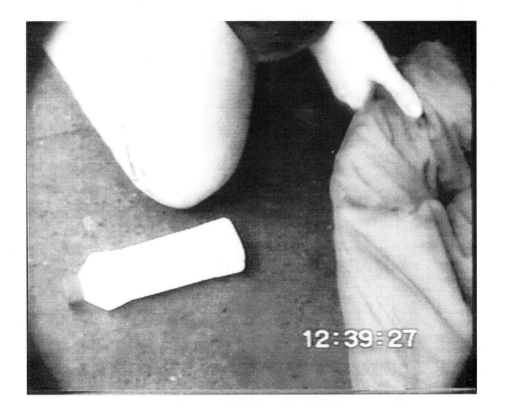

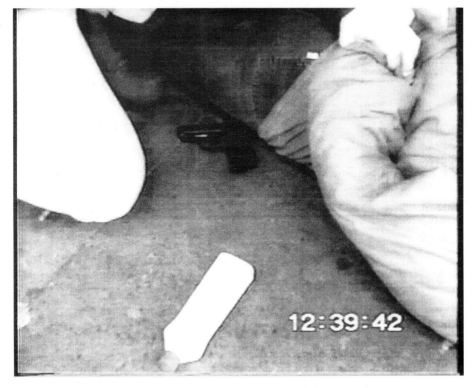

Hickson and Woodruff case: no gun in the top picture and sixteen seconds later a gun has appeared

Neil Putnam, who turned supergrass against his former colleagues in SERCS (South East Regional Crime Squad)

John Yates, the Superintendent who led the inquiry into SERCS. He 'turned' Neil Putnam

The four kilos of amphetamine powder officially declared as seized during a raid on a drugs dealer. Two other kilos went missing

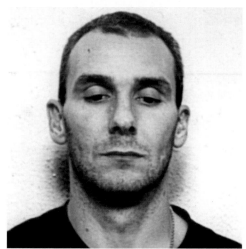

DC Tom Kingston (top left),
DC Tom Reynolds (top right),
convicted of corruption in the stolen
amphetamines case

DC Duncan Hanrahan (above left),
sentenced to eight years for corruption
in 1999

DC Bob Clark (above right), the main
corrupt officer in Putnam's squad

The corrupt DC Austin Warnes on a
park bench with 'celebrity criminal'
Dave Courtney (right)

Sir John Stevens, Metropolitan Police Commissioner

Chief Supt Bob Quick (on the left) took over CIB3 from David Wood. Pictured at an International Police Corruption Conference in South Africa, with Met Commissioner Sir John Stevens (right)

five-year sentence having admitted to appalling crimes, it was necessary to name others as being involved in the crimes. It was suspected that some potential supergrasses had exaggerated their involvement, and to make up the numbers had named other criminals as having been on robberies with them when they had been nowhere near the job. One supergrass, Mickey 'Skinny' Gervaise, even telephoned criminals from prison threatening to 'drop them in it' – accuse them of crimes – if they did not pay money to his girlfriend. No one was suggesting that Garner or McGuinness were demanding money from former colleagues. But the question that had to be asked was whether either or both of them were exaggerating or embellishing the extent of the corruption, not only to minimise their own involvement, but also to keep CIB happy so that they would retain their supergrass status. Garner had been businesslike in the debriefing process, and McGuinness was thought mentally incapable of constructing elaborate lies. But were they telling the whole truth? Could they even be naming innocent officers?

This issue had been raised at a fairly early stage in the questioning of Terry McGuinness. The corrupt detective had just finished describing the Flying Squad officers' thefts of ten-pence coins from two lorries when CIB sergeant Alan Pughsley came to the point.

Pughsley: 'Terry, thinking longer down the line, what can you think may help us to stop people suggesting that all you're doing is trying to minimise your involvement in corrupt activity – that you're just saying other people were involved when they weren't? How can you help to convince us and everybody else that what you're saying is the truth? Will there be documents, or do you think people might have put money in accounts? Are there people out there that can help us? We need to confirm your story.'

McGuinness: 'I accept what you're saying. I honestly don't know who would have put money into accounts because obviously it's the sort of stuff you're not going to discuss with one another . . .'

Pughsley: 'Are you sure it's not a case of you spreading the muck elsewhere?'

McGuinness: 'No, as I've said to you, I do not want to minimise anything for myself. I've done wrong and at the end of the day I'm going . . . I'll take whatever's coming to me and that's basically it.'

Pughsley: 'All the people you've mentioned did what you said they've done, they've stolen cash as serving police officers?'

McGuinness: 'Yes, and if obviously any other officer talks to you, I am confident that he, or one or more of them, will eventually be able to confirm what I am saying.'

The key part of that exchange was in McGuinness's closing words. The corrupt detective knew that he could produce little to corroborate his claims of other officers' involvement. His only chance lay in someone else providing confirmation. But he must have known that the likelihood of that happening was very small. He had only confessed because he had been caught red handed on video stealing drugs. No other guilty Flying Squad detectives would suddenly 'roll over' in the same way as he and Garner had done, because they would reckon that they could get away with it by denying everything. It would be their word against that of discredited, self-confessed criminals. McGuinness could be portrayed as a useless 'meathead' and Garner had retired with mental problems. CIB could mount more sting operations against these other corrupt detectives, but they were unlikely to be caught out because they would be on their guard, knowing they were already under investigation. After Pughsley's pointed line of questioning, McGuinness must have worried even at that early stage about whether he was saying enough to warrant being granted supergrass status.

By early May 1998, McGuinness's interrogation was virtually at an end. He had talked exhaustively about specific corrupt episodes, each involving a limited number of officers, with the maximum on any one occasion being the twelve he said had taken part in one of the coins jobs. The anti-corruption officers then asked him about the various complaints made against him over the years by members of the public, including criminals. Most of these were fairly minor, or where more serious had been unsubstantiated and rejected. There was no talk in these debriefing sessions about fitting up people, the manufacturing of evidence against criminals to gain convictions. But this was perhaps because he had not been asked. However, a question put to him at the very end of his interviews was to cause major problems for CIB3. He was asked: 'Is there anything else you've been involved in or have knowledge of that was not straight – I mean where you've given someone "a helping hand", for example?' McGuinness replied: 'Only what I would call gilding the lily, like you say, where people have been given a helping hand.'

Enlarging on the topic, he said he could not recall any incident in which an innocent person had been fitted up, but went on to say that the

Flying Squad were not dealing with innocent people. They were up against organised villains who were 'bang at it', researching potential robbery targets, doing dummy runs, wearing disguises and carrying imitation firearms. When this type of villain protested about wrongful arrest, said McGuinness, they could be given 'a gobful' or 'verbal' or have something planted on them 'to seal their fate'. He said everyone at his Flying Squad base had known about what were called 'first-aid kits'. When he had arrived on the Squad and had first heard the term used, he had thought that what was being referred to was a straightforward first-aid kit to be carried on operations in case someone was injured. But then he realised that these bags had a more sinister purpose. They contained 'a robber's gear', and included imitation firearms, a balaclava and even wigs, all of which could be planted on robbers. He said there were two possible scenarios in which the kit would be used: 'First, in case a blagger was shot and he wasn't armed or a gun couldn't be found. This was for self-protection, to justify shooting a bloke. Secondly, to give someone a leg-up or helping hand.'

McGuinness said that shortly after he had joined the Flying Squad someone had asked whether he had anything suitable for the kit, and he had brought in a silver-coloured Milbro gat gun. It was a low-powered air weapon that fired lead pellets, but it looked like a real firearm, and it was subsequently planted on a team of criminals who had been looking at a Barclays Bank branch. He recalled another occasion when another team had been looking at a jeweller's. 'On leaving the plot the blaggers walked through a supermarket to a rear service road where the getaway vehicle, a red car, was parked. They were taken out as they got in the car. By the time I got to the car they had all been detained and arrested and officers were milling about.' He said one officer was shouting at one of the robbers, 'Where's the gun, where's the gun? Anyway, this one is down to you and it's got a fucking round in it!' McGuinness then saw a gun on the ground near the robber, and he realised that it had been 'laid down' by the officer. The gun was a 9mm blank-firing Beretta, and McGuinness had seen several of these in the first-aid kits.

The anti-corruption investigators were thrown by these fresh allegations of fabricating evidence which McGuinness had offered only after months of questioning. They appeared to have opened up a totally new area of wrong-doing at his office. But why had McGuinness made these claims at the very end of the debriefing process? Was he himself guilty of gilding the lily in order to ensure he would get a better supergrass deal? Before any further investigation into his claims took place, the debriefers contacted the officer in charge of the case, Detective Chief Inspector Martin Bridger. He decided to question McGuinness himself, to make sure there had been no misunderstanding. McGuinness confirmed to Bridger that everyone knew of the first-aid bags. He said there was no way he was mistaking them for proper medical kits.

McGuinness: 'It was a bag that had certain items in it, paraphernalia in case there was an incident of someone being shot, where they'd made a mistake in good faith. I think the Americans called it a dropsy, to cover the fact that they [the criminals] weren't armed.'

Bridger: 'To later justify police action, that is by shooting someone?'

McGuinness: 'Yes, even though that action may be justifiable. It's to make it a hundred per cent safe.'

Bridger: 'And were they taken out each time you went out on the plot?'

McGuinness: 'I would say the majority of times. It's impossible for me to say that it was there every time, but I would say the majority of times.'

McGuinness went on to say that after Flying Squad briefings prior to operations, most of the senior officers would ask whether the first-aid bag was being carried. He knew of at least three such bags, and named the officers in charge of them. Sometimes they were in the boots of officers' cars, or on the gunships, and 99 per cent of the time, when he was out in the black taxicab used by the Flying Squad for surveillance, he would see the bag being carried in the footwell, next to the driver. The rest of the exchange was dominated by Bridger persistently asking the prisoner whether he was sure about what he was saying. McGuinness would not be shaken. He was adamant that everyone in the office knew about the first-aid kits, and he was prepared to plead guilty to allowing his Milbro gun to be used to fit someone up.

In follow-up interviews with his regular debriefers, McGuinness enlarged on the atmosphere at his Flying Squad base, providing a remarkable insight into the pressures on officers to conform. He explained that there was a hard core of officers who commanded respect and that 'most of the criminality was instigated' by two more senior officers:

In this situation it was impossible not to fall in with the group. Call it peer group pressure if you like. Looking back, there are things I would never have done if I was on my own, but because of this group environment it was a combination of things – misplaced loyalty, fear of letting people down, losing face. You've got to remember I worked with these people day in and day out. Every one of them was a strong person, and despite this we all depended on one another. We would all be on the pavement together facing armed blaggers and, without overdramatising it, your life could depend on your partner. That's the mentality of it. If in certain situations I had been just by myself, I know I wouldn't have done the things I did, but I wasn't. I was part of a group and loved the work, the job, so consequently I just went along with everything. There was a bond you got from being on the Flying Squad that I would say is pretty unique, almost a macho thing. At retirement do's, Christmas do's, ex-Squad officers would get invites and always turned out. It was this very bond that Kevin [Garner] played on when he contacted me about the drugs job. I'm telling you that in the two years I was at Limehouse after the Squad, I never once considered nicking anything or getting involved in criminality. Yet when Kevin contacted me out of the blue, told me about a bit of work, I now know he played on the bond. I couldn't say no. I had to help him out ... I can remember thinking, Terry, don't go through this door, but I couldn't walk away through ignorance, through fear of losing face ...

I feel that all of this came about from the attitudes within the office. I was without any doubt influenced by those around me, strong characters like ...

There is no doubt that within the office these people set a tone of direction. You either fell in with it or you fell out. If you disagreed, what could you do? Go to the detective chief inspector and bitch about the very people he had put in place? I don't think. What options did I have if I saw something going on that I didn't agree with? What would have been the effect on my career if I had said 'no'? I would have been kicked off. The problem I found was once you were dragged in, you were knackered. Nine times out of ten you didn't realise that you were involved.

As an example, McGuinness explained how he had offered up his

Milbro gun as self-protection, knowing that it could be planted on an unarmed person shot by police by mistake.

> The first time I realised that it was going to be used for any other purpose was when I saw it in the footwell of that car. By that time I was fucked. What could I say? After all, I never put it there. I never found it. If I wanted to take it any further, I couldn't go to the DCI. At that time there was nothing in place for me to report to a senior officer, even anonymously. It would have ruined my career, and you know as well as I do that nothing would have stayed anonymous anyway ... People weren't blatantly fitted up. We didn't have to. We were professional enough to work on people month in, month out if need be, to get the job done properly. I'm not trying to paint myself as a saint. Despite everything I've spoken about, I think we were good Old Bill, in that we nicked armed robbers. When I first got on the Squad, robberies were reported in our area at a thousand a year. They were down to 350 a year by the end of 1995. Now that wasn't down to fitting people up, but just to good policing and investigation. I accept that there was bad practice, but to this day I still say the office did a good job.

What McGuinness was alleging about the use of first-aid kits would need to be fully investigated, especially as he claimed that most of those at his Flying Squad base, including senior officers, knew of their existence and of how they could be used. If what he was saying was true, it meant in effect that all these officers were conniving in possible conspiracies to pervert the course of justice. That was a criminal offence. But McGuinness was not finished. He went on to portray an office where serious horseplay and bullying were regular occurrences, with senior officers doing little or nothing to control the practices. These extra allegations would have to be investigated as well, even if they were largely of a disciplinary nature.

McGuinness said that Kevin Garner and another officer nicknamed 'Mental' were always playing practical jokes with imitation firearms or blank-firing starting pistols. Garner would sometimes wear a balaclava and pretend to be mad. He remembered how he had been on the way back to the office carrying a tray of tea when Mental jumped out at him, firing an imitation Beretta, which sounded just like a real firearm. McGuinness said he jumped a mile, spilled all the tea, and shouted at

Mental that he was a cunt. Gunfights like this were a regular occurrence, happening at least once a week, according to McGuinness, and senior officers must have heard the racket but did nothing to stop it, or to prevent the playing of practical jokes on anyone new joining the Squad. One officer, who will be called 'D', was regularly picked on 'because he was basically useless at everything, and everything he did went wrong'. Garner and Mental used to aim blanks at him in the office. The governors turned a blind eye, allowing the boys to let off steam. McGuinness said there was an unofficial rule in the office which decreed that D wasn't allowed in without knocking and asking permission. On one occasion, seeing him standing at the door, McGuinness shouted at him: 'Oi! What are you doing in here?' D retorted: 'What are you going to do about it from there, you fat cunt?' McGuinness said he reached into his desk, took out a Bowie knife whose blade tip was missing, and threw it at D. 'He was like a rabbit caught in the headlamps,' said McGuinness. 'He didn't move and the knife struck him squarely in the chest, blade first. He just shouted, "You cunt, you cunt," and disappeared out of the office.'

As well as the six blank-firing imitation Berettas 'floating round' the office, McGuinness remembered an ornamental sawn-off shotgun and two metal pipes taped together to resemble a shotgun. Another officer had an imitation Magnum .44 revolver with insulating tape on the handle. When that officer left the Flying Squad, he gave the gun to McGuinness, who kept it in his desk. When McGuinness left for Limehouse, the gun was given to another officer. 'I was clearing out my desk when he just leant across and took the gun out of my drawer and said something like, "You don't need that," and then took it. I wasn't bothered 'cos I had no use for it.'

When this phase of McGuinness's questioning finished in May 1998, CIB3 anti-corruption officers put the first-aid kit and horseplay claims to one side while they concentrated on the more serious allegations about the Flying Squad. Although their enquiries into the security van robbery and the other thefts of money to which Garner and McGuinness had confessed were supposed to be secret, information was inevitably leaking out to those termed 'the enemy' – the suspect corrupt officers – and to others, including me. Following my January 1998 *Panorama* programme on corruption within the South East Regional Crime Squad, I was known by many people to be continuing to investigate police wrong-doing, especially that involving the Flying Squad. One of my contacts told me to expect an anonymous phone call from someone who wanted to give me important documents about the Squad. The call came a couple of days later. I was instructed to go to a certain London street where, outside particular premises, I would find a black rubbish bag which would be tied distinctively at the top. Hurrying to the street, I found the heavy bag, carried it to my car and looked inside. It contained more than two thousand pages of police documents concerning the Flying Squad corruption inquiry. These papers, containing interviews, statements and other confidential information, have proved invaluable. To whoever provided them, I give continued thanks.

Some other 'leaks' came from the disclosure of documents to the suspects to which they were legally entitled. The 'enemy' was also starting to hit back at the Met's anti-corruption officers, circulating rumours that some of them had themselves been involved in corruption and other wrong-doing. On a personal level, there was talk of one senior officer having beaten up women. Two others, both married, were said to have had affairs. One was in trouble over an incident with a young woman officer at one of the police training colleges. The wife of another senior CIB officer found two strange men hanging around in the street as she returned from work. Their garden furniture was rearranged overnight. 'I have no doubt that this was intimidation by corrupt detectives or their associates,' the CIB officer told me. 'They wanted to let me know that they knew where I lived, and that I and my wife should watch out.' Another rumour circulated to the effect that an incriminating tape recording had been made of another officer, and that it would be used against him if he ever gave evidence in a corruption trial. Other allegations were made that CIB3 officers were using improper or even illegal tactics during their investigations.

Some of the stories concerned the supergrasses Garner and McGuinness, whom the police wanted to use as witnesses in trials. Garner was said to be mentally ill while McGuinness was viewed as a buffoon, whose evidence was both unreliable and incapable of proof. With their former Flying Squad colleague Keith Green about to go on trial over the cannabis sting in the autumn of 1998, it was said that if they ever gave evidence against him they would be torn to bits in cross-examination. They would be so destroyed that they could never be put forward as credible witnesses in any future corruption trials. Together with the allegations against CIB3 officers, this would effectively mean the collapse of the whole Metropolitan Police anti-corruption initiative. As intended, these suggestions reached Scotland Yard and the Crown Prosecution Service, and they undoubtedly played a part in the prosecution's consideration of how the important Keith Green trial should be handled.

Although Green was pleading not guilty, the police and the Crown took the view that the evidence against him was compelling. The covert video taken by CIB of him, Garner and McGuinness was devastating on its own, with the three of them clearly being seen breaking into 4A Albert Road, Green carrying a police truncheon, and then taking the 80 kilos of cannabis. Then there were the compelling police interviews with him after his arrest in which he admitted that Garner had told him beforehand that they were going to the premises to take property. Although Green was claiming he was unaware that cannabis was to be taken, it was believed that once inside the flat he must have known there was cannabis in the bags, because the smell was so strong, and he was supposed to have been an expert in drugs while at NCIS. Also, he faced another charge, in addition to conspiracy to supply the drugs. The thinking was that if he somehow managed to be acquitted of that, then the second charge, one of aggravated burglary, was bound to stick. With such powerful evidence, the Crown took the view that it was not necessary for either Garner or McGuinness to appear as witnesses. There was no point in them having to face an intimidating cross-examination at this stage in the anti-corruption investigation. They should be held in reserve for the more important trials to come.

Green's mental state appeared to have deteriorated since his arrest. He had been in the Flying Squad for five years, leaving for NCIS after the shooting incident in which he believed he had come close to death. Although he claimed to be suffering from post-traumatic stress, he bore no animosity towards McGuinness, who after the incident was best man at Green's wedding. After he retired from the police on the grounds of ill health, his only job had been part-time rugby coaching. The rest of the time he moped around the house, doing nothing in particular. After his arrest, unlike Garner and McGuinness initially, he had answered all the anti-corruption investigators' questions, but there came a time when he had nothing more to say to them. The officers in charge, Superintendent Dave Wood and Chief Inspector Chris Jarratt, became frustrated with him when he refused to assist them in their wider corruption investigations. He said it was made clear that if he did not co-operate he would be sent to Brixton Prison, where he would have to take his chances with normal criminals. Apparently because of his mental state, he was housed in the hospital wing at Brixton, and he claims that Wood and Jarratt tried to get him to change his mind even there.

The authorities kept up the pressure on him, even after his transfer to a semi-secure mental hospital at Goodmayes, in Essex, where he was to be kept until the trial. A letter from the Home Office's Mental Health Unit stated that Green was viewed as an escape risk:

> He requires treatment in a secure environment where he is not given the opportunity to escape. He is charged with serious offences and, if he is found guilty, the strength of evidence against him and his other defendants is such that he may possibly receive a lengthy custodial sentence. Our concerns about Mr Green are based upon the fact that the drugs allegedly stolen in the crime have yet to be recovered and at the time of his arrest, Mr Green was found to be in possession of forged police warrant cards, a Turkish passport, shotgun ammunition and a considerable amount of cash. A previous application for bail was denied because of concerns by the CPS that Mr Green and his other defendants might attempt to flee from justice. In view of this, there is a need to ensure that there is no reduction in the level of security while Mr Green is in the care of Goodmayes Hospital or receiving treatment.

Two of the hospital's staff travelled with Green to and from Goodmayes for the duration of his trial, one of them sitting with him in the Old Bailey dock. Prosecuting counsel David Waters, QC, gave a straightforward outline of the case, explaining how CIB had set up the sting operation and how two of the three, McGuinness and Garner, had pleaded guilty. The covert video of the three inside the flat, finding the drugs and then carrying them outside to Garner's car, was played to the jury. CIB witnesses outlined what Green had told them in his extensive interviews about how he desperately missed being a police officer and that he had been overjoyed when Garner arrived unexpectedly asking for help in recovering property for a client of his employers, a chauffeuring company. He gained some sympathy from the jury when a detective inspector described searching his home and finding mementos and photographs from his police days all around the house, on walls, tables and shelves. As some of these mementos were shown to and passed around by the jury, Green wept, hanging his head in apparent shame.

When he went into the witness box, his first words to the jury were that he was in a psychiatric unit taking medication four times a day, suffering from continued depression and post-traumatic stress as a result of the 1993 shooting incident. He felt like 'one of the living dead'. Green said that Garner had asked for his help in recovering property because another former Flying Squad colleague had dropped out. Green had agreed, and after meeting up with Garner and McGuinness had asked what the property was, only to be told by Garner, 'Don't worry. Watch our backs – that's all you've got to do.' He said that once inside the flat he had not gone into the bathroom where the cannabis was hidden, but had simply been handed bags by Garner to carry downstairs to his car. He did not know what was inside them and it had never been his intention to supply cannabis. As for burglary, he had believed that Garner was simply acting for someone who wanted their property recovered.

Under cross-examination, Green came under pressure from David Waters, who tried to undermine his story, suggesting that he must have known that there was cannabis present. Had Garner really not told him? As a trained drugs expert, had he not smelled the cannabis in the flat? Green insisted that he had no idea that drugs were involved, and Waters could not go further because he was tied by the rules of evidence. With the decision having been made by the Crown not to call Garner and McGuinness as prosecution witnesses, Waters was not now allowed to change his mind and call the pair to give evidence concerning what they had told Green. Green was found not guilty, and as he left the Old Bailey he was greeted by former Flying Squad colleagues and taken off to a pub for celebratory drinks.

ten

NEW CORRUPTION CRACKDOWN

In recent years we have deployed very sophisticated methods to prevent and detect misconduct, with some success. We have reached a point where I believe that the current framework of disciplinary law and regulations and guidance actually inhibits us making further progress.

Metropolitan Police Commissioner Sir Paul Condon

The not-guilty verdict in the Keith Green trial represented a tremendous setback for the Crown Prosecution Service, and, more importantly, for the whole of the Metropolitan Police's anti-corruption drive. It created fresh ammunition for those critics arguing that the corruption problem was being much exaggerated. Partly to counter this growing criticism, the Met had planned to release to the media the covert video taken at 4A Albert Road. Showing these three ex-Flying Squad officers breaking into a flat and taking cannabis would vividly demonstrate how serious the corruption problem was. However, the Met decided not to release the damning video because of Green's acquittal and associated legal problems.

The trial verdict also provided justification for those Met high-ups who recognised that corruption was a serious problem but who were also arguing that it could not be dealt with satisfactorily through the courts, where juries tended to give the benefit of the doubt to police officers. This group of senior officers wanted corruption dealt with by internal disciplinary procedures or sackings. This would also mean avoiding bad publicity, which they said was causing untold damage to the good reputation of the Metropolitan Police. While it was true that the Green trial and other cases were generating headlines, Sir Paul Condon and those in charge of the anti-corruption initiative had expected such publicity, and took the view that it showed that the Met were facing up to the corruption problem and were tackling it. Keeping cases out of the public eye by dealing with them through internal disciplinary boards was in any event impossible where there appeared to be strong evidence of corruption and of serious criminal acts having been committed, and the police would be failing in their duty to the public if they tried to suppress them. Coupled with this belief in accountability was awareness of a need for 'transparency', a new buzz word in the Met.

Far from shying away from more publicity following the setback of the Green verdict, the force went on the offensive against wrong-doing on two fronts – corruption, and also racism. A few months before, at the Commons Home Affairs Committee, the Commissioner had stressed the difficulties of targeting and prosecuting cunning corrupt cops: 'In recent years we have deployed very sophisticated methods to prevent and detect misconduct, with some success. We have reached a point where I believe that the current framework of disciplinary law and regulations and guidance actually inhibits us making further progress.'

Condon went on to attack one of the police unions, the Superintendents' Association, for what he called a 'very inaccurate and misleading' statement which it had given to the Home Affairs Committee. The Association had said that a previous Commissioner, Sir Robert Mark, had dealt with corruption in the 1970s with broadly the same powers as were available in the 1990s. The suggestion was that the problems facing the current Met hierarchy could be met by simply using these existing measures to the full. Responding to the criticism, Condon listed all the different ways in which 'the pendulum had swung heavily in favour of the bad officers'.

He said:

> Virtually every power which enabled Sir Robert Mark to deal through the disciplinary system with bad officers has been eroded or removed in the intervening years. The burden of proof has now moved to 'beyond reasonable doubt', the same as the criminal system. Officers now have the availability of full legal representation; they did not before and they certainly did not in Sir Robert Mark's time. There was no double jeopardy rule: there is now. We are severely inhibited from using discipline in cases where the criminal system has failed ... Failure by an officer nowadays to answer questions during discipline cases cannot be commented on in the disciplinary process, even though inferences can be drawn in criminal cases. In some ways, by utilising the guidance on sickness and stress, officers can avoid appearing as defendants in discipline cases in exactly the same

circumstances where in a criminal case they would have to appear. Whereas Sir Robert Mark celebrated the ease of using discipline regulations compared with criminal, I believe I am actually faced with a disciplinary system which has as many hurdles, if not more, to clear than convicting an officer in the criminal court. That enormous symbolic power and fear that helped to suppress bad behaviour has actually lifted.

The Home Affairs Committee report, published in January 1998, accepted the need for reform, concluding: 'There is a great deal of justified dissatisfaction with elements of the disciplinary and complaints systems. Improvements to the procedures are necessary if the system is to succeed in dealing with, and if necessary removing, officers who are corrupt or guilty of misconduct, and if the public is to have full confidence both in the system and in the police as a whole.'

The committee said police disciplinary procedures should be as close as possible to those in other walks of life. It supported proposed changes: reduction of officers' 'right of silence'; removal of the double jeopardy rule under which disciplinary proceedings could not be brought where a criminal prosecution had failed; reduction of the standard of proof in less important disciplinary charges to the civil standard – the judgement being on 'the balance of probabilities' rather than 'beyond reasonable doubt'. The committee also recommended changes in regulations that gave some officers too great an opportunity to abuse rules designed to protect officers who were genuinely sick. It wanted fast-tracking of serious cases so that officers would be prevented from being suspended on full pay for months while the full, cumbersome disciplinary proceedings were under way. The committee also declared that disciplinary investigations should proceed despite illness, and the power to reduce an officer's pay after six months' sick leave should be extended to suspended officers.

In December 1998, Sir Paul Condon and his new deputy, Sir John Stevens, held a news conference to launch their new 'Corruption and Dishonesty Prevention Strategy'. It took place as the government was about to approve the new disciplinary powers recommended by the Home Affairs Committee, and with the report of the McPherson Inquiry into the police handling of the murder of the black teenager Stephen Lawrence soon to be published. The two senior officers pledged there would be no 'hiding place' and no 'amnesty' for corrupt officers. 'No one should underestimate our determination to relentlessly pursue and prosecute corrupt and dishonest members of staff, either current or past, and those who seek to entrap our colleagues,' said Sir Paul.

He announced that special integrity tests were to be introduced. These would be of two types. There would be targeted, intelligence-led tests, where CIB would be acting on information that a particular detective or group of officers was corrupt. In such cases, temptations would be put their way, much as had happened in the cannabis sting. Often taking part in these targeted 'tests' would be undercover officers, posing as bent cops or as criminals, offering bribes. There are two kinds of undercover officers, or 'UCs' as they are known to police. The first, Level One officers, are highly trained and belong to a national pool of UCs from which individual police forces can draw. 'Legends' are often provided, with careful briefings being given to each UC, so that he or she understands completely the role they are playing, without necessarily knowing the fuller picture of the targeted operation. Level Two undercover officers can be used as 'market testers', attempting to buy drugs at a house or club, for example. Both kinds of UC face danger, as exposure can lead to physical harm or even death.

The second type of integrity test involved less risk and would not be targeted at individual officers. It could also feature Level Two undercover officers, acting as the so-called 'mystery shopper' used by department stores or other big commercial organisations. Here someone would pose as a member of the public and, for example, go into a police station and raise some kind of problem, to test officers' responses. These non-targeted tests were also to be used to tackle racism. All the Met's officers are expected to adhere to ethical non-racist and non-sexist behaviour, so integrity tests were to be used at police stations where it was thought that racist attitudes existed. One test could involve, for example, an officer from another area having to visit a particular station under the pretext of collecting some documents. While there, he would drop in at the canteen and make racist remarks to see what kind of reaction they received. Another example might involve an officer telephoning a station, pretending he was about to be posted there, and asking for advice on accommodation. A common enough, innocent-sounding request. But in the ensuing conversation, the test caller would say that he wanted to avoid areas with black people, and then gauge the response. Scotland Yard also announced that new recruits to specialist units, such as the Flying Squad and drugs teams, would face intense security screening and vetting.

The Met's measures were approved by the Home Secretary, Jack Straw. A warning had gone out a few weeks before of similar anti-corruption moves on the part of the National Crime Squad, which incorporated the South East Regional Crime Squad. Commander Roy Penrose, who had himself headed successful CIB investigations in the 1980s, called on his officers, many of whom were attached to the squad from the Metropolitan Police, to inform on colleagues they suspected of malpractice. He warned that, as part of the anti-corruption drive, phone calls and pager messages could be monitored, adding that to preserve the secrecy and security of NCS investigations, a 'need to know' policy was being introduced, similar to the 'sterile corridors' system already adopted by the Met's CIB investigators.

Key to the successful operation of the new measures were the police unions. Sitting in the front row at the Met's news conference to launch the new strategy was Glen Smyth, who had recently taken over as chairman of the Police Federation's London branch. He voiced support for the fight against corruption. He agreed to intelligence-led targeting of suspect officers, but warned that he did not want a 'Big Brother' situation arising. There was a world of difference between setting traps where there was justifiable suspicion and embarking on 'fishing trips'. Three years later, in an interview with me, Glen Smyth said that prior to his becoming chairman relations with the Commissioner had largely broken down. He told me that he took the view then, and still does, that there was nothing more undermining to the police service than corruption. 'It leaves a general taint against the whole organisation,' he said.

> We tell people we are a responsible organisation, so we have to behave responsibly. We joined the Met's strategy on the basis that it should be operated fairly, and that the police should have the same rights as the public. Where there was evidence of corruption we wanted to see prosecutions, and if the jury was satisfied, we wanted long sentences. We and the Met are speaking the same truth, but from different standpoints. There was no point in taking a contrary view. You either declare you have a problem, or you face a bigger problem in the future. What I did say to Sir Paul was that CIB had to do the job properly, and they should be seen to be doing the job properly.

Another area where the Police Federation had an apparent change of heart was over libel actions. It regularly used to offer financial help to officers mounting libel actions against newspapers, magazines and broadcasters through its solicitors, Russell Jones and Walker. A threat of libel action from RJW on behalf of an officer would usually entail publishers reaching for their cheque books, trying to settle a case before it got to court, even if the publication or programme concerned could offer a reasonable defence. The problem lay in the cost of defending libel actions. It was said that mounting a libel case could cost £30,000, even before it reached court – and after that about £1,000 a day. Defending an action could cost even more. So, rather than risk the lottery of the libel court, it was easier for the media to try to settle cases at the outset. Much better to apologise for the infraction and pay a few thousand pounds in damages than have to pay £50,000 in costs. It is believed that, up to 1997, the Police Federation had won its last one hundred libel actions in a row, the vast majority, if not all, being settled in out-of-court agreements. But then a national newspaper decided to make a stand.

It happened in 1992, when a group of officers from Stoke Newington police station in north London felt they had been wronged in the *Guardian*, in two articles by the paper's respected crime correspondent, Duncan Campbell. He wrote about allegations of corruption at Stoke Newington, the same allegations outlined in the first chapter of this book which helped lead to the creation of, first, the ghost squad and then the new anti-corruption group, CIB3. Under the headlines 'Police suspected of drug dealing' and 'Disquiet dogs community police station', Campbell reported that eight officers had been transferred to other stations. None of them was named, but five brought libel actions, arguing that their friends and colleagues had been able to identify them with the accusations of drugs dealing of which they were entirely innocent. After a protracted libel trial at the High Court in February 1997, the jury found in the *Guardian*'s favour, deciding that the five officers had not been libelled. It was a landmark decision, greeted as a victory for free speech. But the newspaper's editor, Alan Rusbridger, wrote that the verdict had a downside.

Against all the odds, we won today's case. So why the gloom? Because our victory today was all thanks to the perspicacity and common sense of the jury and no thanks to the court, the judge or the law. We risked hundreds of thousands on the verdict of the jury today. How many smaller papers will take that risk? There was a massive investigation into the Stoke Newington police station. Thirteen cases involving officers were overturned on appeal. Wrongly convicted people were freed. The Met paid out £500,000 in damages. And the Guardian made the mistake of reporting it . . . Our reporting was fair and accurate. Our mistake was to forget the Police Federation. It doesn't like newspapers reporting on inquiries into police wrong-doing or corruption. It employs a firm of solicitors to sue newspapers which try to keep communities informed about what is going on. The latest figures show that in 33 months they fought – and won – no fewer than 95 defamation actions. Their members were richer to the tune of £1,567,000 as a result. Nice little earner for the coppers. A shame about the community being kept in the dark . . . We talk so casually about the right to know and the freedom of the press. But when a decent, honest reporter writes a story that matters, he is given no protection by the courts. That reporter won today. But have the bullies won in the long run? And does anyone much care?

In an editorial headlined 'A victory for freedom', the London *Evening Standard* said:

> The Federation has over the years found that suing newspapers is a profitable option. However, in the long term the Federation is misguided if it thinks it is helping its cause by taking up legal cases such as this. All those who support the police know that public confidence is crucial to the vital tasks they perform. Most officers acknowledge that allegations of police malpractice are a persistent public concern. Allowing even the unfounded suspicion to linger that officers and their representatives wish to hamper legitimate investigation by the press could well make the public believe that police wrong-doing is much more widespread than it really is. When major allegations against the police are made, surely it is sensible if senior officers shout from the rooftops all that they are doing to investigate them, so that the public know their anxieties are being taken seriously. It is now time for the Police Federation to think more of the reputation of the Force as a whole and halt its bullying tactics against the press.'

By coincidence, just a few days after the libel verdict, a former Stoke Newington detective was sent to jail for ten years for drugs smuggling. Incredibly, Ronald Palumbo had gone on multimillion-pound drugs runs to Spain while on bail awaiting trial at the Old Bailey. Palumbo was one of forty-six north London officers against whom allegations were made. Facing charges of committing perjury by fabricating evidence to secure convictions while at Stoke Newington, Palumbo supervised four smuggling runs from Spain involving lorry-loads of cannabis with a street value of nearly £10 million. Cleared of perjury, he was then arrested by Customs officers on the drugs charges, and was finally found guilty at Maidstone Crown Court, Kent.

Losing the libel action cost the Federation an estimated £600,000 in legal fees. Undaunted, the union appealed against the jury's verdict. It was not until July 1998 that it gave up, after the Appeal Court threw out the case. With total costs by then approaching £1 million, disquiet was reported among Federation members about the wisdom of fighting the action. Since then, media lawyers have noticed fewer Police Federation libel actions. This could have been because of the huge costs involved in the *Guardian* case, but the reduction also came at a time of increasing public awareness of police wrong-doing, a change in the union's London leadership, and reform of the libel laws.

Also key to the authorities' moves to root out corrupt officers was the Crown Prosecution Service. CIB had been gathering evidence since 1994, and had dealt with the CPS on a case-by-case basis, as was usual police practice. This involved submitting reports to a CPS lawyer who, after discussions, would decide whether there was enough evidence to mount a prosecution, whether more was needed, or whether it looked as though the best way of dealing with the particular officers was through internal disciplinary procedures. But as the CIB investigations progressed and widened, it became increasingly clear that many of the cases were interlinked, and that the whole inquiry was not only complex, but was also going to take several years to complete. There was also the problem that much of the CIB evidence was intelligence based and difficult or impossible to use in court. Given these circumstances, it was decided to set up a special unit at CPS headquarters in Ludgate Hill, a short walk from the Old Bailey, dedicated to dealing only with police corruption cases. The unit was headed by an experienced lawyer, Robert Drybrough-Smith, supported by Martin Polaine and Carl Holmes. CIB officers were able to discuss cases with them knowing that they were the experts.

Drybrough-Smith was a veteran from the days of the last big inquiry into London police corruption, Operation Countryman. He had been part of the prosecution team in two of the Countryman trials, and also in a spin-off case known as the Christmas Tree corruption trial because a bug had been planted in a Christmas tree in a room in which a criminal had passed money to a detective. In June 1998, Dryborough-Smith was asked to head the new team by the then Director of Public Prosecutions, Barbara Mills. 'I thought it would be interesting,' he told me. 'It turned out to be much more interesting than I had ever thought. The cases we were handling had everything. Legally, they involved so much, ranging from resident informants, sophisticated technical surveillance, to defence challenges under European law. And the facts of some of the cases were sensational on their own, worthy of films or dramas.'

All the lawyers and caseworkers on the new team were positively vetted because of the sensitivity of their new work, and Dryborough-Smith excluded those who mixed socially with the police or who had officers as close relatives. At first, Carl Holmes concentrated on Flying Squad investigations and Martin Polaine on those involving SERCS.

Separately, the Police Complaints Authority also became involved in 1998. In fact, the PCA had been approached at a much earlier stage by the Metropolitan Police, who said they wanted some kind of independent scrutiny of the whole investigation. The PCA had declined, arguing that it had neither the funds nor the staff to supervise what looked like being a long and complex inquiry. Scotland Yard was not unhappy with the PCA's decision. It meant that the Met could get on with their task without outside interference. Later, the PCA did become involved, but only in a limited way. CIB2 officers had been given the job of looking at a number of previous criminal cases and trials that had involved allegedly corrupt Flying Squad officers. In particular, they examined cases in which defendants had made complaints about officers or had claimed in court that they had been fitted up by the Squad's detectives. The PCA then supervised the CIB2 investigations into these past cases. This new inquiry was code-named Operation Goldcard. Of obvious importance to this team of investigators was what Terry McGuinness had said about officers having their own imitation guns and carrying a 'first-aid kit' to fit people up. But when the anti-corruption detectives started to pursue his claims, they were in for a surprise.

Although McGuinness had talked about the guns and the first-aid kit in May 1998, it was not until November of that year that his fellow supergrass, Kevin Garner, was asked detailed questions about his gun. He said he had paid £30 for his imitation weapon so he could join in the office horseplay. 'It came with caps that made a realistic bang when it fired,' he said. 'Some officers mess about with water pistols in general horseplay – that's why I initially bought this gun. The noise made by my gun was not as realistic as the noise made by the other two as their guns fired blanks. It was often a case of creeping up behind people or firing the gun behind people to make them jump. The horseplay would go on for a week and then stop and some time later it would start again. But it would never really go on for longer than a week. It was one way of releasing tension or stress.'

Having seen a television news item about a policeman shooting an unarmed man, Garner said the thought had crossed his mind that it might be a good idea to carry such a weapon with him on jobs, in case he found himself in the same position. But he insisted that he had never actually done so, maintaining that his gun had never left the office. When asked about the use of first-aid kits, he strongly denied their existence, describing the suggestion bluntly as 'a load of bollocks'. The CIB officers were to get much the same denials from others who had served in the same office. While it could be argued that their responses were predictable in that they were unlikely to admit to anything as serious as fit-ups, there was no obvious reason for Garner to deny the practice. Strangely, however, even at that stage, pride may have been a factor for him. He told his anti-corruption investigators on more than one occasion that he and his former colleagues were all good coppers who did not have to resort to fit-ups to gain convictions. Any admissions to noble-cause corruption would have resulted in the destruction of this last vestige of his tattered reputation, as well as that of the others who had served with him on the Flying Squad. Against that, however, Garner had already admitted to much graver offences, and he had also betrayed several of his colleagues. He knew he would be going to prison for about five years, so there was little point in him holding back on something like first-aid kits if they had ever been carried. In addition, he had also been warned earlier that he had to tell the full truth, and that if he was caught out lying he could lose his resident informant status. So, was McGuinness telling the truth, or was he exaggerating to enhance his role as a supergrass?

Whatever the strength of CIB doubts, it did not stop the questioning of more than eighty former and serving officers who had been based with the pair. Those still in the police were given a strongly worded Regulation 163 document setting out the allegations:

> It is alleged that during the time you were attached to the Flying Squad . . . a number of imitation or real firearms were available for use in the following circumstances:
>
> 1 'Horseplay' in that imitation firearms were discharged within the office at other officers.
> 2 In that imitation or other firearms were held within a 1st Aid Kit, whereby in the event of an officer shooting an unarmed suspect, a firearm would be 'laid down' to justify the shooting.
> 3 In that imitation or other firearms were held within a 1st Aid Kit in order to enhance [plant] evidence where suspects had been arrested.
>
> The allegation states that you specifically knew of the existence of the 1st Aid Kit and some or all of the intended reasons for it's [sic] use.
> It is alleged that you colluded in it's [sic] use on operations, and you therefore are guilty of a criminal offence of conspiring to pervert the course of justice.
> It is further alleged under the Discipline Codes that you are guilty of:
>
> 1 Discreditable Conduct in that you acted in a manner likely to bring discredit on the reputation of the Police Service and/or
> 2 Neglect of Duty in that you neglected or omitted to carry out your duty.

Some of the detectives and former Flying Squad officers interviewed over the first few months of 1999 refused to co-operate, particularly those under investigation for corruption after being named by Garner and McGuinness. In prepared statements, these officers denied any knowledge of first-aid kits and refused to answer questions. With them were solicitors from Russell Jones and Walker, the firm used by the Police

Federation which had already been very critical of CIB, suggesting that information about the corruption had been deliberately leaked to the media. The solicitors used the opportunity provided by the interviews with their clients to again attack CIB for unfairness. They said: 'The current allegations are ill-defined and appear to extend back as long as ten years ago. There has been continuing and highly damaging prejudicial publicity concerning CIB's investigations and allegations of so-called police corruption for at least 18 months which has been drawn to the attention of CIB on many occasions to no effect so far. This must call into question the fairness or impartiality of the investigation.'

Some retired officers also refused to answer questions, and CIB garnered little useful information from the serving officers who did talk. The point common to all their statements was that they had been unaware of any bags containing robbers' gear used in the way suggested by Terry McGuinness. Some said he was so thick (many nicknamed him 'One Cell' as well as 'Meathead') that he had confused first-aid kits with the bags carried by surveillance officers containing a change of clothes and basic disguises. One of the first to be interviewed was a detective inspector, who called McGuinness 'indolent'. He said it had taken six months of strenuous effort to move him from the Flying Squad.

Another DI interviewed was someone who had been a sergeant for two years, until June 1994. He had wanted to join another Flying Squad team, and claimed that within two months of his arrival at McGuinness's and Garner's base a detective chief inspector and inspector had called him in and said he was not wanted. The officer believed in more management openness, and there was a personality clash between himself and inspectors who kept a tight control on operations. He said their style was hard but fair, but it became clear to him that not everyone was given as much information as they might have been about why decisions were taken. There were cliques of officers who tended to work together. He was told that they were tough, streetwise detectives, and he was a 'posh' officer with different practices. However, after a particularly successful operation, he felt that he did not need to prove himself professionally to the others, and anyway, he was never going to mix with them socially. The others drank, and there were stop-off places on their way home where they met up socially, whereas he was teetotal and lived in central London. As for horseplay, the detective said he had never witnessed officers playing around with guns, but there were inappropriate comments, banter and general loudness, and he recalled that officers would regularly have their ties cut off with scissors.

The most senior officer to be questioned over first-aid kits and horse-play was a detective chief superintendent who, as a detective chief inspector, had been in charge of the office at an earlier stage. He described his management style as 'hands on'. He sometimes went on operations, but he maintained a distance from the troops, relying instead on his detective inspectors. He said the first time he had ever come across the term 'first-aid kit' was when he read it on the Regulation 163 served on him by CIB. He conceded that such a bag could have been used, but it would have had to have been within a very tight group of officers. The CIB detectives interviewing him did not pull their punches. It was put to him that the office was out of control and poorly supervised, with horse-play involving imitation firearms. The questioning then led on to the very serious matter of the planting of guns on criminals. The detective chief superintendent was adamant that this was not true. He had been the boss and kept things under control. If there were pockets of staff committing offences, then they kept it very quiet, because he knew nothing about it. It was then put to this very senior officer that after transfer to the Flying Squad base he had headhunted a group of people because he knew of their propensity for dishonesty, and was prepared to turn a blind eye to their practices in order to get the job done. He replied that such an allegation was a hundred per cent wrong. If there had been a hint of malpractice, and he had been involved, then it would have been flagged up by judges, barristers and the Crown Prosecution Service at the time. If criminality had been going on, it had been behind his back.

Even those officers named by McGuinness as being honest did not support him. One man, who McGuinness claimed had refused to accept a share of stolen money, said he had no respect for McGuinness and thought him very unprofessional, but he denied ever witnessing any horseplay as described by the police supergrass. Even the detective hit by a knife thrown by McGuinness denied being bullied. Toy guns or water pistols were given, according to McGuinness, to those who had failed firearms courses. However, one officer who had failed denied ever receiving such a gift, though he did say there had been mickey-taking. Another officer described some colleagues scuffling and said he thought McGuinness 'loud' and a bit of 'a buffoon'. Another said he was a 'Walter Mitty' character, never doing much work and telling tall stories. A retired sergeant who had partnered McGuinness for a time said he had never rated him. 'He was just a yob who was a police officer. He was just a bit of a hooligan and everybody knew that. He was treated by most of the blokes as a bit of a joke. He would join in the banter, but because of his lack of intelligence, he didn't realise that quite a lot of the time, he was the joke ... McGuinness was something of a bullshitter. He enjoyed talking about a good job, but you took everything he said with a pinch of salt.'

Although that view of McGuinness was shared by some CIB officers, some of the events he had described as corrupt had indeed taken place. As well as the drugs sting, he was pleading guilty to two other thefts which Garner was also admitting, the ten-pence coins jobs and the switching of counterfeit cash for real money. But as for fit-ups, it appeared that he was on his own. Even Garner had said the suggestion was a 'load of bollocks'.

McGuinness's credibility received a very hefty dent at a later stage in the inquiry. Anti-corruption officers had spent a considerable time reinvestigating the one job where McGuinness was sure that a gun had been planted on criminals after a robbery. He had been so positive, he said, because he had earlier given the gun used, a Milbro, to a colleague. However, CIB investigators discovered that, although the gun found on the criminals looked very similar to McGuinness's, it was in fact a different weapon. McGuinness himself then admitted in May 1999 that he had been mistaken. Later, in April 2000, he pleaded guilty at the Old Bailey to ten offences of corruption, and was given a nine-year prison sentence, reduced on appeal to only seven years. He was never to be used as a prosecution witness in any trial.

Meanwhile, a number of questionable trial decisions had been reinvestigated by CIB, under the supervision of the Police Complaints Authority's deputy chairman, John Cartwright. He had complained over the years about the lack of control exercised over some of the specialist police units, particularly where informants were involved, and had been particularly outspoken in my *Panorama* programme on the SERCS officer John Donald and his colleagues. Donald had been given an eleven-year sentence for corruption first exposed in an earlier *Panorama*, and Cartwright had supervised the resulting CIB investigation. He told me: 'It's very difficult to have deep-seated extensive corruption without someone in management either averting their eyes or being so incompetent that they don't know what's going on. The role of management has

to be examined in these cases.' In 1998, the cases chosen for CIB rein-
vestigation were those where the defendants had claimed to have been
fitted up by Flying Squad officers who were later either charged with
corruption or suspended pending investigations into their alleged
wrong-doing. Cartwright said the importance of so-called noble-cause
corruption – fitting people up – should not be underestimated when
looking at wider corruption. 'There's growing evidence that officers cross
the line,' he said, 'first with noble-cause corruption, strengthening the
case against someone. Having done that once, it's easier to be tempted to
do the same for payment. Noble-cause corruption is an important test.
Once you've succumbed to that it's easier to succumb to worse financial
corruption further down the track.'

Cartwright's observations were based on the corruption investigations
he had supervised for the PCA. Somewhat surprisingly, up to this time
there had been little serious research undertaken into why some police
officers turned corrupt. It was not until later that the first study was
published. Its findings, along with other research, are examined in the
last chapter.

eleven

APPEALS

Bill 'Mad Dog' Hickson and John 'Chainsaw Woody' Woodruff had each been sentenced to fifteen years in prison in 1997 after being found guilty of a post office robbery and of conspiracy to rob others. As notorious 'blaggers' they were ideal targets for 'noble-cause' corruption . . .

Some of the previous cases reinvestigated by CIB under the supervision of the Police Complaints Authority were found to be questionable. Where it appeared that some of those imprisoned had been fitted up as a result of Flying Squad officers' evidence, the cases were sent to the Appeal Court, where Crown Prosecution Service lawyers did not seek to uphold the convictions. Indeed, the CPS sent to the lawyers representing those awaiting appeals a summary of what had been achieved by CIB, as well as disclosing statements relevant to their particular cases. The summary stated that CIB was investigating allegations of corruption, dishonesty and perverting the course of justice allegedly committed by Flying Squad detectives.

'As a result,' it continued, 'approximately 25 officers have either been charged with criminal offences, suspended from duty, or would have been had they not already retired. The Crown currently does not seek to advance these officers as witnesses of truth.' The summary went on to say that there was a larger group of officers who were aware that

> a bag containing items such as an imitation firearm and balaclavas was available, either to protect the position of an officer who had shot an unarmed suspect in good faith (and thereby to provide a justification for his action) or to enhance a case where the evidence against a defendant was circumstantial but not overwhelming ... There is no evidence which suggests that this larger group of officers played any part at any time in the use of the items, but an inference can be drawn that they were aware of their availability and the intended use.

Notwithstanding this, it is alleged they made no attempt to prevent the practice.

The first appeal heard was that of George Ellis and Anthony Zomparelli, whose father Alfredo killed Ronnie Knight's brother David in a bar-room fight. Four years later Alfredo was shot dead in a Soho amusement arcade while playing pinball. Ronnie Knight, former husband of *EastEnders* star Barbara Windsor, eventually admitted hiring a hit man to carry out the killing. Ellis and Zomparelli had been given long prison sentences after a 1996 robbery on the Thomas Cook travel company. Ellis had been cleared by the Court of Appeal of another robbery in 1991 after claiming that police had fabricated evidence against him. At his trial in 1997 for the travel agency robbery, he again alleged that he had been fitted up, this time by the Flying Squad, but the defence failed and he was sentenced to fourteen years' imprisonment.

The Appeal Court heard that three of the officers who had given evidence at the trial were among the twenty-five Flying Squad officers who were no longer regarded as witnesses of truth, having been either charged or suspended for alleged corruption. There were a further six detectives alleged to have known of the existence of the first-aid kit. The main evidence connecting Ellis to the robbery was DNA. Some of his saliva had been found in a balaclava worn by one of the robbers. Ellis claimed that a sample of his saliva had not been properly sealed and was later smeared on the balaclava. The sample had been taken by an officer who, for legal reasons, will have to be called Officer G. For the Crown, John Kelsey-Fry said that the conviction was unsafe, and pointed out that taking the saliva sample had been G's only role in the investigation. Extraordinarily, G had been called from another part of London to perform this one function, according to Ellis's counsel, Stephen Kamlish. The taking of non-intimate body samples was not a specialist job, the lawyer said, being performed routinely by constables. He added: 'It raises the suspicion that he was up to no good.' The Appeal Court quashed Ellis's conviction as well as Zomparelli's.

Terry McGuinness and Kevin Garner were both involved in another case that was referred to the Appeal Court by the Criminal Cases Review Committee. Kevin Martin, Anthony Taylor and Michael Brown had all spent five years in prison after being given ten-year sentences for a raid on a jeweller's shop in which a stun gun was used. It was several months after the robbery before the three were arrested, and from the outset they claimed to have been fitted up. Martin said a stun gun had been planted on him. Garner said he had found it under a cushion on the sofa. Also present during the search of Martin's home was McGuinness, the officer in charge of the case. Another officer there, later suspended, was said to have boasted to Martin that he 'had stitched up guys like you all day long'. A telling comment on the find came from the Appeal Court judges: 'It would be curious if so incriminating an item were to be found so ill-concealed by a surprise raid nine months after the alleged use of that weapon.' There was also no forensic evidence linking the gun found with the one used in the raid. The judges also referred to what they said was the 'surprising' way detectives managed to match Martin's palm print seven months after the robbery with one found on the shop counter. This had happened, they observed, even though Martin had been a suspect for more than six months and his fingerprints were already on police files. McGuinness also showed photographs of Anthony Taylor to a witness shortly before an identity parade. The judges agreed with the Crown that the evidence against the three men could no longer be considered reliable, and they were freed.

Kevin Garner arrested the man whose case was the next to be heard by the Appeal Court. In 1996 Abraham Shakes was sentenced to eight years' imprisonment for conspiracy to commit an armed robbery the year before at a Dairy Crest depot. The Flying Squad were tipped off about the robbery, which was to take place when a security van arrived. When it looked as though the robbers had launched their attack, the waiting police moved in. Dramatic police video footage shows Garner leading the way, his outstretched arm pointing a gun, chasing someone round the security vehicle. Photographs were taken of Shakes lying on the ground, handcuffed and face down, with a revolver by his side. Another photo showed Shakes standing with a bruised face, held triumphantly by Garner with his gun in a holster on his belt. At his trial, Shakes, who had previous convictions, claimed that he had only been at the dairy to collect crates to jack up a car as he knew the depot was closing down. Disputing much of the police evidence, he claimed that the gun had been planted on him. Police said the weapon had been stuck in his waistband. But Shakes was wearing loose-fitting jogging trousers which would not have been able to hold the heavy gun. He also said that, as some of the police surveillance footage showed, he was an unlikely robber. He had a withered left arm which was virtually useless, and the video showed him even having difficulty performing simple tasks such as shutting a car door. Shakes's disabled arm was recalled by Garner prior to the appeal, when he was asked what he remembered about the job. He said: 'I recall I nearly shot him because he wouldn't take his hand out of his pocket. I thought that he could have a gun in this pocket.' He admitted pistol-whipping Shakes to the ground, but denied planting a gun on him. The appeal judges quashed Shakes's conviction. Later he was awarded £100,000 compensation for his injuries and the time he had spent in prison.

There was an even more dramatic arrest video in another of the appeal cases, and it was to play an unexpectedly important role. Bill 'Mad Dog' Hickson and John 'Chainsaw Woody' Woodruff had each been sentenced to fifteen years in prison in 1997 after being found guilty of a post office robbery and of conspiracy to rob others. As notorious 'blaggers' they were ideal targets for noble-cause corruption. Both men had been jailed for twelve years in the 1960s for armed robberies. Then Woodruff was given an eighteen-year sentence in 1979 for being part of a gang that waylaid a security van, cut into it with a chainsaw, and stole more than £1 million. Later, Hickson was arrested after a £6 million robbery on a security van in 1983 and received a six-year sentence for handling stolen cash.

At their 1997 trial, police had said the pair had been watched carrying out reconnaissance on post offices for a year, and were thought to have taken part in seventeen robberies, netting them up to £300,000. Police had heard that they were going to rob a particular sub-post-office, so had set up an ambush. Police video taken from a vantage point on the other side of the road shows frightened shoppers running from the post office. Woodruff and Hickson then emerge like a couple of elderly friends, the former wearing a surgical collar as disguise. 'They're out!' a police officer is heard shouting on the video. 'Attack! Attack!' The film then shows several armed Flying Squad officers surging to the other side of the road and attacking Woodruff and Hickson. Subsequently the camera operator moves across the road and films the pair on the ground. Beside Hickson on the pavement is a gun and a washing-up-liquid bottle containing ammonia.

It looked like an open-and-shut case, with police testifying that the gun pictured had been found on Hickson and that a weapon had later been found on Woodruff. However, at their trial the pair argued that it had not been a robbery, but simply theft. They explained that they had been set up by a police informant who had told them the money was there for the taking at the post office. All they had to do was walk inside, wave a gun around, and the money would be handed over. They said they agreed to do the job and were given a gun by the informant. The weapon had been carried by Woodruff, not by Hickson. The pair's story was not believed, and they were found guilty.

However, they decided to appeal after learning that Officer G had been suspended and then charged with corruption, and that others in the arresting team were also suspended. G had given evidence at the pair's trial about the role of the informant, and he had also witnessed the discovery of the gun on Hickson. When CIB anti-corruption officers reinvestigated, they found discrepancies in the prosecution case. G and another officer had said that the gun had been found on Hickson when he was lying on his back on the pavement. But the video showed him lying on his front, and there was no sign of any gun being found on Woodruff at the scene. A custody officer at the police station to which the two were taken said that the gun had not been found in Woodruff's pocket until he was being booked into a cell. Two of the arresting officers said they had found the gun on Woodruff outside the post office, but because it had been cocked they believed it unsafe to handle, so left him with it after handcuffing him. If that had been the case, said the custody officer, then they should have told him and he would have approached Woodruff in a different way. It was beginning to look to CIB as if the pair's story could be right. Had some of the arresting Flying Squad officers planted the gun on Hickson, having failed to find a weapon on Woodruff at the scene? The story that two of them had found Woodruff's weapon and allowed him to keep it until their arrival at the police station looked unlikely, because it would have represented a breach of police rules. The two were served with disciplinary notices by CIB, alleging that they had 'attempted to pervert the course of justice, falsified evidence, and failed to secure safely a firearm . . . The allegation is these officers gave false evidence as to the time and place when they found the gun on Mr Woodruff.'

As the date of Woodruff and Hickson's appeal approached, I was given a copy of the police video of the arrest. By then I had done several pieces for the BBC on police corruption in London, and one of

Hickson's relatives wanted me to examine the video to see whether there was an explanation for a gap of about two minutes on the timer in the bottom right-hand corner of the screen. It was easily explained. The operator had filmed the initial arrest from the other side of the road from the post office. He had then switched off the camera while he left an observation post and crossed over to film the pair on the pavement. But what intrigued me on viewing the video was a much smaller break of only sixteen seconds. This was a crucial gap, and it had been missed by everyone in the case. The camera angle barely changes, but the timer jumps by sixteen seconds. In that short time, a gun suddenly appeared on the pavement next to Hickson. Before the camera is switched off, there is no gun, but when it is switched back on, there it is. What a remarkable coincidence that the weapon should be found when the camera was not rolling, and when Hickson was on his front, not on his back as G had said. All the camera operator could tell CIB about the gun was that it had not been there when he started filming. He had not witnessed it being found and he could not explain why the camera had been switched off for just a few seconds.

The existence of another police video recording the arrest scene was unearthed by CIB detectives just prior to the appeal being heard. Whether it gave a full picture of what had happened outside the post office will never be known. It had disappeared in mysterious circumstances. CIB had discovered a note relating to this second video in their thorough trawl through the vast amount of documentation relating to the case. Shopkeepers in the area had complained of threats and intimidation from local youths, so, in response, the local police had launched Operation Shutter. Three video cameras were set up to cover the shops, and one of them, on private premises, covered the area near the post office. The local police were aware of the Flying Squad operation, and after the arrests of Hickson and Woodruff helpfully gave a copy of the video to the Squad. The paperwork showed that the tape was taken to a Met police laboratory from where it was collected later by a Flying Squad detective constable. What then happened to it is unclear. No further trace of it could be found and the DC was in no position to help CIB. He was facing corruption charges for another alleged offence.

However, more evidence was found that the gun had been planted on Hickson and had come from a first-aid kit. Police notes relating to the arrest and the events leading up to it had been scoured for clues. In G's notes, written on 10 January 1996, a week before the post office raid, were four words, one of which was key: 'Speak Bob re: Kit'. Although the words had been crossed out, their implication was clear, according to the defence in their grounds for appeal: 'Having regard to what is now known about G, an inference can and should be drawn that on 10 January, G had in mind to plant an imitation firearm upon Hickson.' With the Crown no longer able to put forward G and others as witnesses of truth, the Appeal Court quashed Hickson and Woodruff's convictions, but they were sent for retrial on lesser charges. A few weeks later, at the Old Bailey, the pair were freed after the judge declared that a fair trial was impossible because any proceedings would be affected by 'the stench of corruption'.

Officer G's reference in his notes to the 'kit' had a much wider significance beyond the Hickson and Woodruff case. The discovery of that one word appeared to provide confirmation of what Terry McGuinness had said about a 'first-aid kit' being used to fit up criminals, to 'gild the lily', as he had put it. It did not provide positive proof that such a kit had been used against the pair, but at least it represented circumstantial evidence. Although McGuinness had never been written off by CIB, this new evidence went some way to restoring some of his reputation. He had, it was argued, never said that he himself had planted evidence, but he thought that others had. Former Flying Squad officers have told me that they share the view of the ex-detective chief superintendent, who said that while he had no personal knowledge of such a kit, he could not rule out its existence.

One retired officer told me that it needed just two officers with total trust in one another to plant a gun or some other kind of robber's gear on a criminal. Others in the arrest team may genuinely have seen nothing happening, and if they did, or suspected that something had been planted, what were they supposed to do? They were part of a tight-knit group, loyal to one another, with their lives sometimes in the hands of their colleagues in violent situations. Could they really be expected to grass on their mates, especially when they knew that whoever had been fitted up was 'at it', and deserved to be convicted? According to this retired detective, CIB's questioning of the dozens of Flying Squad officers could have been more productive if the officers had not been cautioned beforehand, and not warned that anything they said about the first-aid kit could be used in evidence against them. But CIB officers had no choice in the matter. They had been given evidence by McGuinness suggesting that everyone working out of his office knew of the kits, and the rules therefore dictated that cautions had to be given when any of these officers was interviewed. It is doubtful, anyway, that CIB would have received direct confirmation of the existence of any first-aid kit without offering some kind of immunity, which they could not do. Without immunity or some kind of deal, if any of these Flying Squad officers had said they knew that such kits had been used, they would have been admitting to knowing that a very serious offence had been committed, and they would have been prosecuted, with all the consequences, including sacking and the loss of a large part of a valuable police pension. Even if some kind of off-the-record chat had been possible, such was these officers' distrust of CIB that they could never be sure that whatever they said would not be leaked to their colleagues, either deliberately or inadvertently.

Although McGuinness was never to appear as a prosecution witness in any trials, he came close to being used by the Crown Prosecution Service and CIB over the 'coins jobs'. But it was decided not to go ahead with charging any of the other officers allegedly involved in stealing the ten-pence pieces from the two lorries because there was too little evidence to corroborate what McGuinness and Garner had said. There was also a further problem. Because there had been two incidents, and they had occurred years before, the pair had difficulty remembering which officers had been involved in which incident. They made mistakes. CIB took the view that these were understandable, and wanted to jog their memories by showing them contemporaneous documents. These would go some way to showing which officers had been on duty or in the area. But CIB's request for permission for the move was vetoed by the CPS.

Another case where separate corroboration did exist involved Garner alone. It looked to the CPS as though it would be successful. Two officers were charged and a prosecution started. It seemed that this would be the first trial arising out of the Flying Squad supergrass confessions, and the first in which Garner would be giving evidence.

Garner had told the CIB3 officers that he had been involved in switching two amounts of counterfeit 'funny money' for cash seized in police raids. He knew who the target was in one case, but not in the other. CIB3 believed it was an Essex businessman, Stan Goodman. Goodman had approached me in 1998 having learned that I was a journalist interested in police corruption. He explained how he had been on trial on three occasions, each time being found not guilty after alleging he had been fitted up by police. Fed up with what he called persecution, he was about to sue the Metropolitan Police. In the first of his three trials he was charged with possession of counterfeit money, no less than £26,000 worth out of a total of £40,000 he said was kept at his home as a cash deposit for a property for his ageing father. Goodman claimed that all the money had been genuine when it was seized by police, who accused him of being involved in printing counterfeit notes and producing pirate videotapes of popular films. He said that corrupt officers must have switched it. This first trial took place in September 1996, over a year before the cannabis sting that led to Garner's confessions. Goodman's barrister, David Nathan, had a field day when cross-examining one of the main prosecution witnesses, PC Robert Dawson. He was the officer who had examined the £40,000 seized from Goodman and taken to a police station. When Dawson counted the money, he saw no reason to believe it was anything but genuine. But some of the notes produced in court were quite clearly crude forgeries, with many of them even carrying the same serial number. A bundle of £20 notes was handed to Dawson, and Nathan commented that they were not good forgeries:

Nathan: 'Just have a look at these. They look like gloss photographs, do they not?'

Dawson: 'Perhaps, yes, I would say that.'

Nathan: 'Just look at that bundle, please. Look at the serial numbers on those notes. Take any one at random.'

Dawson: 'They are the same.'

Nathan: 'Take another bundle. What is the serial number?'

Dawson: 'It is the same.'

Nathan: 'And you would agree, they do not feel like twenty-pound notes, do they?'

Dawson: 'Well, I wouldn't say that they don't feel like it . . .'

Nathan: 'How many forged notes did you spot that night when you counted out forty thousand pounds?'

Dawson: 'I didn't spot any.'

Nathan: 'How many identical serial numbers did you spot?'

Dawson: 'I wasn't looking at serial numbers. I was just counting the money.'

Nathan: 'You cannot fail, I suggest, to notice the serial number. If you just put the notes down one after another – you are a policeman. The numbers are the same. How many did you spot?'

Dawson: 'I didn't spot any. I wasn't looking for it.'

Nathan: 'Let me make it plain to you, Mr Dawson, as I do not want you to be under any illusion. I am going to be suggesting that a crooked police officer has substituted forged for genuine notes while those notes were at a police station.'

Dawson: 'That is nothing to do with me. That hasn't happened . . .'

Nathan: 'There are a number, are there not, Mr Dawson, not to put too fine a point on it, of very serious problems in relation to this forty thousand pounds?'

Dawson: 'There are, which I can't account for.'

Nathan: 'You cannot possibly say that exhibit is the same as the exhibit you bagged and sealed on 20th February?'

Dawson: 'I can't now, no.'

Nathan: 'You cannot possibly say that the exhibit has not been interfered with, can you?'

Dawson: 'I can't, no.'

Nathan: 'You cannot possibly say that notes have not been substituted, can you?'

Dawson: 'I can't.'

Nathan: 'And if they have been, it means, does it not, that someone at the police station is extremely dishonest?'

Dawson: 'Someone.'

Summing up the position, David Nathan addressed the judge: 'Your Honour, to put it crudely, if your Honour will permit me, Mr Goodman's case is that he has been fitted up, set up, exhibits have been interfered with, tampered with . . . It is a very, very broad attack on the integrity of this whole investigation.' The prosecution barrister then threw in the towel: 'There can be no doubt upon any view, even if there is an explanation for what has happened, that the integrity of those exhibits in this trial has been impugned in a way which in my view cannot be restored. The effect of that on the whole of the case against is such that the proper course here is for the prosecution to offer no further evidence and that is the course that I propose to take.'

Goodman's second trial for video piracy also collapsed without the defence even having to put their case in full. At the third, in March 1998, Goodman appeared charged with trying to bribe two police

officers to drop driving offences against his son. Once again, David
Nathan spelled out Goodman's position:

> Two juries on two occasions were directed by a judge to find Mr
> Goodman not guilty. From that moment the buck now passes to the
> police. Forty thousand pounds in cash, in that man's loft, seized by
> the police was tampered with at a police station. At this very court in
> the late summer of 1996, when the money, then in police possession,
> was examined, it was not the same as when police seized it. That is
> what happened. They will not give it back. They have had forty
> thousand pounds of his money. They have prosecuted him. They have
> destroyed his work. They have destroyed his son's work. They have
> seriously affected his life.

The jury acquitted Stan Goodman, apparently choosing to believe him
rather than the two police officers who said he had tried to bribe them.

Goodman told me that his chief persecutor was an officer with
SERCS, DS Barry Toombs, the officer in charge of the counterfeit
money and video piracy cases. Although I had never heard of him, when
I made enquiries he was described to me as an amiable buffoon, a poor
detective who in the late 1980s had tried to join the Flying Squad. He
was rejected because, according to his then detective superintendent:

> It is now abundantly clear that he is no longer suitable for service in
> so demanding a branch as SO8 [Flying Squad].
> 1 He clearly fails to appreciate the results of his actions in Crime
>   Squad duties, overreacting and constantly making wrong decisions.
>   He has demonstrated a complete lack of understanding in respect of
>   informants participating in crime.
> 2 He is found to be indiscreet.
> 3 He has created a world of fantasy in which he lives. He is a single
>   man but to his colleagues he states he is married with children.

After that devastating report on his unsuitability for the Flying Squad,
Toombs somehow bounced back with his next posting, indicating the
quality of some of the officers then working there. Until 1993, Barry
Toombs actually worked for CIB – the Complaints Investigation Branch!
He then worked as a DS at Leyton before joining that other élite team of

police officers, the South East Regional Crime Squad, which became part of the National Crime Squad.

One name stood out as I looked though Goodman's voluminous papers: Detective Sergeant Dennis Miller of the Flying Squad. According to police records, he had been called to the police station by Toombs to look at the money. All I knew about Miller at that stage was that he had been suspended along with several others after Garner and McGuinness's confessions. What was puzzling was why a Flying Squad officer, normally dealing with robberies, should have been called in to what at that stage looked like a video piracy case. I also knew that Kevin Garner had admitted to an offence involving counterfeit currency. I did not know the details, but I put two and two together and concluded that Garner's admission related to the Goodman case. Goodman's money had clearly been switched after it had arrived at the police station. Had Miller and Toombs been involved?

I started preparing a long piece for BBC2's *Newsnight* on Scotland Yard's anti-corruption drive, which would focus on Goodman's story, and the difficulties he had encountered during his fight for justice. With the programme virtually ready, Scotland Yard was approached for a comment. A very senior officer asked us to delay broadcasting indefinitely because we were interfering with an on-going CIB operation. Knowing that legally we would be prevented from broadcasting anything if officers were charged, he warned that if we did not agree to the delay then officers would have to be charged immediately. It was decided reluctantly that the BBC would have to comply with the request. But before there was a chance to inform Scotland Yard, we learned that Dennis Miller and Barry Toombs had both been charged with stealing Goodman's money. Effectively, we were gagged.

It took more than a year before *Newsnight* was legally able to broadcast the Stan Goodman story. During the wait, more emerged regarding what had been discovered during the CIB investigation into the whole affair. CIB2 had, in fact, started an inquiry in 1995, when Goodman had complained after his arrest that he was being fitted up. Little appears to have been done, however, until the autumn of 1997, when the investigation was taken over by Detective Superintendent John Coles of CIB3, one of the three senior and much-respected detectives brought in to develop proactively the intelligence gathered by the ghost squad over the previous two years. Coles, a very bright detective, went on within four years to command Scotland Yard's organised crime group, which includes the Flying Squad. In 1997, although not directly involved in any enquiries into the Flying Squad, he knew of his colleagues' investigations and that Miller was alleged to be one of the corrupt officers.

After Garner had 'rolled over' following his arrest for stealing cannabis in December 1997, he talked extensively about DS Miller. He claimed that Miller asked him whether he could obtain £20,000 of 'funny money'. Garner quoted him as saying it was for his mate Barry Toombs, an officer in the Regional Crime Squad, who was pointed out to him in a pub. Garner said he contacted a criminal friend, who agreed to get him the fake money. When the criminal handed the fake cash over, it was all in £20 notes for which he charged Garner only between £2 and £4 each as they were what he described as 'shit' – poor copies of the real thing. Garner said he gave the money to Miller, who was unconcerned about the quality, and that he received £1,000 for his trouble.

Armed with this information, Coles interviewed Toombs and Miller on more than one occasion during the first few months of 1998. Both officers denied any wrong-doing. Toombs described how he had called in the Flying Squad because he thought the £40,000 could have come from a robbery. Miller, whom he had known for several years, had arrived at the police station and they had looked at the money, with Toombs at one stage standing away from Miller, who had his back to him for a time. At his interview, Miller provided a written account prepared beforehand of what had happened at the police station, and it differed from Toombs's version, even down to which of the police station's rooms the money had been examined in. Coles told Toombs that Garner had stated 'that he provided to DS Miller counterfeit currency which was to be used in a job with his mate, who he refers to as Toombsy . . . The suggestion is that it was this particular case that we are investigating that this passing of counterfeit currency was all about.'

As Coles enlarged on Garner's allegation, Toombs's solicitor, Lawrence Kelly, interrupted, making comments that were to be repeated by many of the lawyers representing suspect officers. He said that Garner's motives in making statements could be crucially important to Toombs, 'particularly if Mr Garner's trying to give evidence in consideration for receiving a lighter sentence for his drug dealing offences or his counterfeit currency offences'. Toombs protested that he was an honest officer. Although several complaints had been made against him, none of them was for dishonesty. 'There's no way I'm involved in substituting counterfeit currency for genuine currency, there's no way.'

While Toombs was prepared to answer every question put to him, Miller adopted the exact opposite position. After reading aloud his account of what had happened at the police station, Miller refused to answer any questions after advice from his solicitor, Rod Fletcher, of Russell Jones and Walker. 'I've no further response,' Miller replied to all of Coles's questions. At a later interview, after asserting his innocence, he replied 'no comment' on twenty-eight occasions.

The two officers were charged with conspiracy to steal £26,000 and both appeared at Bow Street magistrates' court in central London. Coles faced problems as he continued trying to gather evidence against the pair. CIB accepted that the money had been switched, but it emerged that other officers could have had access to it. The evidence pointed to the swap having been made by one or both of the officers charged. But both strongly denied it. Their accounts differed, and no other officer came forward to say that they had seen anything amiss. Dawson told Coles that he was not a hundred per cent certain that all the money he counted was genuine, and there was also a problem over Garner's evidence. He said he had provided £20,000 of 'funny money' but £26,000 of Goodman's cash turned out to be counterfeit while in police hands. Where had the rest come from? Goodman himself presented a further problem. He was needed as a witness at any trial of the pair because he would give evidence that the £40,000 had all been genuine. But charging the pair meant not only that the BBC programme about the affair was put on hold, but also that Goodman's civil action against the Met would be delayed. On legal advice, he refused to give evidence. This was partly because he had already been cleared of counterfeiting at his own trial, but also because he was in something of a catch-22 position. If he did give evidence at Toombs and Miller's trial, and the pair were cleared, where would that leave his civil claim against the police?

After assessing all the evidence, the Crown Prosecution Service decided not to go ahead with a prosecution. This was for two connected reasons. First, it was feared that inconsistencies in the differing accounts of what happened to the money would be exploited by defence lawyers. That, coupled with the belief that juries were notorious for giving police officers in the dock the benefit of the doubt, led the CPS to conclude that there was not 'a realistic prospect of conviction'. But the case was not entirely dropped. It was 'discontinued', which meant a trial could still go ahead if further evidence came to light.

The decision gave the green light to Stan Goodman's civil action against the Met for malicious prosecution and his claim for damages for psychiatric injury and financial loss. Although CIB believed he was a victim of police corruption, the Met lawyers wanted to defend the case if he would not agree to accept a reasonable amount of compensation. Goodman had legal aid and turned down various offers of compensation from the police. He believed a jury would find for him and award him more than was on offer from the Met. But there was also another important factor. He told me he wanted a public platform from which to expose police corruption. He never got it. Shortly before the civil trial was due to start in May 2000, Scotland Yard upped its offer to £200,000. Goodman's lawyers thought it a reasonable offer given all the circumstances, and under the rules this meant that his legal aid would have to be withdrawn. This was because it was deemed not to be in the public interest to spend large amounts of public money on legal aid for a long trial simply to increase, possibly, the amount of public money that would be paid to a plaintiff. The decision upset Goodman, who was thirsting for revenge for the injustice he had suffered. He decided to continue on his own, without lawyers. The trial started with all the might of the Metropolitan Police ranged against him. It was a hopeless task. After two days, he gave up. He was forced to accept the £200,000 offer.

The Goodman case highlighted the continuing conflict within the various authorities as to how allegedly corrupt officers should be tackled. Certainly, corruption existed. But conservative elements argued that it was not on the scale estimated by the Commissioner, and even if it was, launching high-profile trials was not the best way of dealing with bent cops. The acquittal of Keith Green demonstrated the difficulties associated with putting police officers on trial, and it was argued that the reputation of the Met as a whole would suffer through bad publicity resulting from further trials in which police washed their dirty laundry in public. It was suggested that a better way of handling the problem was to keep it 'in house', allowing the wrongdoers to retire early or by dealing with them through disciplinary hearings. Sir Paul Condon and his supporters disagreed. Where there was good evidence of corruption, officers should be put on trial. This would demonstrate to the public that the Met was indeed rooting out the cancer. If serious police wrong-doing was dealt with at disciplinary hearings, it would be hiding the problem away, as the proceedings were held in private with access denied to the public and journalists. This represented an injustice to the public.

What CIB needed after the decision to abandon the prosecution of Dennis Miller and Barry Toombs was another case, one with evidence so strong that convictions would inevitably follow. This would prove once and for all that corruption was a serious problem and that the Met was tackling it effectively. CIB eventually got that case, but not before they endured more setbacks.

Dennis Miller and Barry Toombs remained suspended for more than a year after the pay-out to Stan Goodman, then both officers appeared at separate Scotland Yard disciplinary hearings. Miller, the subject of many complaints, was 'required to resign'. This meant that he could leave the police with his pension intact. Toombs was reinstated in December 2001 after the disciplinary proceedings against him were ended.

As a result of the CIB investigations that followed Garner and McGuinness's confessions, several other Flying Squad officers were charged with various other corruption offences. Some are still awaiting trial, while others face disciplinary proceedings.

twelve

PROBLEMS AND DIFFICULTIES

'I risked my life to help the police with some of the most important cases of recent years. Now I am being thrown to the wolves.'

Geoffrey Brennan

The two former Flying Squad detectives Kevin Garner and Terry McGuinness were not, in fact, the first Met officers to turn supergrass. That distinction belonged to a former detective, Duncan Hanrahan, who had left the Met in 1991 on an ill-health pension. After working for others as a private detective, he eventually set up his own company, 'Hanrahan Associates Ltd, Security Consultants and Investigators'. His business cards featured an apparently prestigious-looking address near Marble Arch in the West End. But it turned out to be just an accommodation or mail-box office. Hanrahan was devious and corrupt, and his contacts included other suspect detectives and former officers.

In February 1997, Hanrahan made a move that was to lead to his downfall. He telephoned a south London police officer, Detective Chief Inspector Peter Elcock, who was number two in one of CIB's area offices, dealing mainly with the less serious complaints. Hanrahan told Elcock that his wife was interested in joining the area complaints team. Could he meet him for lunch to discuss the possibilities? Elcock agreed, but was puzzled about the call. Instead of a lunch-time drink in the local pub, the invitation was to a fairly expensive restaurant, Luigi's in Dulwich. Elcock discussed the call with his boss, Detective Superintendent Tom Smith. By sheer coincidence, Smith had heard the name Hanrahan just a few days before, from me. I had gone to see him at Norbury police station because he had expressed an interest in reinvestigating the particularly brutal south London murder of a private detective whose life ended with an axe embedded in his skull. The dead man had known officers suspected of corruption and some of them were friends of Duncan Hanrahan (see Chapter 14 for the full story). I had mentioned

Hanrahan's name to Smith, so when Elcock told Smith of the call, the senior officer was intrigued. CIB was contacted and Elcock was given the go-ahead for the meeting. He was given authority to pretend to be a corrupt officer, but he was warned that Hanrahan had to be allowed to make the running. Elcock was not to act as an agent provocateur.

During the lunch Hanrahan hardly mentioned his wife, Linda. It was clear he had used that story as a pretext to get the officer on his own in congenial surroundings. Hanrahan told Elcock he was working as a private detective and turned the conversation to mutual former colleagues, naming some officers known to be the subject of corruption rumours. When Elcock did not say anything derogatory about them, Hanrahan judged that the time was right to ask for a favour. He said he had a client facing car fraud charges who wanted help. For £1,000, could he possibly have a look at the prosecution papers against the man? Playing his role of bent cop cleverly, and not wanting to appear over-eager, Elcock did not agree immediately. Instead he raised problems. He said it would be difficult for him to march into whichever police station was dealing with the matter and demand the papers. But if Hanrahan's client was to make a complaint against the police, then the matter would be referred to Elcock and he would be entitled to have a look at the documents. Hanrahan agreed to the plan, and they arranged another meeting.

At the second meeting, Hanrahan was joined by his company's co-director, Martin King, another former detective who had left the Met in dubious circumstances. King had contacts with men involved in major robberies. He had owned a snooker club, restaurant and nightclub; currently he owned a detached house in south London and lived in a large flat close to Harrods, where he often took his police contacts for lunch. Among his friends was a former Met police commander. King's children went to private schools. But the reality was that he fenced stolen works of art and acted as a middleman between criminals and corrupt police officers. King and Hanrahan's conversation at the second and subsequent meetings with Elcock suggested that the two former officers belonged to a corrupt group of serving and former officers. Access to the PNC, the Police National Computer, represented no problem for them, and their contacts in other government departments provided more confidential information.

All of their meetings were secretly tape-recorded, causing further worries for Elcock, who already had concerns about his role. His story was that he was nearing retirement and the extra money would boost his pension, and also help pay for his daughter's forthcoming marriage. But he was given no special training by CIB for his undercover role. Normally an easy-going, confident character, he was hit by nerves each time he went for one of these meetings. Sometimes he wore a secret microphone which transmitted their conversation to CIB listeners in a nearby van. On other occasions he wore a body-set, comprising microphone and recording equipment. Only rudimentary instructions on operating the equipment had been given, however, and he feared discovery, which could have resulted in appalling, violent consequences. 'I was always worried that they would suspect me,' he told me later. 'I had to be very careful with what I said. I had serious decisions made about how far I could go. It had to come from them. But I didn't know who I'd meet or what danger I was in. I asked CIB what happens if they find the recording equipment on me, and the best advice I was given was "If they find it – run!"'

Hanrahan paid £1,000 to Elcock in a pub car park and then did not appear at later meetings, leaving his partner King to deal with Elcock. In effect, Hanrahan was King's errand boy, meeting police and then, if they showed interest, introducing them to King. The criminal was completely taken in by Elcock. In one taped conversation, the DCI added credibility to his role by pretending that he was concerned about being arrested, getting 'nicked'.

'. . . See, I could get fucking nicked,' said a worried-sounding Elcock.

'Pardon?' replied King.

'You know I could get fucking nicked, if it all goes dark.'

'Look, I'm saying to you, I'm on your side, whatever.'

'Yeah?'

'I'm protecting you.'

'Yeah?'

Not having dealt with corrupt officers before, Elcock had little idea of what the going rate was for what he was being asked to provide. When he suggested that £2,500 was too low a price for sabotaging a prosecution, King immediately upped the amount.

'I mean, if he's out of the whole lot,' said Elcock, 'it's gotta be worth at least two and a half grand.'

'Well, yeah,' King responded. 'We'll go for five.'

For providing information and documents, Elcock was paid a total of

£7,500. More came after King said he could return a Henry Moore statue, worth £100,000, stolen from a Mayfair gallery. Elcock registered King as an informant and took him to Scotland Yard with the statue. The criminal received a reward of £10,000. There was also a payment of £3,000 from the Met's informants fund, and £1,000 of that was given by King to the officer. There were promises of 'five or ten gee' more for other help, but the Yard decided to end the operation after the stakes became too dangerous. The end came after Elcock was told that if particular papers could not be obtained, a witness in a forthcoming trial would have to be killed. The proposal was that Elcock would lure the witness to the top of a block of flats, where a hit team would then take over and push the witness hundreds of feet to his death. Elcock told CIB of the plan, and Scotland Yard decided to move in. All the main players were arrested. Surprisingly, given the strength of evidence against him, Hanrahan applied for bail at his first appearance at Bow Street magistrates' court. At the hearing, promising him work if he was released, was Sid Fillery, another former detective who featured in the 'axe-in-the-head' murder investigation (see Chapter 14).

Hanrahan and King, confronted with all the evidence against them, decided to plead guilty. Two criminals for whom they had acted, Ray Brown and Mark Mahoney, fought the case, but were found guilty. Judge Giles Forrester commended Elcock: 'There is no doubt, from the facts of this case, that over a three-month period, he performed a delicate undercover role to an exceptionally high standard.' King was sentenced to nine years' imprisonment for two counts of conspiracy to pervert the course of justice and three of corruption, but the Appeal Court reduced the total to six years. Brown's sentence of three years was reduced to twenty-one months, and Mahoney's five to three and a half.

Clearly, King, in his fifties, knew a lot about police corruption. Attempts were made to persuade him to talk to CIB officers. But he belonged to an old school. Like a 'staunch' criminal to whom grassing was anathema, he refused to co-operate. Not so Hanrahan, however. A younger man, aged forty, he was made of weaker stuff, and had the nickname 'Drunken Duncan'. He took little persuading before agreeing to turn supergrass in the hope of receiving very lenient treatment and a drastically reduced prison sentence. After supposedly telling all in a series of debriefings with anti-corruption officers, Hanrahan was sent to Parkhurst on the Isle of Wight, one of the country's two prisons with a special supergrass wing, where the inmates are kept separate from other prisoners. However, while following up leads provided by Hanrahan, CIB officers began to suspect that he had been withholding information. Confirmation of this came shortly before he was due to be sentenced, when Hanrahan confided in another inmate on the supergrass wing that he had only told investigators what they already knew, or what was incapable of corroboration. The other supergrass passed the information about Hanrahan's deception to CIB, which learned that he had also been passing on information about an on-going covert police operation. CIB officers confronted him, threatening to withdraw their support and to throw him out of the witness protection scheme. This would have been a terrible blow to Hanrahan. He had been made bankrupt, his marriage was in ruins, and he feared retribution from those he had implicated in corruption. He was hoping for a new identity from police and their help with finding a job and accommodation when he came out of prison. Faced with losing the deal, he explained to CIB that he had been too scared to tell all previously, because of the violent reputations of some of his connections. He then confessed to leaking information about the covert operation, and owned up to more corruption, identifying others involved.

His eventual sentencing at the Old Bailey in March 1999 produced surprises with the public naming in court of more allegedly corrupt former officers. This unusual tactic was deliberate. I understand that those named were under electronic surveillance, and their reactions to the resulting unwelcome publicity were being monitored. Outlining Hanrahan's deception with CIB, prosecuting counsel John Kelsey-Fry said that he had been exposed as a complete fraud, who had tried to avoid opening up 'a can of worms'. But he had also aimed 'to frustrate the police and pull the wool over the eyes of the court'. According to the lawyer, Hanrahan was now admitting to having had corrupt dealings with a serving officer and another former detective, Nigel Grayston, who also features in Chapter 14 of this book. Hanrahan was said to have paid Grayston money for information and to sabotage prosecutions. On one occasion, Hanrahan paid £1,000 to have charges against an estate agent involved in an alleged affray dropped. Grayston said that a colleague handling the case would say it was a 'load of bollocks'. The case was dropped, but the estate agent refused to pay, claiming he would have been acquitted anyway.

Kelsey-Fry also singled out two other former detectives as corrupt, both of them serving officers when they were involved with Hanrahan. They were DC Chris Carter and DS Len Guerard, who had been stationed at Heathrow Airport. He claimed the pair had been involved with another officer, suspended for other alleged wrong-doing, in stealing a large quantity of Ecstasy tablets from a shop in Chiswick, west London, and had also been involved in planning a £1 million robbery at Heathrow. The lawyer described how a courier who regularly passed through the airport carrying £1 million in cash from Lebanon had been robbed in August 1994. The crime had been investigated by Carter and Guerard. Carter had suggested to Hanrahan that the courier's firm could provide protection to safeguard against any future robberies. But according to Kelsey-Fry, the former officer was now saying that Carter and Guerard were involved with him in a plot to rob the courier, although he described it in its early stages as not serious. However, Hanrahan's partner, Martin King, brought in a criminal gang from Grove Park in south London who were prepared to carry out the robbery, using stun guns on the courier. Kelsey-Fry alleged that King, Hanrahan and the two officers went to Heathrow to commit the robbery on two occasions. On the first, the courier did not arrive, and on the second there was what he described as a 'falling out' between the Grove Park men and the others, and the robbery never took place.

Hanrahan pleaded guilty to a series of eleven offences, including conspiracies to rob, steal, supply drugs and pervert the course of justice. Judge John Blofeld said: 'The offences strike at the very roots of justice, and must be deterred. If society has a future, as it does, the police force must be above corruption, with heavy sentences for those found out.' Hanrahan was sentenced to a total of eight years and four months.

One of those who was shocked by what had been revealed at the Old Bailey about Hanrahan's corrupt activities was another former officer who had kept in close contact with Hanrahan since their days together on a CID course at Hendon Police College. As a detective sergeant, Alec Leighton had been suspended and was under CIB investigation after *Panorama*'s exposure of John Donald's corruption in 1993. He had been in charge of Donald, but had always denied knowing of his corrupt activities or being corrupt himself. While still suspended and preparing to start up his own private security company, Leighton had worked with Hanrahan Associates, but he became disillusioned. They received very good instructions from very good clients, but Hanrahan was 'always looking for an angle to exploit an investigation and bleed it dry for money, by fair means or foul. It was usually foul.' The pair broke up, but after Hanrahan's arrest, Leighton claims he received regular feedback about the supergrass's debriefings by CIB.

'Anyone who has met or worked with Duncan will say he was always considered to be a relatively harmless Walter Mitty character with a very sick sense of humour,' said Leighton in a briefing note about Hanrahan. 'I do not know anybody who can believe that CIB have taken what Duncan has said seriously ... I was aware that the inexperienced senior CIB officers dealing with him hung on his every word and saw a lot of mileage in him. The more streetwise and experienced lower-rank detectives considered him to be the total fabricator that he was always known to be.'

Ignoring the fact that Hanrahan had pleaded guilty to eleven offences, Leighton continued to pour scorn on his former colleague, particularly over the Heathrow robbery plot. He recalled that he had been working with Hanrahan at the time and had been involved in trying to provide security for the Lebanese businessman-courier. Leighton said that he had enquired about hiring two experienced protection officers and had costed leasing or buying a vehicle that could have a safe welded into its boot. The Lebanese was also interested in finding out the prices of body armour, electronic listening devices and other security equipment.

In his notes, Leighton wrote:

> During the time I was trying to pull all the information together to quote for the job, Duncan said something, which at the time, and up until very recently, I considered to be one of his sick, stupid and infantile jokes. He said that we should run the job for a few weeks, and then rob the security vehicle. As mentioned, I considered this to be one of Duncan's stupid inane comments that he was prone to making. There was another time that he mentioned the robbery again when in company, but again I considered it to be in jest, in accordance with his sick mind. It wasn't until I read an article in a newspaper when he was sentenced that I saw reference to the robbery again. I couldn't believe that he was now using his own sick joke to the detriment of others, to wriggle his own way out of a situation that he had been

responsible for creating. But Hanrahan was always such a Walter Mitty. Even his ex-wife used to say that he had an 'O' level in embroidery.

Chris Carter and Len Guerard vigorously denied any involvement in a Heathrow robbery plot and CIB and the Crown Prosecution Service took the view that there was insufficient evidence to charge either of them. However, the alleged theft from a Chiswick shop of Ecstasy tablets, worth at street prices up to £600,000, was a different matter. CIB obtained what they believed was enough evidence to mount a prosecution against the pair. However, the case was to backfire spectacularly against CIB – not just once, but twice. It was to cost the CIB detectives dear in terms of their reputation for scrupulous fairness. It was also a very long, time-consuming, complicated operation.

The story of CIB's failure started after Hanrahan told the anti-corruption investigators that the drugs theft had involved three police officers and a group of criminals, all of whom he named. The latter included Steven Warner, a man associated with the notorious London criminal family the Adams. CIB thought that, if caught, Warner could become a valuable supergrass. So anti-corruption detectives targeted him in an operation involving the use of undercover officers. One calling himself 'Dave' approached him and was sold a kilo of cocaine for £29,000. Further business was discussed, with Warner declaring that he could supply 20 kilos at a time. A few days later, Warner told 'Dave' that he wanted someone 'permanently sorted', which the undercover officer took to mean that he wanted the man killed. 'Dave' then introduced Warner to another undercover officer, 'Mike'. When the two met, Warner checked that 'Mike' was not carrying a tape recorder and then said he wanted the man 'six feet under'. The price for the contract killing was agreed at £10,000, with a deposit of £500 to be paid. At a later meeting, Warner paid the deposit to 'Mike' and handed over a Browning gun and details of the victim, his house and his family. The man had to be done 'good and proper', he said.

When arrested and interviewed, Warner did as expected and confessed to a string of serious offences, which were listed when he appeared for sentencing at the Old Bailey in July 1999. These included supplying cocaine to 'Dave' and soliciting 'Mike' to commit murder. The court was also told that he admitted conspiracy with Hanrahan to arrange for a consignment of Ecstasy tablets to be stolen by serving police officers from the Chiswick shop. CIB officers hoped that Warner would give evidence for the prosecution at any trial mounted for the theft of the Es. But that prospect faded when the judge gave him a total sentence of only seven years, having been told of his contrition and of his co-operation with the police. Warner reckoned that seven years was a good result. Why should he make trouble for himself by going into the witness box and giving evidence against his associates? However, CIB were not dependent on Warner. Once again using undercover officers posing as drugs dealers, they mounted what was in effect another entrapment operation. This time the target was the manager of the Chiswick shop, Jason Proctor, who had continued to deal in drugs after the theft of the Ecstasy tablets. He too was arrested and eventually agreed to give evidence.

The trial began in October 2000, but it was on the same day as the Hatfield train crash, which dominated the news, resulting in virtually no media coverage for the proceedings. Four men were in the dock, all denying conspiracy to steal Ecstasy tablets. They were the former detectives Chris Carter, aged forty-seven, and Len Guerard, fifty-two, and a serving officer, Detective Constable Colin Evans, who was suspended after allegations of corruption while with the Flying Squad. The jury were not told of this connection. With the three, who were on bail, was Vincent Arneil, who had a criminal background and was in custody.

Outlining the prosecution case to the jury, Orlando Pownall alleged that Arneil had ordered a large number of Ecstasy tablets from Jason Proctor, who managed a pine furnishing shop. Arneil had no intention of paying for the drugs. He contacted Duncan Hanrahan and the pair discussed different ways of stealing the drugs once they had arrived at the shop. Eventually, said Pownall, Hanrahan recruited DC Chris Carter and DS Len Guerard, who obtained a warrant to search the pine shop, pretending that they had genuine information to the effect that there were stolen cigarette lighters on the premises. The two enlisted the help of another Heathrow officer, DC Colin Evans. The three detectives then 'raided' the shop. In the basement, in a large cardboard box, were forty thousand Es with a street value at that time of about £600,000. According to the prosecution, Evans stayed on the shop's ground floor with the manager while the other two detectives went to the basement and found the box. It was taken upstairs and then carried outside, where it was put into Hanrahan's van, parked near by. The tablets were then sold and the proceeds shared among the alleged thieves.

Pownall told the jury that after his arrest Hanrahan turned supergrass and admitted a number of offences, including the pine shop Es conspiracy. Steven Warner had pleaded guilty. Another man, John Walter, had also admitted his part in the conspiracy. Pownall said that Hanrahan, Walter and Proctor would be giving evidence. He outlined Hanrahan's history, acknowledging that he had lied and recognising that they, the jury, might be reluctant to convict anyone on the uncorroborated evidence of such a man. But, he went on, there was an abundance of independent supporting evidence which proved that what he was saying was true.

However, when the prosecution witnesses were called, they proved to be unsatisfactory. Hanrahan admitted that he had lied in the past and lawyers for the four defendants showed him to be devious and unreliable, ready to do anything to try to save his own skin. Similarly, Proctor admitted that he had lied to police when first arrested and he was accused of further lying, it being suggested to him that there had been no theft at all at the pine shop, and if there had been that he himself had stolen the Es with criminal associates, and then falsely claimed that police officers were responsible. At times, he reacted angrily to the defence lawyers. When the defendants gave evidence, they did so confidently, sticking to the accounts they had given to CIB officers at the time of their arrest. Guerard described Hanrahan's story as 'a pack of lies'. He recalled him as someone known to be 'dodgy', with the nickname 'Drunken Duncan'. He remembered the search of the pine shop because Carter had told him that he had been telephoned the night before by Hanrahan who had informed him that there were stolen cigarette lighters in the shop. The information was of interest because they had been investigating the theft of lighters from one of the Heathrow shops. He declared himself innocent of any wrong-doing during the search. Carter said that after receiving Hanrahan's phone call he met him and the pine shop was pointed out. A search warrant was obtained and Evans was recruited because he was on the early shift at their base. He said the search was carried out without incident. Nothing was found, and Hanrahan, who had been outside in his van, was told this later. Evans confirmed that he had stayed with the shop owner but had also searched drawers without finding anything.

The jury was confronted with a mass of opposing evidence. On the prosecution side were self-confessed criminals who admitted to having lied. On the other side, the defendants were police officers with unblemished records who had gone into the witness box and given reasonable accounts of what had happened. The verdict was inevitable: not guilty.

The prosecution's failure came as a blow to the anti-corruption investigators. DC Colin Evans remained suspended for some time before being allowed to retire. But CIB, instead of licking their wounds and abandoning Carter and Guerard, were far from finished with the pair. It had been information from Duncan Hanrahan which had led to the two officers being charged over the theft of the Ecstasy tablets, and his evidence had clearly been found unreliable by the jury. But information about another apparent disappearance of drugs allegedly involving the pair had also come to light. Hanrahan had no connection with it, so his lies would not have to be exposed again, and, on the surface at least, the information seemed more credible as it came from police officers, not criminals. One of Carter and Guerard's former colleagues at Heathrow, Constable Adrian Daniels, had come forward. He told CIB of an incident in 1994 in which, during a raid on a drugs dealer, a bag of what looked like a kilo of 'speed' (amphetamines) worth several thousand pounds had gone missing. Following the raid, only a tiny amount of the drug had been logged in at the police station. CIB detectives contacted other officers who had taken part in the raid, and also traced the drugs dealer, who had fled abroad. They all broadly supported suspicions that Carter and Guerard, in charge of the raid, had disposed of the drugs. The pair were charged with conspiracy to pervert the course of justice and with blackmailing the dealer, and they appeared again in the dock at the Old Bailey in September 2001.

This second prosecution also received almost no publicity. Just as their first trial had passed without notice by virtue of opening on the same day as the Hatfield train crash, so it was with the second, which started in the immediate aftermath of the attacks on the World Trade Center in New York and the Pentagon in Washington. Orlando Pownall again led the prosecution team against the two former detectives. Outlining the case, he explained that the 1994 raid had been on a drugs dealer, Kirk Lawrence, who lived in a caravan on a nursery in west London. Pownall said that Lawrence alleged that Guerard told him, after finding the amphetamines, 'you look after us, and we'll look after you'. He had not complained when only a fraction of the drugs find was registered, and was happy when charges were eventually dropped against him. Lawrence was asked to turn informant and felt he had no alternative. Given the pseudonym 'Arthur Askey', he was to claim that the defendants threatened him with arrest for another offence unless he paid them £2,000. According to the prosecution lawyer, Lawrence eventually handed over £1,000, leaving the country a few months later 'to escape the pressure being exerted by the defendants and the risk to which he was exposing himself by informing on others'.

While there was little additional evidence to support Lawrence's claim of blackmail, CIB, with legal advice, believed they were on much stronger ground with the other charge of conspiracy to pervert the course of justice. Carter and Guerard had been charged with that particular offence because it was not known with any certainty what had happened to the drugs. Their disappearance effectively meant that the course of bringing Lawrence to justice had been interfered with, so justifying the charge. Although Lawrence was a criminal, the allegations of wrongdoing over the drugs were supported by four of the pair's former police colleagues.

Continuing his prosecution summary, Pownall said that Adrian Daniels, the constable who had alerted CIB, saw one of the defendants with a bag containing the drugs, but when he next saw it back at the police station, two of his other colleagues had it, and the bag contained considerably fewer drugs. He asked them what had happened to the remainder and they replied that they did not know, as they were not in charge of the job. Daniels alleged that a few days later the defendants followed him on to a balcony of the crime squad office at Heathrow and told him to keep his nose out of their business. They said they had poured the missing drugs down the sink because Lawrence, the dealer, had 'rolled over' and become an informant. Pownall said three other officers had noticed the reduction in the number of drugs. One claimed he was told by the defendants that they had flushed the drugs down the toilet in order to turn the dealer into a grass. Another was told by Guerard: 'This is how you get informants. You ditch some of the drugs and the prisoner doesn't get a long sentence and he helps you out with information.'

However, when the four officers gave evidence for the prosecution, there were differences in their accounts of what had happened. One of them admitted she had only made a full statement of what had happened after coming under pressure from CIB. Daniels was picked out for particular criticism by defence lawyers. He was said to have borne a grudge against the pair and was not to be trusted because he had himself breached police rules and been disciplined for not disclosing to the Met that he had financial problems resulting in a county court judgement against him. That 'offence' had resulted in him being 'strictly admonished' by the Met for 'thoroughly discreditable conduct'. The defence also pointed out that the paper trail relating to the drugs was faulty, as there was no record of who had actually registered the find at the police station.

When the two defendants went into the witness box, they protested their innocence, giving their evidence confidently, just as they had done at their first trial, having an answer for everything flung at them by the prosecution. One of Carter's explanations was particularly devastating to the prosecution and CIB, and must have had a telling effect on the jury. An important part of the case against the pair had been an event two days after they had been charged. A video of the incident had even been shown to the jury. Describing it, prosecuting counsel Orlando Pownall said that one of the four officers giving evidence for the prosecution, Richard Souter, who had by then retired, had been shopping at his local Sainsbury's supermarket with his young son. Sitting by the doors were the two defendants. It was not their local supermarket, said Pownall. Carter got up and told Souter, 'We can't talk to you, we're on bail.' Souter was in the shop for more than an hour and Carter and Guerard were still there when he left. 'Unsurprisingly, you may think, he felt a bit flustered,' Pownall told the jury. 'While he was at the till, packing his shopping, Souter noticed the defendants standing a few aisles away. Carter looked at him and winked. Although Souter did not feel threatened by the defendants, it is submitted that their appearance in the shop two days after the charge was no coincidence. Why did they remain in the shop for so long without apparently making many purchases?' the counsel asked rhetorically. 'They were trying to intimidate Souter as they knew he had revealed the truth about their activities in 1994!'

It was a strong charge. But someone had not done their homework, as became clear when Carter explained why he had been at the supermarket with Guerard. He declared that neither of them had tried to intimidate Souter. Far from it not being Carter's local Sainsbury's, he was able to show that he visited that particular store regularly and had a loyalty card to prove it. He went there to help his aged mother do her weekly shopping. His mother, complete with a full basket, was pointed out to the jury on the video. Carter also explained that Guerard was with him because he had phoned him beforehand as they needed to discuss the forthcoming case. The supermarket had simply been a convenient place to meet. Furthermore, when they saw Souter, aware that it could cause problems, they telephoned their solicitor, asking for advice on what to do. They were told that as long as they did not speak to Souter they could stay at the store.

Much play of CIB's supermarket disaster was made by Carter's barrister, Geoffrey Cox, in his closing speech to the jury. Cox had stood as a Conservative candidate at that year's general election, failing to get elected. Although he can be flamboyant, he is also very persuasive, marshalling his arguments fluently like any good politician. Knowing, however, that the prosecution case was not dependent on the supermarket incident, Cox concentrated on attacking the most important evidence against Carter and Guerard – the accounts of the four main police witnesses. The differences between them were exploited to the full. Although Cox stopped short of a full attack on the officers, he maintained that their recollections of events seven years before were simply shaky and unreliable. They raised so many doubts, he said, appealing to the jury and pointing at the two defendants, that they could not possibly be convicted.

The trial of the two former officers had lasted four weeks. It took the jury just over four hours to reach their unanimous verdicts: not guilty of conspiracy to pervert the course of justice and not guilty of blackmail. Carter and Guerard hugged each other, thanked the jury, waved to their relatives and friends in the public gallery, and left the dock. Their ordeal was over. Their innocence had been established.

Other CIB operations also ran into problems and ended in failure. There were other acquittals too. The various defendants protested their innocence and their friends and colleagues joined them in declaring that the Met's anti-corruption effort was misplaced and that the number of corrupt officers had been greatly exaggerated. The investigating detectives blamed their difficulties on the fact that some of the suspects, as police oficers, knew how the system worked, and they were defended by top lawyers. While CIB officers were dealing with the problems thrown up by Duncan Hanrahan's failure to turn full supergrass and tell the whole truth, in the same year, 1997, another high-ranking CIB officer was wrestling with what was acknowledged by police and lawyers to be a much greater 'can of worms'.

In the early 1990s, John Coles had been a detective chief inspector targeting top criminals, producing 'intelligence packages' which were then handled by various specialist units. Promoted to superintendent at the end of 1996, he was summoned to a meeting with the Deputy Commissioner, Brian Hayes, and Roy Clark, then in overall charge of the ghost squad and CIB's proactive teams. He was told that a new unit was being set up the following spring, to follow up and develop the ghost squad's information, and he would be running the intelligence side. But in January 1997 he was informed of a change of plan. Superintendent Dave Wood was to be in charge of intelligence-gathering, and Coles was given what was described to him as a nightmare case, a terrible mess involving a criminal businessman, Geoffrey Brennan, and two detectives, Inspector John Redgrave and Constable Michael Charman. As detailed in Chapter 3, Brennan had stolen £400,000 given to him by a Chinese-American businessman in a mobile-phone deal, and in 1994 had claimed to the ghost squad's head, Roger Gaspar, that he had paid Redgrave and Charman £50,000 to protect him, by providing a cover story that he was helping Scotland Yard in an investigation into drugs dealing, arms running and money laundering. Relations between Brennan and the ghost squad soured as he learned that a separate police inquiry into the theft was closing in on him. It culminated in his arrest in November 1996. Although he had admitted on tape to stealing the £400,000, when charged he replied: 'I am not guilty of this offence. At all times I acted with the knowledge of the Metropolitan Police as part of a police operation . . . Prior to attending here [a police station] I had protection status. That's now changed. My family are in jeopardy.' Shortly after this declaration, he said he approached Charman for help, and told the officer that he and Redgrave had been under CIB investigation for more than two years.

As Superintendent Coles read through the papers in the case and listened to the Brennan tapes, he wondered whether Brennan had manipulated CIB from the very outset. Had his life really been in danger when he first approached Gaspar, claiming that his role as an informant had been discovered by a violent criminal? Could the story have been invented by Brennan in collusion with the criminal, so he could obtain

PROBLEMS AND DIFFICULTIES

further protection from the police inquiry into the theft? Coles knew that fraudsters such as Brennan were capable of constructing elaborate stories to extract money from their victims, and they knew roughly how far they could push the law. Brennan would have known that his confession to the theft would almost certainly never be used against him in court because Gaspar had not cautioned him, and there was unlikely to be any separate evidence to corroborate any corrupt payments to detectives. Coles' suspicions were largely confirmed in January 1997 when the clever Brennan, worried after being charged, counter-attacked on two fronts, muddying the situation even further.

First, he contacted the Police Complaints Authority to withdraw his allegations against Redgrave and Charman. He claimed he had been put up to blackening the pair by his old handler, the Flying Squad detective sergeant Chris Smith. He said that Smith had 'had it in' for Redgrave and Charman since the 1980s, when all three had worked on the huge Brink's-Mat robbery inquiry. Smith strongly denied both claims, but Brennan also alleged that Smith and other officers had been moonlighting for a private security company he was running, and he issued a complaint against Gaspar too. His claims meant there would have to be a fresh inquiry into the whole affair, and that his prosecution for the theft would have to be postponed.

As if that were not enough, Brennan also set out to cause Scotland Yard maximum embarrassment, aiming to have the case against him dropped altogether. Just days after contacting the Police Complaints Authority he approached the *Mirror*, which ran a story under the headline 'Bent Coppers Shopped Me To Gangsters'. It said: 'Brennan joined a huge undercover operation to trap American mobsters who wanted to sell Ulster Protestant terrorists an arsenal of machine guns and explosives. Plans were made to switch cash to a secret police bank account while Brennan introduced an undercover cop into the crooked American cartel.' Brennan was quoted as saying: 'I risked my life to help the police with some of the most important cases of recent years. Now I am being thrown to the wolves.'

The day the *Mirror* published the story, Redgrave and Charman were suspended, their homes having been raided three days before. From the outset the pair have denied receiving money from Brennan, or indeed, any corruption at all. The two also denied involvement with newspapers at that time. But Brennan himself approached the *Sunday Times*, claiming that detectives had pressurised him into incriminating innocent police officers. The resulting story, splashed on 2 March across the newspaper's front page, with a further whole page inside, confused the picture even more. Under the headline 'Yard Loses £½m in Mafia Arms Sting', it related how two Scotland Yard detectives had been suspended over the disappearance of nearly £500,000 from a secret police bank account, set up to stop the American Mafia selling weapons to an Irish terrorist gang. The newspaper said it had seen hundreds of pages of intelligence documents 'at the heart of one of the most sensitive policing operations in recent history'. Although the newspaper did not name Redgrave and Charman, it said they were claiming to have been the victims of the Met's zealous anti-corruption campaign. 'They say that everything they did – including placing money, which they believed to have been stolen or earned from drugs sales, into the secret police account in London – was approved by senior officers.'

The stakes had been upped, but Geoffrey Brennan's fight was far from finished. He was the main source for a second *Sunday Times* story in August which said that Scotland Yard detectives were earning tens of thousands of pounds moonlighting as private eyes, illegally bugging members of the public, and selling highly sensitive police secrets. Brennan was pleased that the newspaper singled out Chris Smith in its front-page story: 'Chris Smith worked for Brennan while a detective sergeant on the Flying Squad. According to Brennan, Smith was paid £100 a day for his help during a three-month spying operation on a private house in Sussex ... They placed miniature bugs in holes drilled through a downstairs window and connected them to voice-activated tape recorders.' Brennan told the newspaper that Smith had used police equipment during his moonlighting, which had earned him £20,000-30,000. In a later story, Brennan was quoted as having decided to speak out about corruption because he was being unfairly targeted by police officers: 'It's a vendetta. They are trying to silence me by making trumped-up charges. I'm being persecuted because of the information I have ...'

Brennan's tactics of creating maximum confusion and embarrassment were working. Superintendent Coles was having difficulty finding a way to cut a path through all the allegations and counter-claims over Brennan. Coles set out all that had happened over the previous four years in a report for the Crown Prosecution Service. He submitted it in

January 1998, asking for advice from a senior lawyer, one of the Treasury counsel who advise the CPS and prosecute on their behalf in major cases. Three months passed before Coles met the senior Treasury counsel Nigel Sweeney, who eventually concluded that without Brennan's co-operation the chances were that a prosecution of Redgrave and Charman would fail. By that stage, however, Coles received what looked like a lucky break. It arose out of a series of Old Bailey trials in which seventeen people were sentenced to a total of more than 130 years in prison for their part in violent robberies.

Coles heard that one of Charman's friends, a CPS caseworker called Debbie Cahill, was enquiring about Chris Smith's involvement in the trials. Smith had by then retired from the Flying Squad, but as one of the officers involved in the prosecutions he had been called to give evidence. In the witness box, subjected to defence lawyers' cross-examination over his moonlighting, he admitted that he had indeed been working for Brennan while still employed by the Met. Having learned of Smith's admissions, Cahill asked CIB for more information about what had been said, querying whether it would have any adverse effect on another trial she was handling in which the former DS could have been involved. Luckily, someone in CIB recalled that Coles had been dealing with Chris Smith and forwarded the query to him. Thinking about what could be behind the request, Coles concluded that Cahill was trying to gather material for Charman with which to discredit the CIB investigation. He also realised that her request provided him with an opportunity to mount a sting operation. It would be aimed at Charman, but could ensnare Redgrave too.

The plan was to give Cahill confidential documents, bug her home and find out whether she passed them on to Charman. The superintendent ran his plan past Treasury counsel Nigel Sweeney and received his approval. The CPS caseworker lived in a bungalow in South Benfleet, Essex, which meant that Coles had to apply to that county's Chief Constable for permission to bug her home. Having obtained the authority, he installed an ISD, an intrusive surveillance device, in the bungalow, ready to be activated later. Calls on her office phone were also intercepted. Then, knowing that she would be attending a CPS case conference on the forthcoming trial, Coles arranged for her to be given a copy of his interview with Smith. The document was specially marked. From listening to the bugs, the anti-corruption detectives learned that Cahill had invited

Charman to her home. The officer went there, glanced at the documents, and then suggested that Redgrave should also see them. Cahill invited him for dinner. That evening, a team of CIB officers led by Coles waited in a car park near the bungalow, monitoring the conversation inside that was being picked up by the probe microphone.

The sting was working, but with Redgrave involved the situation had changed. John Coles could have tackled it in various different ways, but the plan he favoured was one whereby the bug in Cahill's home would not have to be disclosed. Redgrave would be given the document or a copy of it, and arrested as he drove away from the bungalow, but at some distance from it. Coles had a uniformed officer with him in his team. He knew from the probe that Redgrave had been drinking, so he planned for the uniformed officer to stop him for some traffic misdemeanour as he drove home, and arrest him on suspicion of drunk driving. He would then be searched and the incriminating document would be 'found' on him. It was hoped that Redgrave would not suspect that a sting had taken place and that he would put the problem down to a chance, routine police stop. That way, the bug could stay in place and more interesting conversations could be picked up.

Whether the plan would have worked was never discovered. Further conversation from inside the bungalow horrified Coles. Redgrave was clearly examining the document because he was commenting on its contents. But instead of his taking it away from the house, there was talk of destroying it, with concern being expressed about fingerprints. Cahill was heard remarking: 'Yeah, we'll go stick it in the barbeque and burn it.'

This threw Coles into a dilemma. He had planned to let events take their course, but if the document were destroyed, valuable evidence that Redgrave and Charman had seen and handled it would be lost. He reckoned that Cahill must have breached the Official Secrets Act by showing the document to the two officers, and that they, because of the talk about destroying it, were also committing an offence – conspiracy to pervert the course of justice. Fast, surprise action was essential. Coles was the only one of the CIB team in the car park who knew where Cahill's bungalow was, so he led the way, smashing the front door open with the uniformed officer. The sound brought Redgrave running to the hallway, where he stopped in his tracks on seeing Coles. 'I thought you were villains,' he gasped. The CIB team found the documents crumpled up, as though ready for destruction. Cahill and the two officers were arrested, taken to police stations and later charged with conspiracy to pervert the course of justice and with breaches of the Official Secrets Act.

However, the three protested their innocence, arguing that there had been no conspiracy and that the bugging and the way they had been arrested had been unlawful and out of all proportion to the alleged offence. A female magistrate at Bow Street agreed. Although describing Cahill's taking home of the documents as 'improper and unprofessional', she said that there had been no aiding and abetting by Redgrave and Charman over any breach of the Official Secrets Act. 'I do not find the disclosure was likely to impede the detection of offences.' As regards the second charge, conspiracy to pervert the course of justice, it was alleged that the three defendants had sought to destroy the document, using their knowledge of its contents to obstruct an investigation. But in response to that the magistrate declared: 'I find insufficient evidence of a tendency to pervert the course of justice and insufficient evidence of conspiracy.' She threw the case out. Very unhappy, CIB and the CPS then took the unusual step of appealing against the decision. Convinced that talk of burning the document amounted to a conspiracy to destroy evidence, their lawyers went to a High Court judge and argued that the charges should be reinstated. The judge refused.

The legal decisions dealt a body blow to CIB. What had appeared to be a sound proactive investigation, after the allegations made by Geoffrey Brennan, had failed. Not only were Coles and his team back at square one, but also their position was made much worse by the fact that Redgrave, Charman and Cahill decided that they were not going to go quietly. They wanted justice – recognition that they were innocent – and made official complaints about the treatment meted out to them. Other prosecutions were also to fail, and CIB was to come under sustained criticism from, amongst others, Members of Parliament. Before that, however, there were to be major successes.

thirteen

SERCS

*He was asking me if I had any debts and things like that. I
said I had credit cards and I owed money on them. And he
very blatantly turned round and said, 'Well, don't worry
about that. A few months here and we'll have all your debts
cleared. You won't have any debts and you'll have money ...'
The corruption was despicable. There was no way out. I was
in it up to my neck. We felt we were untouchable. No one was
going to find out we were stealing.*

Neil Putnam, on joining the élite South East Regional Crime Squad

Although Duncan Hanrahan was the first of the police corruption supergrasses, within months he was followed in 'rolling over' by Kevin Garner
and Terry McGuinness. However, the next of the police supergrasses to
go into the witness box at the Old Bailey was Detective Constable Neil
Putnam, who had served with the South East Regional Crime Squad.
The evidence he gave against his colleagues in this other élite group
proved devastating. It boosted the fortunes and credibility of Scotland
Yard's anti-corruption campaign which had taken such a battering after
Hanrahan. Putnam served much of his time in prison with Kevin
Garner, in the supergrass wing at Full Sutton in Yorkshire. The pair were
similar. They were of the same age and both say they became corrupt in
the same year, 1991, largely because of peer pressure after joining their
respective squads. They each named more than a dozen officers as
corrupt. But while Garner and his Flying Squad colleagues dealt with
robbers, Putnam and the SERCS detectives stole from drug dealers,
reselling seized cannabis, cocaine and even opium.

Neil Putnam's police career had started so well. Born in 1957, and
brought up in Walworth, south-east London, after passing O-level
GCEs he decided on a career as a policeman. He applied to become a
Met police cadet, but was rejected because he was not tall enough.
After two years working fitting window blinds, he reapplied and was

accepted. During training at the police college at Hendon in north London, his take-home pay was £38 a week, considerably less than the £125 gross pay he had been getting as a fitter. But it did not matter. 'I really wanted to join the police service,' he told me. 'Being a Londoner, I believed that through joining, I could give something back to London, as I had strong morals that had been instilled in me through my upbringing. The money was not an issue. I joined because I wanted to do some good.'

The story of Neil Putnam's descent from do-gooder to bent cop is based on a long exclusive interview with me, on his police statements and his evidence at the Old Bailey. During his four years as an ordinary PC, Putnam's only encounter with anything remotely corrupt came while on road traffic duty when the 'golden hook' was lowered his way after a road accident near Croydon. Putnam explained that the golden hook – a reference to a breakdown lorry's towing hook – operated when a vehicle was so badly damaged that it needed to be towed away.

> The police officers would recommend a tow-away service, a garage, to the driver, who was usually so shocked by what had happened that he'd take the officers' word for it. But, of course, the officers had an arrangement with the particular tow company, and the officer would be paid later. On this one particular occasion, I was dealing with one aspect of the accident and the driver and another officer were dealing with another part. And a couple of days later, this officer came up and said, 'Here you are, here's a five-pound note for you.' I said, 'Oh, where's that from?' and he replied, 'From that accident the other day.' I mean, I had heard stories of the golden hook but it was the first and only time it happened to me. Five pounds doesn't sound a lot now, but in those days it was quite a lot of money. With it, I used to get my meals out of the canteen, and a couple of packets of cigarettes, and it would last me for a week.

On becoming a detective in 1981, Putnam was posted to Notting Hill. Within a few days, he again entered that grey area verging on corruption. He was taken out by a senior detective for a tour of the famous Portobello Road area. At its northern end, away from the antique and art shops, are fruit and vegetable stalls, and the senior officer told the young Putnam that he was going to 'collect the rent'. Putnam learned what he meant as they walked north along Portobello Road. 'He promptly went to different stalls and other places where he collected bags of fruit and vegetables and other bits and pieces,' Putnam told me.

> We stopped at a pub and he told me to wait outside while he went in. It wasn't even opening time. When he came out, he seemed quite happy with himself, and then we went back to Notting Hill. I never saw him pay for anything, or get any money, but the words he used to start with were that he was going to collect the rent. Did I see it as wrong? Yes, I saw it as wrong at that time, but I wasn't looking at it as bribery or corruption or anything like that. It was more like he was receiving gratuities for something, a tip for something. I don't know what went on in the pub, but I was a brand-new detective and I wasn't going to turn round and start pointing the finger at a senior officer. I wasn't going to blot my copybook by making accusations.

At Notting Hill, heavy drinking was the CID norm, and Putnam joined in. 'It was the done thing,' he said. 'If you wanted to be accepted, and you wanted to be part of the culture, then you made sure you were in the pub and you bought your round with everybody else.' However, alcohol and money problems began to cause difficulties for Putnam. He had married young, when only seventeen, and by the time of his next main posting, to the area drugs squad at Croydon in south London, he and his wife Gail had three children and mounting credit-card debts. Putnam made no attempt to sort out his life. Instead, he and some of his new colleagues formed the 'gallon a night club'. Putnam was out drinking at least three nights a week, returning home drunk, abusive and sometimes violent towards Gail. But he enjoyed the work, much of it on surveillance, and although there were great temptations, he said there was no corruption.

> It was a mixed team of uniform and CID officers, who worked for each other, working for an end goal. We achieved our goals and it was a very happy time for me. There was always the opportunity for corruption because when you're dealing with drugs and raiding crack houses in Brixton and so on, there would always be copious amounts of cash lying around. But it never entered anyone's mind. It was an honest, decent squad with honest, decent officers.

Putnam's ambition spurred him to apply to SERCS, the South East Regional Crime Squad, which he believed to be the best of the élite squads, dealing mainly with the drugs world. On joining, he found the atmosphere completely different from what he had been used to before. At Croydon there had been proper supervision by inspectors and sergeants. The senior officers went out on jobs with the detective constables, and there was mutual trust and respect. Putnam was disappointed with his new squad: 'I found that SERCS was fragmented, disorderly and with a lack of discipline. Everything was muddled and people seemed to be going off and doing their own thing, without anybody binding it all together. The senior officers seemed disinterested and there was a lack of respect for the sergeants.'

On his very first day with this élite group there were two surprises. First, there was the arrogance. Reporting for duty at his new base at the old East Dulwich police station in south London, Putnam was asked how he had travelled from central London. After replying that it had been by bus, he received a scathing response: 'Regional Crime Squad officers don't get buses. No, we drive everywhere!' His next surprise came with mention of corruption. After introductions, Putnam was invited by his new team back up to central London, to a pub in the City. There, one of his new colleagues asked him some pointed questions. 'He was asking me if I had any debts and things like that. I said I had credit cards and I owed money on them. And he very blatantly turned round and said, "Well, don't worry about that. A few months here and we'll have all your debts cleared. You won't have any debts and you'll have money." I knew that he was talking about ways of making money corruptly.' The conversation went no further at that stage. But just a few weeks later, he was recruited into the ranks of the corrupt.

It happened during Putnam's first big job with his new squad. In September 1991, the SERCS team mounted a large-scale operation after being tipped off that drugs smugglers were flying a plane loaded with 200 kilos of cannabis resin from Spain. The planned 'drop' for the cargo, worth about £600,000, was a farm near the Ashdown Forest, deep in the Sussex countryside. But the aircraft missed the exact site and dropped the drugs near by. Dealers on the ground, watched by the SERCS team, waited until nightfall before moving in to gather the drugs parcels. The detectives then pounced, arresting three of the gang and seizing the drugs. One of Putnam's colleagues, DC Bob Clark, asked him whether he could borrow his holdall. Putnam handed it over, thinking it was to be used to transport some of the drugs to a police station. In fact, unknown to Putnam, Clark used the bag to take several thousand pounds' worth of the cannabis for himself, to sell it on illegally. Two weeks later, Clark handed £300 to a surprised Putnam. 'You're caught unawares, on the hop,' he told me. 'You're not expecting it and suddenly this money is just thrust into your hand, and the words are "That is for you", and it's there, it's on you, and you have a split second to make your decision. In that split second I made the wrong decision. I remember thinking, well, Christmas is coming. I had three children. It's not going to hurt. I don't know what it's for, but I'll take it anyway.'

Putnam said it was a fortnight later before he realised what the money was for. 'I was working in the equipment room and I saw my holdall. I could see chippings of cannabis inside. I was really angry and I thought they've used my bag to steal drugs. That was when I realised that Bob Clark was stealing drugs and selling them on, and then getting the pro-ceeds of the sale . . . I was disappointed but I felt I couldn't do anything, because I'd already accepted the money. I'd actually spent it.' Putnam, like Kevin Garner on the Flying Squad, was trapped. He still wonders, with hindsight, whether Clark really needed the holdall, or whether it was a clever ploy by the cunning detective to suck him into corruption. After Putnam had taken the £300 without query, Clark would believe that he could be relied on to keep quiet. Any doubts he may have had would have been dispelled by the second test – leaving the bag with the cannabis traces inside for Putnam to find. The new squad member could have complained at that stage. The fact that he did not protest meant that he could be counted on as a willing partner in future corruption. If Clark had indeed reached that conclusion, he was right. Putnam told me: 'I wanted to succeed on the Regional Crime Squad. I wanted to be accepted, and I thought, well, if that's the way I've got to succeed here to be accepted – to be part of the team – then I've got to go along with it.'

The East Dulwich SERCS team frequently got together after work and on days off. They called themselves the 'Groovy Gang'. Meanwhile, Putnam's drink and money problems grew worse and he moved out of the family home. From being a happily married man who had joined the police with such high ideals, he now found his whole life in chaos. And then came more corruption. The team were tipped off that a drugs courier was to collect 100 kilos of cannabis from a vehicle parked at a golf course in south Croydon. Putnam, posing as a taxi-driver, kept the courier under surveillance as he drove into the course's car park. Once the drugs had been transferred to the boot of the dealer's van, Putnam called in the rest of the waiting team. The dealer was arrested and his drugs were put in the back of the black taxicab being driven by Putnam. According to Putnam's account, Clark asked him if he knew anywhere quiet near by, and he replied that there was a parking area in some woods not far away. They drove to it. Putnam knew what was going to happen and made no objection. Clark got out of his car and into the back of the cab with the big bag of drugs. In order not to leave fingerprints on the cannabis blocks' clingfilm wrappings, he pulled the sleeve of his sweat-shirt over his hand and lifted out about 20 kilos, worth at that time more than £30,000. Clark put them into another holdall which he carried to his car, ordering Putnam to return to the police station to log in the remaining drugs.

The following day, Putnam said he went to Clark's home and was given an envelope containing £2,000, his share for helping to steal the drugs, which had already been passed on for recycling. Clark confirmed what Putnam had suspected. The drugs had gone to the informant who had tipped him off about the car park deal and the earlier aircraft drop. The informant's code-name, Jack Higgins, disguised the fact that it was a woman, Eve Fleckney. A small, attractive, sensual woman, she was also Clark's lover. For years, Fleckney had mixed with big-time robbers and drugs dealers. She turned informant herself after her home was raided by SERCS officers, including Clark, and £60,000 in drugs money went missing. Arrested, and owing the money to dealers, Fleckney was in deep trouble. She says she was offered a deal. If she became an informant, the police would ensure that she did not go to prison. She would receive rewards for her information and would therefore be able to pay back the £60,000 she owed. Fleckney agreed to the deal and Clark became her main handler.

Regional Crime Squads depend on good intelligence. Sometimes it is NCIS or Customs providing the information, but each SERCS team tries to develop its own network of grasses. The East Dulwich team was no exception, and were viewed as being particularly successful. Fleckney became unquestionably one of the team's most productive informants, if not the most important. Work dried up when she was out of the country for some months. Her relationship with Clark blossomed. Strict guidelines apply to police-informant relationships, purportedly as a protection for both sides. While it is accepted that informants have to mix with criminals, they are instructed not to play a major part in any crime. And an informant's police handler is told to keep the relationship on a professional basis, with a senior officer in a supervisory role as 'controller'. From virtually the start, Clark and Fleckney flouted the rules. Fleckney was a major drugs dealer in her own right, and Clark was her lover, although at the same time he was living with a policewoman. Fleckney and Clark spent nights together at expensive London hotels, and would meet on short holidays or trips. Clark liked *The Simpsons*, and would register himself as Bart Simpson. Fleckney became pregnant, by Clark, she claims, and had an abortion. The relationship was also corrupt. Clark gave seized drugs to Fleckney who then recycled them to dealers. She shared the proceeds with the bent detective, who passed on some of the cash to his colleagues. The pair would benefit twice from their treachery, as Fleckney also gave Clark large portions of the rewards she received from Scotland Yard for her information. The pair shared, for instance, £6,000 for her tip-off about the Sussex aircraft drop.

Although Putnam found Clark cold and arrogant, he was a willing participant in the corruption, believing that he could not untangle himself, even if he had wanted to. 'There was no way out,' Putnam told me, adding that there was no one with whom he could confide: 'I couldn't have spoken to my senior officers within the Regional Crime Squad, because I didn't trust them myself. I didn't know who else was involved in the corruption. The only place I could have gone to was CIB, but I didn't trust them either at that stage. They were known as the Muppets. Anyway, I wanted to preserve what I had. I didn't want to go to prison, lose my job and everything I had.'

I asked Putnam about *Panorama*'s exposure in 1993 of the corrupt relationship between a criminal 'informant' and the detective John Donald. Donald had been suspended after the broadcast, along with others from the SERCS office at Surbiton, which was next door to Putnam's at East Dulwich. It was this programme which helped kick-start the whole Met anti-corruption campaign. Putnam knew some of the Surbiton detectives well, and given the similarities between what had occurred there and what was happening at East Dulwich, I asked him if the programme had had any effect. 'I've got to say that it didn't have any effect at all,' he replied 'It didn't worry anybody. All the attention was on

Surbiton. No one came to us from the Regional Crime Squad head office to speak about it or to check up. We were ignored, and it didn't curb any of our activities. Things just carried on. It was as though the programme had never happened. I know they tried to change things at Surbiton, but the rest of the regional crime squad seemed to be immune.'

'So, if there was corruption at Surbiton and East Dulwich, how widespread do you think corruption was at that time?'

'I think it was throughout the London region, at all the branch offices. At least somewhere within every branch, there was at least one officer who was corrupt.'

'You were corrupt. Did you talk about it with the others involved?'

'Not really, because I didn't want to know what they had done. It was like a protection for myself. I believed that if I didn't know, then I couldn't tell. By the same token, I wouldn't mention what I had done or what money I had received. Maybe it was naivety on my part, but I thought I was protecting myself, and in a way protecting other people . . . I mean, for an officer to become an informant against other officers is a horrendous step to take, because he faces being ostracised throughout the police service. Since the day I joined, there's been this musketeers' attitude. All for one and one for all. You just don't grass up your mates.'

That secrecy meant that Putnam only definitely knew which of his colleagues were 'wrong 'uns' if they had taken part in corrupt activities together. One taking a lead role was Chris Drury, who joined the team in 1993, rapidly becoming Clark's willing lieutenant. Although a weaker character than Clark, and with a cocaine habit himself, he made clear he was 'up for it'. Putnam himself had moved back in with his wife, but he was becoming more corrupt. He was not only sharing in the proceeds of Clark and Drury's activities, he was himself stealing. In July 1994, Putnam, Clark, Drury and others raided the home of a fraudster, looking for cash. Putnam said he will never forget the sight when he forced his way through the front door: 'The thing that struck me straight away, and it was incredible, was the amount of money. Everywhere you looked there was just money, cash.' The team divided into pairs, going into rooms together. 'Bob Clark came into the bedroom where I was with another officer, and he was holding a police property bag, and he turned round and said. "Any money you find, just put it in the bag, because I'm the official exhibits officer." Well, we knew that Clark and Drury were up to something because Clark only volunteered to be an exhibits officer if he could actually steal something. I can't remember which of us said it, but it was something along the lines of "they're amassing fortunes in there. We won't get a fair slice of it." So we decided to keep back £1,000 that we had found ourselves.' In addition to that money, Putnam alleged he received another £400, a share of the money gathered by Clark as 'exhibits officer'. By that stage, thieving was part of Putnam's life. 'I was in it up to my neck,' he told me. 'We felt we were untouchable. No one was going to find out we were stealing.'

The corruption continued. It was not until 1996 that the team's nefarious world started to fall apart. The first cracks had appeared a year earlier after Eve Fleckney betrayed a drugs dealer who regarded her as a very good friend. He was known as 'Guildford John' and had dealt in drugs for years, since his days as a hippy. Fleckney was a regular customer, and in January 1995, having picked up 10 kilos of cannabis in London, he delivered some to her, and then travelled on to Aldershot. But en route a car shot in front, blocking him in. Two men got out and came towards him. Guildford John thought he was about to be robbed by rival dealers. He was right. But the two men were police officers, in an unmarked car. Fleckney had tipped off Clark, who had decided to steal the drugs with Chris Drury. The pair slammed John against a wall and searched him, finding only a little money. Having identified themselves as police officers, they found the cannabis in the boot of the car. They took the drugs, with a street value of about £27,000, freed John and let him keep his money as well. The pair reckoned, correctly, that the dealer would be so grateful, having avoided arrest and years in prison, that he would not complain. In fact John didn't make any official complaint, but the first person he telephoned afterwards was Eve Fleckney, who, unknown to him, had betrayed him. Not knowing whether she had been busted too, he asked whether she was OK, and when she replied positively, he outlined what had happened to him after he had left her. The treacherous Fleckney told him that she would help him in any way she could.

While pretending to help, Fleckney continued to pass information about Guildford John to her lover Bob Clark, who had by that stage transferred to the Flying Squad base at Tower Bridge. She told the corrupt officer that Guildford John stored his drugs at a 'safe house' in a picturesque village in Surrey. Clark passed the information to Drury, and in April 1995 Drury, Putnam and two other detectives raided the premises. The couple living there were close friends of John, but they had no large amounts of cannabis. There were only a few ounces of hashish for their own use in the house. Believing there was more, the three other officers searched the overgrown garden and an old van while Putnam continued looking inside the house. He found £800 in an envelope, hidden in a drawer. The male occupant asked Putnam about doing a deal. He would admit that the few ounces of the drug were his, but as it was just for his personal use, could he simply be cautioned rather than prosecuted? Putnam went outside to consult Drury, telling him of the £800. 'Can it be nicked?' asked Drury. The two officers went back inside, and Putnam told me what happened next: 'We told him that that unless he gave us the £800, we would arrest him, seize his cannabis and everything that went with it. If he gave us the money, we'd leave the cannabis where it was, walk away, leave him alone and never see him again. He handed the money over.'

Putnam said he shared the money with Drury and Clark. He claims to have been conscience stricken later about stealing the money from the couple, money they had saved, most of it for rent. 'I'd lowered myself lower than I could ever possibly go. It was despicable. It's difficult to put into words actually how bad I felt, because, you know, I really felt it was the lowest point I could possibly go. I just hated myself.' These feelings did not stop Putnam engaging in more corruption. He received £250 for a cocaine deal and £500 for stealing some amphetamines. But unknown to Putnam and the others, the incident at the house was to lead to the corrupt team coming under investigation by CIB. The tenant had made a note of the registration number of the unmarked police car in which the detectives had left, and told Guildford John what had happened, describing the officers to him. John realised that the description of one of them, Drury, matched that of one of the two men who had robbed him of the drugs just a few weeks before. At that stage he did nothing more about either incident. But he did a year later, after other SERCS officers arrested him as he unloaded boxes of cannabis from the boot of his car.

While being driven off to the police station, the laid-back John made what he described to me in interview as a flippant remark, referring back to the earlier theft. 'The police officers were quite hyped up, and I wanted to calm the situation down. They were asking the normal questions, so I said, "Oh, you're not going to do the same as the last guys did?" The inspector in front said, "What do you mean?" and I said, "Oh, you're not just going to take the pot and let me go, then?" The inspector was really affronted by this and started getting angry, saying, "Are you suggesting that we're corrupt officers?" I replied, "No, I'm not suggesting you're corrupt. It's just what happened to me last time."'

He then related what had happened to him and his friend. The SERCS officers called in CIB. But this was 1996, before the creation of the proactive CIB3. The anti-corruption officers who dealt with this complaint were from CIB2. They interviewed John and also saw the tenant, but it was made plain to both men that there was little chance of the investigation getting anywhere. John told me: 'I got the impression that although they would have to act upon this information, they weren't very hopeful of it going any further because I was a known drug dealer making allegations against police officers, and generally people just aren't going to believe me.'

John was given a four-year prison sentence for drug dealing. While he was on remand, CIB2 officers saw him twice, taking statements, and then, three months after being sentenced, he was seen again:

> I had got the impression that their motivation wasn't there, and then they came and said there was nothing they could do. They were going to drop it. They said there wasn't evidence. They didn't really go into it with me, but they did say that we were criminals and we were questioning the integrity of the police and obviously it would not go down too well with any jury. They seemed to be more interested in me being an informer for them. They offered me various inducements to see whether when I came out of prison I would help them and be an informer, but I said no, I'm not interested.

Unknown to John and the anti-corruption detectives, Putnam and the other bent officers had taken steps to ensure that the inquiry would founder. As was then the custom, they had been served with the Regulation 163 notices, telling them that a complaint had been made which was being investigated. Straight away, Putnam and the others met at a pub in Croydon, the Cricketers, to discuss what to do about their theft of money from the premises. 'We basically put together, or hatched together, a set of lies to protect ourselves from prosecution,' Putnam told me. 'Our story was that there was no drugs in the property; that we'd

195

never taken any money; that there was no money; that everything that was being said against us was a lie; that the man there was making it all up; that we were going to blacken him that he was a drug dealer; and we would say how could they [CIB] take the word of a drug dealer against honest officers.'

The strategy worked as far as Putnam was concerned. He was told that the inquiry was over. However, a serious investigation was under way into his corrupt colleague, DC Bob Clark. He had been under suspicion since the previous year over his relationship with Eve Fleckney. When Clark left SERCS for the Flying Squad, he should have handed over his drug-dealing female informant to another SERCS detective, because his new team concentrated on robberies, not drugs. Unusually, he kept her as his informant, and it was suspected that the relationship was corrupt. Confirmation of that came from a separate investigation into Fleckney herself. For eighteen months she was targeted as a major drugs dealer by SERCS officers based at Surbiton. In charge of the operation was Detective Inspector Martin Bridger, the same officer who had arrested Guildford John and heard his complaint about having had drugs stolen from him by two officers. Fleckney's home had been bugged, and in conversations with her then partner, another drug dealer, she mentioned getting help from her detective friend 'Bob'.

By that stage Clark had been told to break off his informant relationship with Fleckney. He knew that she was being targeted by SERCS and decided to warn her. He engineered what he hoped would be a final meeting with her, ostensibly so she could be paid an outstanding reward by a Scotland Yard officer. The meeting, in a park in Dulwich, was monitored by a SERCS surveillance team. When the Scotland Yard officer had handed the cash reward to Fleckney, he walked off, leaving the pair together in conversation. The hidden watchers were unable to hear what was being said but Clark was doing most of the talking, and when they left the park, separately, it became obvious what Fleckney had been told. Previously, she had shown no sign of suspecting that she was under observation. But immediately after the meeting that changed. When Fleckney drove off, she went through a series of anti-surveillance measures aimed at throwing off anyone following her. These tactics included driving twice right the way round roundabouts and doubling back the way she had come. However, she appeared not to have realised that there was a tracking device on her car. The following day, police deregistered her as an informant. Nothing could be proved against Clark, but a few weeks later he was quietly removed from the Flying Squad and forced to return to basic CID duties at Streatham.

Eventually, in 1997, Fleckney was arrested and remanded in custody, charged with major drug dealing. DI Bridger visited her in prison, hoping to persuade her to talk about her corrupt relationship with Clark. She refused to co-operate. There was nothing in it for her. Later, however, abandoned by Clark and given a hefty fifteen-year prison sentence, she changed her mind. By then it was 1998 and several months since the formation of CIB3 and an influx of keen, experienced, younger detectives to the anti-corruption team. DI Bridger and the head of CIB3, Chief Superintendent Dave Wood, thought it was worth visiting her in prison. 'She was continually tearful,' Wood told me. 'There was no doubt in my mind, and she expressed this, that she had been in love with Bob Clark. She'd had a couple of abortions as a result of the affair she'd had with him and still had a close affection for him.' Nevertheless, hoping that she would get her sentence reduced, she decided to co-operate, her head taking over from whatever love lingered in her heart for the corrupt officer. She turned informant.

To supervise what would be the new corruption inquiry into the activities of the East Dulwich SERCS officers, another detective was called in. He was John Yates, the highly regarded superintendent in charge of the north-west London murder squad. Yates told me of his shock when he started researching the allegations:

> I was stunned, and I use the word carefully, at the scale of the corruption. I had never imagined that officers could behave like that, behaving with such impunity, being so openly corrupt and getting away with it. But there's also, running at the back of my mind, that here was a woman with a fifteen-year sentence, with very much to gain from providing us with information and intelligence. I kept a very open mind about her throughout. It was a fairly dynamic relationship in that she's a very strong character as you would imagine her to be, because of the environment she had been operating in. It was a constant battle of wits for me to remind her of her responsibilities as a resident informant [supergrass] and that she was a credible witness. My job was to go out there and find the independent corroborative evidence that would back up what she was saying.

Yates had a team of twenty-five detectives working for him. Unlike CIB2 investigators, they were hand-picked, highly skilled officers, all thoroughly vetted. They concentrated initially on investigating Bob Clark and Chris Drury, the two officers Fleckney had told them were most heavily involved. It was decided to suspend them. They were treated like major criminals and raided at six o'clock in the morning. Somewhat surprisingly, given his cleverness, and the fact that there had been an earlier investigation, useful evidence was found at Clark's home. It showed that his relationship with Fleckney had gone far beyond what was allowed between an informant and a handler. When he answered the door to the anti-corruption officers, he was wearing a dressing gown taken from an expensive hotel where Fleckney said they had spent the night. There were also gifts she had given him. Yates had expected Clark to have tried to cover his tracks. That he had not done so Yates put down to Clark's arrogant belief that he would never be brought to justice:

'The template of a corrupt officer is that they are arrogant. They believe they'll never get caught. The crimes they indulge in are, to an extent, victimless. What's involved are drugs and dealers' profits being stolen. These people are unlikely to complain. If a complaint was made, it would be difficult to get evidence. It would often come down to a criminal's word against that of a police officer. So Clark and the others operated in a framework where the possibility of getting caught was negligible, and if they were caught, they'd probably get off.'

Yates's team also raided the homes of the others from the SERCS East Dulwich team. But different tactics were used. Clark and Drury were too far down the road of criminality to co-operate with the inquiry. The others were viewed as having been on the periphery and would be useful for intelligence. They would be suspended, but they would also be asked if they wanted to talk about others' corruption. They would be given time to think about their position and told they could approach the anti-corruption team later. In fact it was Yates himself who raided Putnam, but this was not because the superintendent had any prior intelligence or suspicion that the detective constable had been involved in serious corruption. All that was known about his role was that he had been present when £800 was allegedly stolen from the Surrey house. In particular, Yates had no idea that Putnam's outlook on life had totally changed a couple of years before. Not only was he waiting for the CIB knock on his door, he was also ready to confess.

Putnam's wife, Gail, had become a born-again Christian early in 1995 and Putnam had followed suit later in the year, in December. Although to protect himself and his family he had continued to lie in 1996 about the Surrey affair, he said the burden of guilt was hurting him by 1997. He had moved from SERCS, back into uniform as a home beat officer at Penge. Part of his duties was to talk to young people about the dangers of taking drugs. 'I kept thinking what a hypocrite I am. I'm trying to tell these kids one thing and yet I knew I was a drug dealer. I was as bad as the people I was criticising.' Another part of his new job was to take young constables out to show them around. He remembers one man just out of police college asking for advice on how to deal with officers in a corrupt situation. 'I replied that you should inform a trusted senior officer straight away, or you ring the "whistle-blowers'" hot line at Scotland Yard, regardless of the circumstances, regardless of what's going to happen to you. After telling him that, I thought to myself, again, what a hypocrite I was, giving him advice like that.'

In January 1998, a *Panorama* programme I presented on the widening investigation into police corruption within SERCS and NCIS caused Putnam and others great worry. While the original 1993 *Panorama* on the John Donald affair had not disrupted the East Dulwich team's corrupt activities, he said the follow-up programme caused 'alarm bells to ring all over . . . People were panicking. I mean really panicking. They knew that things were coming to a head. There had been rumours beforehand of ghost squads and proactive teams of detectives around London, and it seemed that it was now happening, and it caused a lot of people a lot of fear.' Putnam had heard that Clark and Drury had been raided and he knew he would be visited too, but when Superintendent John Yates arrived it was still a shock. Putnam was angry with Clark and Drury and angry with himself.

'Putnam struck me immediately as a very nervous character,' Yates told me. 'The first thing he mentioned as we came through the door was some unsolicited comment about there being two of them. It didn't take a genius to work out that there could be opportunities there, but I had no idea of the scale of what he would eventually admit.' Yates took Putnam outside, talked to him about CIB3, and told him about the belief that corrupt officers could be divided into two categories – the meat-eaters and the grass-eaters. 'He started talking about carnivores and grass-eaters,' Putnam told me. 'The meat-eaters were the main players, the main corrupt people, those taking the prize cuts. I'd never heard the expression before. He felt I was a grass-eater, as were most of my friends. We were lower down the scale. He said he wanted the carnivores. He left me in no doubt that he wanted Clark and Drury.' Putnam made no immediate response. But after being suspended later in the day, he talked to his wife about his corruption. He faced an agonising choice. He knew that if he kept quiet it was likely that there would be insufficient proof against him and his corrupt colleagues. They would stay free men. But if he told the truth he would go to prison, and by turning against his colleagues he would become that most hated of people, a grass. Putnam took the step that was to change his life for ever. He decided to confess. 'My whole world was collapsing around me and there was nothing I could do about it. It was just that ... I wanted to tell the truth.'

Through a senior officer, arrangements were made for Putnam to have a meeting with Yates at a room in a hotel near Gatwick Airport. He had decided to try to minimise his own role in the hope that he would still get a reduced prison sentence. He also wanted to protect his friends. As Yates appeared to want only Clark and Drury, Putnam thought he would give them to him. But the others involved would be left out of the picture. Although Yates did not know that what Putnam was telling him was incomplete, he was delighted: 'He was actually confessing to stuff that I didn't know about, and also corroborating an issue that I felt we didn't have a chance with. I was staggered, absolutely staggered that we had this jewel who was going to provide us with the inside track on the corrupt activities of the squad.'

Because Putnam had made serious allegations against fellow officers, he faced possible retribution, so it was decided to hold him at a secret location. After being taken home to collect clothes and having bidden a tearful farewell to his wife, he was whisked off to a police station with special cells at Folkestone in Kent. He was to spend months there. The first few weeks were taken up with daily questioning, but it soon became clear that he was not telling the whole truth. So Yates warned Putnam that he would be dumped out of the protected witness system if he did not deliver up all his corrupt SERCS colleagues. 'Here was a man clearly ashamed of what he'd personally done,' Yates told me, 'and ashamed of what it would do to his family and of what it did to the Metropolitan Police. I made it quite clear that if he didn't tell us everything, his credibility as an informant would be minimal. In the days after that, a whole catalogue of serious criminality came out.'

Much of Neil Putnam's evidence about stealing drugs complemented what Eve Fleckney had said about recycling those same drugs, given to her by Bob Clark. She and Putnam were both to give evidence at the Old Bailey, but not before Fleckney caused problems as an unwilling witness; in the witness box she refused to answer questions about her relationship with Clark. Fleckney was a worried woman, fearing for her life. She had told anti-corruption officers: 'I am concerned that during the time I've been working with Clark he has made threats to me, that if I told anyone, and it all came out about what we were doing, then I would be shot. He told me this on many occasions. Although he never said it to me in an aggressive way, I knew that he was serious. He never said it after any event in particular, but said it many times. It was a sort of ongoing thing, and I still believe this even now.'

Fleckney explained to the court that police had assured her that she would be giving her evidence in secret, in camera, so she had been shocked to discover just moments before entering the witness box that it would be in the full glare of publicity. She refused to continue. Although the trial went on, it was clear that the prosecution case was considerably weakened without her. Eventually, she agreed to return to court, having struck a deal with the authorities to the effect that she would be screened from the public gallery while giving evidence, and that the media would be banned from printing a photograph or sketch of her. The trial was halted and then restarted again with a fresh jury.

Both Fleckney and Putnam were subjected to days of gruelling cross-examination by defence lawyers. Describing Fleckney as a lying and deeply manipulative drugs trafficker, Clark's QC, Alun Jones, attacked her from every angle. He ranged from claiming that she was only giving evidence in order to obtain a five-year reduction in her fifteen-year sentence to attacking her for deceiving the jury by wearing clothes that made her look like a primary schoolteacher. But, sometimes tearfully, she gave as good as she got, insisting that she had been in love with Clark, recycling drugs for him on many occasions. Jones described the other main witness, Putnam, as a self-confessed bent policeman and a drunken wife-beater. His handling by the police came under particular scrutiny, it being alleged that he had only agreed to co-operate because the police had offered him illegal inducements, including financial help with mortgage payments. Putnam denied it, revealing that his wife had been forced to sell the family home because they could not afford to keep paying the mortgage. It was also alleged that keeping Putnam for months on his own in police cells had been a breach of prison rules for resident informants. In evidence, Yates said the rules had not been drawn up with police officers in mind. He said it was a unique situation, and that he and other CIB officers had been on a 'learning curve' throughout the inquiry. Yates was embarrassed to learn from defence lawyers that some of the more junior officers did appear to have broken some other rules. The defence lawyers claimed that the cumulative effect of these amounted to Putnam being given favoured treatment in order to keep him happy about giving evidence. However, if these were breaches, they were undoubtedly minor. The fact that they were picked on and amplified indicated increasing desperation on the part of the defence, which found itself trying to fight strong prosecution evidence.

The infringements had only been discovered towards the end of Putnam's evidence, when he revealed that he had kept a diary of his time in CIB custody. He handed the book to the court, to be scoured by the defence. They found the first favour had occurred during Putnam's journey to police cells in Folkestone. According to the regulations, refreshment stops can be made when prisoners are being transported for long distances, but on no account should they be given any alcohol. However, it emerged from Putnam's diary that his escort had stopped for a snack lunch in a pub, and because they knew that Putnam would not be allowed a drink again for a long time, he had been bought a pint of beer. This was hardly an inducement to Putnam, but Yates had been unaware of it, and when challenged about it while giving evidence he had to concede that it had indeed been a breach, although a minor one. The same applied to two other incidents. These related to witness protection officers taking Putnam with them when they test-drove two new cars. What the jury made of this nit-picking is not known. But Clark and Drury were each found guilty of most of the charges. Clark was cleared of the 'golf course' incident.

Sentencing Clark to twelve years' imprisonment and Drury to eleven, the judge, Sir John Blofeld, said the pair were arrogant, wanting power and prestige: 'Both of you took the view that the law was for lesser mortals than yourselves. You did whatever you wanted whether it was inside or outside the law.' Clark, in particular, had manipulated his superior officers at SERCS, and they, in turn, had not exercised adequate supervision. Prior to conviction, both men had been suspended, receiving full pay, like all the other officers suspended as a result of CIB enquiries across south-east England. In Clark's case, this amounted, with various allowances, to £32,000 a year. It also emerged that he had had substantial joint equity in his house – about £125,000 – but after it had been searched, before his arrest, he had signed a form of pre-nuptial agreement with his common-law wife, reducing his liability in the house to under £10,000. At a separate hearing, in February 2000, the judge gave Eve Fleckney and Putnam sentences of only four years each for their part in the corruption. Putnam had confessed to sixteen separate episodes of wrong-doing.

The first trial was followed by another involving three other SERCS detectives: Sergeant Terry O'Connell, forty-three, and Constables Tom Reynolds, thirty-nine, and Tom Kingston, forty-two. The three all denied their part in stealing 2 kilos of 'speed' – amphetamines – from a dealer. Once again Putnam was the main prosecution witness, although by then he had been released from prison, having already served most of his sentence in police custody. He described how the dealer's home had been raided just after the delivery of 6 kilos of the drug. Putnam said he had gone into the kitchen where the drugs had been found by O'Connell and Kingston. Kingston handed him 2 kilos of the drug, worth several thousand pounds, and told him to take them to DC Tom Reynolds at his home. Putnam did so, and said Reynolds later gave him £500.

A curious, unexplained episode was revealed during Putman's cross-examination by defence lawyers. In a statement before the trial, Putnam had said he thought Sergeant O'Connell was involved in the conspiracy to steal the drugs. But by the time he appeared in the witness box, the story had been watered down. Putnam now told the jury that he thought O'Connell was not involved and, furthermore, that he was an honest officer who, if he had realised what was happening, would have done something about it. Why Putnam had changed his mind about O'Connell's role was never fully explored. The sergeant's lawyers were obviously pleased with what Putnam had said, and did not want to question his motives and risk him contradicting himself by saying something detrimental about O'Connell.

But it also emerged that during Putnam's time in police cells at Folkestone he had received an unusual visit from DCI Chris Jarratt, who had nothing to do with the investigation into his claims. CIB's system of so-called 'sterile corridors' was supposed to keep each inquiry team apart. But Putnam told the court that Jarratt, then head of CIB's protected witness scheme, had visited him on a Friday evening, which was unusual in itself. Putnam said he was told by the officer that Terry O'Connell had been a good friend of his, and he could not believe that he had done what Putnam was alleging. Putnam said he could tell from Jarratt's tone and demeanour what he was getting at. He took it as a veiled threat, he told the court, and complained about it the next day to the two protection officers who visited him. What then happened, if anything, is unclear, as the issue was not explored further when the two protection officers gave evidence. However, I raised it later with Chris Jarratt, and he expressed surprise, exclaiming that no one had mentioned the matter to him at all, and that my account of what had happened was the first he had heard of it. He confirmed that O'Connell had been one of his closest friends, the two having worked together on the Flying Squad. He said that friendship would have been acknowledged when he had visited the prisoner, but he maintained that he would not have said anything that allowed Putnam's interpretation of the event. Jarratt added that he felt he should have been told what Putnam had said, instead of having to learn it from me.

Somewhat surprisingly, given what Putnam had said about O'Connell, the jury at the Old Bailey found all three defendants guilty. Kingston and Reynolds were each jailed for three and a half years for stealing and selling amphetamines. O'Connell was given a two-year sentence for acts intended to pervert the course of justice. That second trial was to have been followed by a third arising out of the raid on the fraudster's house during which, according to Putnam, detectives had stolen a large amount of cash. But because all but one of the officers charged with that offence had already been convicted, there was doubt about whether it was in the public interest to go ahead. The remaining officer was Terry Broughton, who had been co-handler, with Clark, of Eve Fleckney. He denied involvement in any corruption and the case against him was eventually dropped.

Amongst others branded as corrupt by Putnam was a detective who was severely criticised at the McPherson Inquiry into the death of the black teenager Stephen Lawrence. He was Sergeant John Davidson, a Scotsman, with the nickname 'O.J.', which stands for Obnoxious Jock.

In statements to anti-corruption officers, Putnam alleged that Davidson had been involved in thieving goods after the hijacking of a lorry in 1994, and had behaved corruptly the following year over a cocaine deal. Davidson had retired from the Met and went to run a bar in Spain. He was arrested in 1999, but always denied the allegations and was never charged. However, CIB officers knew that Davidson was facing criticism at the Lawrence inquiry, so as part of the disclosure process sent details of the allegations to the judge in charge, Sir William McPherson, aware that the inquiry was exploring the issue of alleged corruption during the police investigation into the tragic murder. The allegations were not disclosed to the Lawrence family or their lawyers.

The five officers convicted in the two trials in which Neil Putnam gave evidence appealed against their convictions and lost. However, there was a concession during the hearing from the Crown's lawyer, Orlando Pownall, who had prosecuted at the Old Bailey. He said that the initial police debriefing of Putnam and some other interviews should have been recorded, either on tape or with full contemporaneous notes. The fact that this had not happened meant there had been breaches of PACE, the Police and Criminal Evidence Act, and of the CPIA, the Criminal Procedure and Investigations Act. The three Appeal Court judges said in their ruling in 2002 that although the police had breached the law, they had not done so deliberately, and no injustice had resulted. Bob Clark and Chris Drury were more successful in their appeals against the length of their sentences. These were reduced from twelve and ten to ten and eight years respectively.

As had happened after the Flying Squad corruption came to light, a number of people convicted by SERCS officers' evidence launched appeals. One such was Billy Pope. He had been sharing a flat with Eve Fleckney in 1990 when they were raided by a team that included DC Bob Clark. Fleckney had claimed that police took £60,000 in drugs money from the flat. After being found guilty of having a shotgun at the flat and possessing drugs, Pope had been given a seven-year prison sentence. He had denied owning the shotgun or the drugs, and said he had been fitted up by police and their informant, David Norris, some of whose devious double-dealing is described in Chapter 3 of this book.

Putnam joined the SERCS team at East Dulwich just after Norris – their star informer – had been shot dead by contract killers, hired by criminals who wanted him permanently silenced. Norris was rumoured to have had corrupt relations with the police, confirmed for Putnam when he was told by one of his new colleagues that Norris had been 'a good earner' for the squad. Putnam could tell anti-corruption officers little more about Norris, but Fleckney knew plenty about him. She told CIB detectives and the Old Bailey jury that it had been Norris who had instructed her to take the shotgun home in 1990. It had not belonged to Billy Pope, who was charged and convicted for its possession. The £60,000 she believed police had taken from the flat had also been hers. It was the proceeds of two or three weeks' drugs dealing. After accepting the police offer of bail if she turned informant, she said that Norris was fed to her by police, and he started supplying her with large quantities of drugs, mainly cannabis, at cheap rates. She sold them on, saving the profits in order to repay the £60,000 she owed dealers. Fleckney told the court that there could only be one way Norris was able to supply such cheap drugs. They must have been seized by police and given to him to resell. She explained that after Norris's death she had started to do the same for DC Bob Clark. When Pope learned what Fleckney had said in court, he complained to CIB, pointing out that she had provided proof that he had indeed been fitted up by Norris and police officers working together. At the time of writing his case was being looked at by the Criminal Cases Review Commission and I understand it is likely that it will be referred to the Court of Appeal. CIB was also investigating at least one other case of alleged fit-up involving Clark.

Putnam, the CIB investigators and the judge hearing the cases all blamed poor supervision at SERCS for the fact that corruption had been allowed to flourish at East Dulwich. However, lack of supervision was only partly to blame in another important CIB corruption case to be heard at the Old Bailey, which involved others known to Putnam. Fairly traditional police methods had been used to bring Clark, Drury and the three other corrupt officers to justice. The next case involved mounting a long-term secret surveillance operation, ending in a sting. It was aimed at discovering whether police had played any part in events surrounding the dramatic murder of a private detective.

fourteen

MURDER AND THE DETECTIVE AGENCY

They are alert, cunning and devious individuals who have current knowledge of investigative methods and techniques which may be used against them ... Such is their level of access to individuals within the police, through professional and social contacts, that the threat of compromise to any conventional investigation against them is constant and very real.

Murder investigation report on a private detective agency

One of CIB3's most important proactive operations was mounted shortly after the big influx of detectives into the anti-corruption team's ranks early in 1998. A private investigation agency was targeted. Bugs were planted in its offices because those working there were linked to a network of suspect corrupt officers and ex-detectives. Some were suspected of involvement in events surrounding a murder. But no one had ever stood trial for the killing of the agency's partner, Danny Morgan, found slumped in a pub car park with an axe embedded deep in his skull.

To get to the bottom of the murder mystery, the new anti-corruption team enlisted the help of the then Deputy Commissioner, Sir John Stevens. Their suspicions were set out in a secret document sent to him by CIBIC, the CIB Intelligence Cell. Although worded tortuously in police-speak, its message was clear: 'You are aware of our efforts to achieve evidential opportunities to establish the reality of current and past corruption activities involving ex-Detective Sergeant Sid Fillery and his partner John Rees. Additionally, we are wholly sighted of the need to establish once and for all whether or not Fillery and/or Rees were involved in the Morgan murder . . .' What CIB wanted was to plant bugs and probes to listen in to potentially incriminating conversations at the detective agency. CIBIC needed Sir John's authority for the listening devices. Once they had received his go-ahead their bugging operation was to last several months. During that time anti-corruption officers deliberately fed a story about the murder to a national newspaper, knowing that it would provoke discussion among those working for the agency and, hopefully, result in vital evidence emerging. The whole operation ended with the arrests of twelve men, including two serving officers and some ex-detectives, for corruption and conspiracy to pervert the course of justice.

The sequence of events that led in fits and starts to CIB's covert operation began with the horrific murder of Danny Morgan in March 1987. Morgan, a Welshman, was a private investigator, in partnership with Jonathon Rees, in a private detective-security company called Southern Investigations, based at Thornton Heath in south London. During the evening of 10 March, he had been drinking at the Golden Lion public house in Sydenham. Later that night he was found next to his BMW car, dead, with an axe sticking out of his head. Theft did not appear to be a motive as the murdered man had £1,000 in his pocket. The axe was a common brand, costing £4.50 at any hardware store. Sticking plaster had been wrapped round its handle as a precaution, ensuring not only that no fingerprints would be left but also helping the wielder of the axe to keep a grip in case his hands became sweaty or wet with blood. The savage murder looked like a professional job – a hit. Suspicion soon fell on Morgan's partner, Rees. He had been one of the last to see the Welshman alive, and associates said there had been increasing animosity between the pair.

Southern Investigations had been set up in 1984. Although joint partners, the two had different approaches to investigative work. Rees looked and talked like a policeman, and mixed with detectives. Through his contacts he was able to access the Police National Computer for information. He was a freemason, like many officers at that time. Among the detectives he knew was Sergeant Sid Fillery, and two other officers who have already featured in this book, DC Duncan Hanrahan and DS Alec Leighton, of SERCS, named as a suspect in the John Donald corruption affair. Morgan preferred to work on his own. Married, with two children, he was financially successful, owning a Jaguar and an Austin Healey as well as the BMW. He could be boastful and, according to some, was a womaniser. Rees did not like the way he treated women clients, while Morgan disapproved of Rees's close relations with the police.

Something causing particular friction in the weeks before the murder arose from an incident the year before. Rees was providing security for a car auction company in Charlton, south London, following a £20,000 robbery there in February 1986. Some of his police contacts were helping, 'moonlighting' while off duty. While not amounting to corruption, such work was in breach of police disciplinary codes. On 18 March, it was Rees's job to bank the takings, £18,200. He took the money to a Midland Bank branch's night safe, only to find that he could not open it, someone having superglued it shut. Rees decided to take the cash home. But he claimed it was stolen from him on his doorstep after a noxious liquid had been squirted in his face. The local CID officer who investigated the alleged robbery was none other than DC Duncan Hanrahan, who went to see Rees in hospital. No one was ever caught, let alone prosecuted. Hanrahan did not even bother to make any enquiries at Rees's home or with his neighbours to see whether anyone had witnessed the attack. He later told murder investigators that he thought that Rees had either been set up by someone who had known his movements or had been involved himself. Also believing the attack to have been a sham, the car auction company demanded its money back, holding Rees responsible for its loss. Rees agreed to pay the money back, and wanted to take it from Southern Investigations' account. But his partner, Morgan, resisted, arguing that the auction work had been unwise and was nothing to do with him. Why should he suffer from Rees's mistake?

It was not until more than two weeks after Morgan's death that police investigating the murder learned that the car auction company was pursuing a civil claim against Rees for the loss of the money. The company had written to three officers present at the auctions on various dates and wanted to interview them, but none of them had told the officer in charge of the murder investigation, Detective Superintendent Douglas Campbell. One of the three, Sid Fillery, was even on the murder team, under Campbell, who was furious when he found out. Fillery had taken a statement from Rees the day after the murder and had accompanied him to the mortuary to identify Morgan's body, where the pair had to wait until the pathologist removed the axe from his head. Campbell was also worried as it appeared that some of the company's documents were missing. He arrested the three police officers, along with Rees and two others. A year later, at the inquest into Morgan's death, Campbell told the coroner that there had been insufficient evidence to charge anyone over wrong-doing during the murder investigation or in events leading up to it.

Another witness at the inquest also spoke in dramatic terms of ill feeling between Rees and the dead man. Kevin Lennon, an accountant at the detective agency, said Rees wanted his partner to leave. Rees had thought of arranging for his police contacts to arrest Morgan for drink-driving, so that he would lose his private investigator's licence and be forced to leave the firm. Lennon told the court that six months before the murder Rees had told him he had found the perfect solution to the problem, saying: 'My mates . . . are going to arrange it.' He claimed Rees had said: 'These officer friends of mine will either do it themselves or arrange for someone that is on a pending charge to do it, and in return they will drop the charge.' Rees and Fillery also gave evidence, both denying any wrong-doing, with Rees disputing Lennon's version of events. The coroner, Sir Montague Levine, said the case left 'lots of room for disquiet', adding: 'In all the evidence, it must be said here and now that there has not been one single shred of evidence to link anybody who gave evidence in this court with the killing of Daniel Morgan. No blood, no fibres, no fingerprints.' The verdict of the inquest jury was unlawful killing.

No charges were brought at that stage against any of those arrested in connection with the murder. Jonathon Rees complained about his treatment by police, and this was investigated by another senior officer. After the initial murder inquiry and the inquest, this amounted to the third major examination of the crime. The complaint was held to be unsubstantiated. Two of the three police officers who had been arrested then sued the Met for 'false imprisonment'. They were later to receive substantial damages in an out-of-court settlement. But there was no official complaint from the third officer, Sid Fillery. He left the police, stepping defiantly into the murdered man's shoes. He joined Southern Investigations, working alongside Jonathon Rees.

Desperately unhappy with the turn of the events, Morgan's brother Alistair and his mother, Mrs Isobel Hulsman, also complained about the police handling of the investigation, claiming that Danny could have been murdered because he was about to expose police corruption. It appeared that he had spoken vaguely about going to newspapers to tell what he knew of police wrong-doing. If true, this could have been in connection with police officers moonlighting, accessing the PNC or doing other favours for the agency. It had also emerged that Morgan had known a detective who had been found shot dead, with a shotgun by his side. The verdict on DC Alan 'Taffy' Holmes, like Morgan a keen follower of Welsh rugby, was suicide. It appeared that he had been approached by anti-corruption investigators because of his links with very senior suspect detectives, but rather than disclose or give evidence against anyone, he had killed himself.

The Morgan family's concerns were referred to the Police Complaints Authority. In July 1988, it announced that there was to be a fresh investigation into the murder and police conduct during the first inquiry. Hampshire Police were in charge of this fourth investigation, which cost more than £1 million. Its terms of reference were to investigate allegations that police were involved in events surrounding the brutal murder of Daniel Morgan. After taking 1,600 statements, the Hampshire review concluded that there was no evidence to suggest police involvement, and no evidence that anyone on the Met's murder team had deliberately tried to hamper the original investigation. However, in February 1989 Hampshire arrested and charged two people with the murder. They were Rees and a bodyguard called Paul Goodridge. But their prosecution was halted a few weeks later when the Director of Public Prosecutions stepped in to 'discontinue' proceedings. Rees and Goodridge then sued Hampshire and the Met, alleging malicious prosecution. Goodridge claimed he had only been charged to scare him into divulging information about Rees's involvement. Years later, in a brief court hearing, Hampshire accepted that there had been no basis for believing that Goodridge was involved. The bodyguard, in turn, accepted that Hampshire had not been motivated by malice.

Meanwhile, Southern Investigations continued its enquiry work, with Sid Fillery working in the murdered man's place. The detective agency did not shut up shop immediately after the murder, and Rees, although a suspect and under surveillance, continued to be seen meeting with police officers. Among them was the corrupt DC Duncan Hanrahan and also DS Alec Leighton, who had told murder investigation officers in a statement that he had been friendly with Rees and through him had met Morgan on several occasions. That statement was made seven days after the murder, and two days later Leighton was seen by other investigators chatting to Rees in a pub. In another statement, Leighton admitted discussing the murder with him and telling him about his earlier interview, but maintained that there had been nothing sinister in this. Told by officers that he had caused embarrassment to the inquiry, he agreed to try to avoid Rees in the future. However, the contacts did not stop, and during the Hampshire inquiry into the murder Leighton was required to make yet another statement. In this, the detective sergeant disclosed that he had seen Rees about eight times since the murder. The meetings had continued even though Leighton had been transferred to the Serious Crimes Branch at Scotland Yard. He told Hampshire police that, during the meetings, Rees gave him information about drugs and a murder.

Although Leighton was suspended in 1993, suspected of corruption after *Panorama*'s exposure of DC John Donald, his contacts with Rees and Southern Investigations continued. A keen freemason, he was seen with Rees, Sid Fillery and Duncan Hanrahan in a Croydon masonic hall at a 'Brothers in Law' luncheon club. Leighton's car, a Ford Cortina fitted with police radios, was also used by one of the agency's security guards. A patrolling policeman had seen the guard sitting in the car outside a building site in the middle of the night. Thinking it looked suspicious, he had asked who owned the car and was told it was Southern Investigations. Checking on the registration, the policeman found it belonged to a detective. Its use for private work breached police rules. The driver was arrested, handcuffed and taken to a police station, suspected of having stolen the vehicle. After various officers were contacted, the story that emerged was that Leighton, too drunk to drive, had given the keys to Hanrahan, who had by then left the police and was working with Sid Fillery. The car had then been used that night by the agency's security guard.

Later, while suspended and receiving full police pay, Leighton started working for Hanrahan, joining his company Hanrahan Associates. He then formed his own private investigation and security company, Mayfayre Associates. Working with him was another ex-detective who had been dismissed. Later, this former officer successfully appealed against his sacking and was reinstated, but after a day back at police work he went sick and was allowed to retire. Leighton also retired. His name was constantly mentioned during the trial of the corrupt DC John Donald and the criminal Kevin Cressey, who had paid £20,000 in bribes. Others in the SERCS team at Surbiton were said to be frightened of Leighton's power. He was described as the unit's 'real gov'nor'. It even emerged that one officer, DC Pat McCarthy, was so worried about important documents going missing from the office that he breached police regulations and took them home. He was given the nickname 'Paranoid Pat'.

The trial and sentencing of John Donald to twelve years' imprisonment in 1996 attracted considerable publicity, and provoked more interest in police corruption. The following year there were newspaper stories about Geoffrey Brennan and his dealings with allegedly corrupt officers in south London (see Chapter 3). Hanrahan was arrested in a sting operation (see Chapter 12) and named another former detective, Nigel Grayston, as corrupt. Grayston also did work for Southern Investigations and has always denied allegations that he was involved in any corrupt activities. Sid Fillery was at Hanrahan's first court appearance at Bow Street magistrates' court, offering to stand by him and give him a job if he received bail. He remained in custody. At the end of 1997, Sir Paul Condon had spelled out the severity of the corruption problem facing the Met, and subsequently there had been the successful sting operation against former members of the Flying Squad.

It was in this heightened atmosphere that Morgan's brother Alistair and his mother again started to press for a fresh investigation into the murder. It coincided with increased concern about Southern Investigations' activities, with the Met suspecting that serving and former officers were leaking information about police operations to the agency, which was then selling it on to newspapers. It was believed that Southern had played a part in setting up newspaper stings. It not only hired out expensive electronic listening devices to the media, but also delivered sting 'packages'. These kept everyone happy, apart from the victims, but who cared about them? Such a sting could take place, for example, if the agency received information from one of its police contacts that someone was dealing in drugs. Southern would then mount its own sting, planting drugs on the man or arranging for someone to pretend to want to buy drugs. A newspaper would be tipped off to be at the sting to obtain evidence. On the eve of publication of the story, the newspaper would hand its evidence over to the police, who would then move in and arrest the criminal. The newspaper got its exclusive. The police were happy because they were seen to be catching criminals. Southern was paid for its help, and the agency passed on some of the money to the officer who had supplied the original information. This kind of scam worked for a while, and no one seemed too concerned. But that view was to change.

First, some of the cases fell apart on reaching the courts. The victims set out how they had been fitted up, and the authorities criticised police and newspapers for their tactics. But more importantly, Southern also started to become involved in gathering scandalous information about personalities and establishment figures, including politicians and members of the Royal Family. They sold the stories to the highest bidder, and it proved to be profitable work. Perhaps fearing for the future, Southern was also starting to try to undermine the Yard's crackdown on corruption by spreading stories and rumours about some of those associated with it, blackening their names and questioning CIB tactics. By early 1998, Scotland Yard decided to act.

The Morgan family's fight to bring the murderers to justice was being helped by their respective MPs, the then Cabinet minister Chris Smith for Alistair Morgan, and Richard Livsey for his mother, Mrs Hulsman. There had been meetings in 1996 with various officers from the Met and Hampshire. These culminated in early November 1997 at a Scotland Yard meeting between the Morgan family, their MPs and the Commissioner, Sir Paul Condon, who was with Roy Clark, the Deputy Assistant Commissioner overseeing the anti-corruption drive. Condon promised that his officers would review the case. Alistair Morgan followed up the meeting with a series of phone calls to Roy Clark, pressing him for action. Morgan kept suggesting that the only way to get evidence was to plant a bug in the agency's offices. Clark kept responding: 'I hear what you say.' A bugging operation was under way by June 1998.

I have obtained a series of internal Metropolitan Police documents setting out the sequence of events leading up to the operation, with reports on its progress. Some are headed 'Secret' and others are simply 'Restricted'. Many of them have been redacted, that is to say, they have large chunks and even whole pages scored through with a thick black felt-tip pen. Some even have dates removed, including what appears to be the first document, addressed to DAC Clark, and stamped 'Secret' in red ink at both the top and bottom of the page. The sender's name is also deleted, but it is probably from someone on the ghost squad. It says: 'For a considerable period of time, there has been much spoken about DS Sid Fillery and his business partner John Rees being involved in corrupt activities involving serving police officers.' The document went on to say that rumours were continuing to circulate about events leading up to and surrounding the Morgan murder. 'A recent operation has produced a surfeit of intelligence that indicates Rees is liaising with ex-DS Alec Leighton and [name deleted]. He uses the latter as conduit for PNC checks and police intelligence trawls. This relationship certainly provokes current police corruption.' Following receipt of the secret document, Clark sent a memo to Detective Superintendent Chris Jarratt, the head of CIBIC: '. . . the intelligence indicates that Fillery and Rees are co rrupters of police officers and participants in organised crime.'

It was in June 1998 that the head of the Metropolitan Police's Specialist Operations, Assistant Commissioner David Veness, gave permission for anti-corruption officers to secretly enter the Southern Investigation offices at 2 Grange Road, Thornton Heath. His authority specified that if practicable a bug should be planted there and then, but if necessary a second visit could be made at a later date. The CIB technical officers who were to break into the offices at the rear of the building, above a garden, faced three main problems. First, they did not know the layout of the premises. Second, finding a suitable place to deploy a listening device often proved difficult. Third, the principal occupants, Rees and Fillery and some of their associates were aware of the CIB interest, and they were also security conscious. CIB had to be very careful not to leave the slightest indication that anyone had been inside the offices, let alone planted a bug. 'They are alert, cunning and devious individuals who have current knowledge of investigative methods and techniques which may be used against them,' said a report. 'They use some of the techniques in their own daily activities. Such is their level of access to individuals within the police, through professional and social contacts, that the threat of compromise to any conventional investigation against them is constant and very real.'

A heavily redacted report dated July 1998 said that CIB entry and deployment at the office had been 'thwarted'. Further permission was sought and obtained, but there were still difficulties the following month when the Deputy Commissioner, Sir John Stevens, became the authorising officer. By October these difficulties were overcome and a bug was in place. 'On this occasion,' said a report, 'the deployment went well and without compromise. The equipment put into place is performing effectively.' However, although the bug was working well, the conversations it was picking up were muffled by background noise. Another entry was made and a probe listening device installed by drilling a hole from outside. Separately, a video camera was installed and a 'hide' constructed for the necessary receiving and recording equipment. In addition to the recording equipment inside the premises, permission was sought and given to tap telephones there.

By February 1999, the various devices were clearly working well. A report said that Rees had been heard discussing CIB activities, particularly those of Detective Superintendent Jarratt, who was heading the operation against the company. In fact, that report was prepared by Jarratt, who wrote about himself in the third person. He stated that Rees, Fillery and their associates were believed to be sabotaging police investigations and prosecutions on behalf of clients.

> Product already obtained confirms that Rees harbours ill-will against CIB3 personnel. In scanning intelligence around police corruption in London, it can be stated that Rees and Fillery are a crucial link between the criminal fraternity and serving police officers. There is nothing that they do that in any way benefits the criminal justice system ... I see the ongoing intrusion as crucial to our efforts to control corruption within the Met. Should we be able to successfully arrest and prosecute Rees and Fillery for corruption matters, it will be seen within police circles as 'untouchables' having been touched, and will put off many who are currently engaged in malpractice, and, indeed, those officers who may be contemplating committing crime.

The report also said that limited monitoring had already shown that visitors to the premises had asked Rees to obtain blank police charge sheets for a scam; that he had agreed to pervert the course of justice over a theft and was waiting for police to give him information about the desecration of the street memorial to the murdered black teenager, Stephen Lawrence.

In April 1999 there was at last a conversation inside the office about the Danny Morgan murder. According to a monitoring report, Duncan Hanrahan's imprisonment had sparked off a discussion: 'Fillery is particularly concerned at what Hanrahan might have told police about the association between them, and whether Hanrahan has given information about the murder of Daniel Morgan ... Clearly Fillery is concerned and feels more vulnerable around this issue than many others discussed.'

Transcripts of some of the tape recordings made by CIB3 during the next few months are revealing over what is discussed in the Southern Investigations office about the anti-corruption inquiry. In one whispered telephone conversation, Rees appears to be explaining that Hanrahan has passed information to them about CIB3's questioning, and who they are interested in. Rees says CIB3's targets are 'Fillery, number one, me number two and you number four'. Rees went on: 'Hanrahan said what they [CIB] want to do is fuck us all. He said they keep talking about the fucking Morgan murder every time they see me.'

A report in May said a serving police officer was passing information to Rees about the Yorkshire Ripper, Peter Sutcliffe. Information was also coming in about two high-profile prisoners being held in Belmarsh top-security prison – Kenny Noye, awaiting trial for a road-rage murder, and David Copeland, the London neo-Nazi nail bomber. Information from police working on the inquiry into the murder of the TV presenter Jill Dando was also being received and re-sold to the national media. There was discussion about someone inside Buckingham Palace giving information, including a tip that the marriage of two prominent members of the Royal Family was in trouble. Particularly worrying for the anti-corruption officers, the report also said that Rees and Fillery were 'currently working on a smear campaign to discredit senior police officers of CIB3'. The then new head of CIB3, Detective Superintendent Bob Quick, who had taken over from Dave Wood, noted that Rees and Fillery were 'extremely concerned' about the adverse publicity over the murder of Daniel Morgan. His report said the name Southern Investigations had been changed to Law and Commercial so that it would not be continuously linked to the murder investigation. (For the sake of consistency, this book will continue to refer to the agency by its original name.)

The June monitoring report said that two former officers, Alec Leighton and ex-DC Nigel Grayston, had arranged meetings with Rees and Fillery away from the office, so they could discuss business face to face. And into the frame came another police officer, DC Tom Kingston, who was at that stage suspended and charged with drugs trafficking, along with other officers named by Neil Putnam, as detailed in the previous chapter. The report alleged that enquiries with Barclays Bank had revealed that Rees and Kingston could have been involved in money laundering by placing £170,000 into a bank account, claiming the money had come from a client's overseas business account. In another transcript of a conversation, Rees tells someone over the phone that Kingston is in the office with him. Kingston then tells Rees to tell the person on the other end of the phone 'If he's got any scandal on Putnam . . . I wanna kill him.'

In another discussion, Kingston says that in addition to awaiting trial on drug charges he is also facing disciplinary charges for doing a PNC check. The call to PNC headquarters from his police station was tape-recorded and anti-corruption investigators, having identified him as the caller, asked him to provide voice samples. Kingston refused. He also says that he suspects his home telephone is tapped, but claims he is not too worried, as evidence obtained that way is not admissible in court. The pair then talk about how easy it would be with new computer equipment to reproduce a police warrant card. Kingston alleges that Nigel Grayston, after being forced out of the police in 1997, used to borrow Kingston's warrant card when he went out on private enquiry work. Just before leaving the office, Kingston says his contact with the Special Escort group is doing work for CIB, ferrying their supergrasses around the country, but he is not given the identities of those he is transporting. Rees asks Kingston to pass on a message to his contact: 'Tell him to keep his ears open, if he hears anything about the old Morgan murder.'

It took anti-corruption officers little effort to work out that Kingston's contact was one of his best friends, and that he was passing, through the suspended detective, sensitive information from a confidential police publication called the *Police Gazette*. Kingston was then selling it to a reporter with a Sunday tabloid newspaper, a regular visitor to Southern Investigations. 'It is likely that journalists and private investigators who actively corrupt serving police officers would receive a long custodial sentence if convicted,' said a CIB report on the wider inquiry. 'There will be a high level of media interest in this particular investigation, especially when involving journalists. The Metropolitan Police will undoubtedly benefit if a journalist is convicted of corrupting serving police officers. This will send a clear message to members of the media to consider their own ethical and illegal involvement with employees of the Met in the future.'

However, before that interesting issue of police-journalist relations could be pursued, another remarkable conversation in the agency's offices was picked up during the bugging operation. It led to another huge proactive investigation, ending at the Old Bailey in 2001 with heavy jail sentences for three people, one of them a serving detective.

The refocusing of CIB's efforts in respect of Rees and Fillery came after Simon James, the thirty-five-year-old son of a jeweller, walked into Southern Investigations and asked Rees for help. He explained that he was separated from his wife, Kim, a former page-three girl, who was now a fitness instructor and part-time model. The pair were in the middle of an acrimonious custody battle over their young son. James was only allowed to be with his boy at weekends, but he wanted full custody, especially because he was worried that the boy could come to some harm. Enlarging on his concerns, he told Rees that he suspected his wife was mixing with drug dealers and could be dealing drugs herself. James asked Rees to investigate his wife's lifestyle and gather evidence that would help discredit her, so he could gain custody of the boy. Rees was happy to oblige.

It was at their second meeting, in mid-May, that the pair started to hatch a conspiracy. Rees began the discussion with news of a preliminary investigation on Mrs James: 'One of our surveillance team is a police motorcyclist on the drugs squad, and he works for us on the side. It's a couple of years before he retires from the squad. He did a check on her, but there's nothing on the files. There are no reports about her. She doesn't come up associated with any drug dealers.' However, James was not reassured. Convinced that his wife was involved in drug distribution, he suggested that she may not have shown up in police records because she was fairly new to the game. Anxious not to lose someone who could be a lucrative customer, Rees makes another suggestion: 'There is another option available to you now, rather than just surveillance. Through our contacts, we have her turned over.' Realising what is being proposed by the private detective, James hesitates: 'I think the only way is to watch her for a while, to see what happens, rather than go steaming in, and finding there is nothing there. I don't want to jump the gun. To be honest with you, I don't want my little boy around this.'

'Well, that's right,' Rees responds. 'If they go in, if there is some gear in there, obviously it's going to be a small amount, so she will get her collar felt. It'll frighten the life out of her. If there is nothing in there, we can make it, we can frighten the life out of her anyway. If you want I can have her banged up for a weekend.'

James again expresses concern about his little boy, who is just fifteen months old. Working on his client's anxiety, Rees says: 'Sometimes there's danger from these low-life people. If she loses a bit of gear, and she might be carrying £50,000 worth, the villains say you owe us £50,000, and if you don't pay us, we will chop that child's legs off.'

Appalled that his son could be injured, James agrees to the private investigator's next suggestion. Having asked how secure Kim's flat is, Rees then muses about what his police contacts could do: 'I just wondered ... We can do things.'

James: 'I'm not being funny. I'd rather you talk to me straight.'

Rees: 'One thing is that they can have a look. They lump it up. They are Old Bill, but they are burglar Old Bill – that's what they do. They go in a place, have a look around, plant bits of electronic ...'

James: 'Next Thursday, she is going to be away for the night.'

Rees: 'I just wonder if it might be worthwhile, going in and planting some gear. Now, having said that it's done, it's available, but it costs.'

James: 'I realise that, but to be honest with you, where my little boy is concerned, I don't give a fuck ... I mean, I'm not averse to doing anything.'

Rees: 'I mean, we put ourselves in this. What we are doing is fraught ... Me and you could end up doing porridge as well, if we get caught out.'

James: 'Yeah, I mean, you're professionals. That's why I have come here ...'

Rees: 'All right, I'll have a chat to our people today.'

The next day the pair again discussed planting drugs in the flat. On the tape transcript, Rees says that a Class A drug, such as cocaine, should be found, as that carries a bigger sentence for possession than cannabis. The drugs should be in a bag with Mrs James's fingerprints on the inside, which would show that she knew what was there. This can be achieved, explains Rees, by getting a plastic bag that she has handled, simply turning it inside out and putting the drugs inside. The private investigator again warns James that the operation will be costly as police will be involved. 'I'll warn you now that they will want a sizable drink, to make sure it's done properly, because you only get one stab at this, and it needs to be managed properly. The ultimate goal is that she [Kim] goes away [to prison] and stays away, and is never ever . . . or the only way she gets access to that child is supervised access for the rest of her life.'

After agreeing to the plan, Simon James leaves the office and Rees then has a discussion with the suspended DC Tom Kingston about someone who could mount a burglary. They talk about their mutual friend, the ex-DC Nigel Grayston, who they say is running around like a headless chicken. Later, Rees and Sid Fillery discuss involving Grayston, whom they refer to as 'Boysie'. After another two days, Simon James returns to the office and pays over £7,500 in cash, some of which is to be used to buy the necessary cocaine. However, there is a change of plan. Instead of putting the drugs in Kim's flat, they are to be planted in her car.

The conspiracy to fit up Kim James with drugs presented CIB with a dilemma. The second purpose of their covert surveillance at Southern Investigations was to gather evidence about the Danny Morgan murder. But little more had been discovered about it during the bugging operation. And now another serious crime was taking place. If police stepped in and arrested the various participants, the surveillance would have to be called off as, by law, the existence of the bugging equipment would have to be disclosed to those arrested. That would spell the end of the murder investigation. But there was also concern about making premature arrests before the drugs were planted, it being argued that such a course would probably result in the conspirators wriggling out of any prosecution. They were reckoned to be so clever that it was necessary to arrest them only after a lot of evidence had been accumulated, so that the risk of them escaping conviction was negligible. There was also another factor. The full extent of the conspiracy and exactly who was involved were still unknown. But delaying the arrests gave rise to another problem – what to do about the innocent victim, Kim James. Should she be told by CIB what was going on? The risk in so doing was twofold. First, she could refuse to participate and the operation would have to be called off. Second, even if she agreed to go along with the CIB team, under the strain of acting a difficult role she could inadvertently confide in someone and that could then lead to the conspirators discovering the CIB plan. But if the fit-up was allowed to go ahead and she was then arrested and charged with possessing cocaine, how would she react? The shock could have a very harmful effect on her. After weighing up all the different issues, CIB decided to let the drugs crime go ahead, without telling her.

From their continued monitoring of the detective agency's offices, anti-corruption officers learned that another suspect south London detective had joined the plot. DC Austin Warnes had been forced to leave SERCS earlier in the year under a cloud for dealing with a particular informant. Although already suspected of wrong-doing, Warnes, now with local police, agreed to feed information into the police intelligence system to the effect that Kim James was a drugs dealer, along with another woman. On 8 June, Warnes filed an intelligence report, what police call a Crimint, saying that the part-time model made regular runs in her car to deliver cocaine to West End nightclubs. He said the information came from one of his informants, who would provide updates on when the next drugs delivery run was due. Believing until then that the plotters were intending to plant cocaine in the flat, CIB had already installed a secret video camera in the entrance to Kim James's block of flats. After the change in the conspirators' plan, CIB approached people living in a flat opposite her block. They asked for permission to set up a police observation point so they could use another video camera capable of filming in the dark. The flat's occupants agreed, and from their new vantage point officers were able to observe and video movements around Kim's car, which was usually parked outside her block in the street. The watchers did not have to wait too long.

Under the cover of darkness, late on 12 June, a figure was seen approaching Kim James's car. After looking around to ensure that he was not being observed, he forced a door open. He then left the car only to return a few minutes later, apparently carrying something. After spending more time at the car, he then walked away. The CIB team then set in motion the next phase of their pre-planned operation. They searched the car, found some wraps of cocaine, and replaced them with a harmless white powder. On 15 June, the corrupt DC Warnes updated his earlier intelligence report. He told a detective sergeant in a conversation secretly tape-recorded by CIB that Kim James would be driving to the West End with thirty to forty wraps of cocaine that same evening. He suggested that her flat and her car should both be searched. The detective sergeant quickly passed on the information, and officers from a tactical support group raided the flat. None of them was aware of the CIB involvement. The anti-corruption team kept them in the dark, not knowing exactly how many police were working with Southern Investigations and not wanting anything of their secret operation to leak to any of them. Kim and her young son were in the flat when the police raided. As the officers made a thorough search for the drugs, Kim protested her innocence and, realising that her husband was in some way behind it, told the police: 'He's trying to take my child. I know he is.' Finding nothing in the flat, the officers then searched her car and found the drugs. Kim collapsed. After recovering, but still in a distraught state, weeping, she said that her husband had access to the car, and he must have planted the drugs inside. Instead of being held in custody, she was given bail.

The next day, totally unaware of the CIB operation, Kim telephoned her husband, accusing him of framing her. He denied it, but surprised that she was not in custody, and beginning to panic, he contacted Jonathon Rees at Southern Investigations to find out what had happened. After trying to calm him down, Rees was heard by CIB telling his partner, Sid Fillery, 'that fucking bitch is still running around with the kid'. Rees tried to contact former officer Nigel Grayston, apparently the conduit between the agency and Warnes. Rees wanted Grayston to sort the matter out, but he was away on holiday. Events then began to move fast, with mounting unpredictability and chaos. CIB was losing control of the situation.

Simon James had managed to get access to his boy for a few hours, but instead of returning him to Kim he took him to Wales, saying that his wife was unfit to be looking after him. Mrs James's lawyer immediately went to the High Court family division and explained that Simon James was suspected of being behind the drugs find, and that he had taken the boy. A judge issued an order for the boy's return and demanded a full inquiry into the police handling of the drugs affair. Scotland Yard was contacted and a detective inspector in charge of Warnes was instructed to find out more from the DC about the original information and about Simon James in particular, as it was being claimed that he had planted the drugs.

Meanwhile, over at Southern Investigations, Rees was telephoned by a very angry Grayston, who had returned from holiday and had heard that explanations were being demanded from DC Warnes. By that stage Simon James had returned the boy and had gone to see Rees, who told him what was happening as a result of his wife's complaint. 'She's screaming stitch-up,' Rees told James. 'She's screaming that you're the only person who had access to her car . . . She's lashing out in all fucking directions. Now what's happened is that my man [Warnes] has just been called into the office by his DI who says he wants to see all the informant's information. My friend's DI doesn't know what the fucking hell is going on and he's actually ranting and raving and saying what the fucking hell's happened here? He wants to see the informant.'

A little later, Rees related to Fillery what 'Boysie' had said on the telephone: 'Boysie said his man had just been called in by his DI who said they'd just had a fucking order from the fucking High Court. This fucking man had kidnapped the fucking kid and this woman's saying she was stitched up by her husband who planted the gear in her car. The DI's saying he wants to see the fucking informant and that he's got to go and see the judge . . . Boysie's panicking.'

'Well, you're not Boysie's informant,' observed Fillery.

'He's saying, "My man could lose his job,"' said Rees. '"My man could get fucking nicked." He's screaming down the phone. He's going, "Where's that cunt [Simon James]. I wanna know where he is. I'll fucking do him."'

Rees went on to explain to his partner that someone was ready to pose as the informant, in case the detective inspector continued to insist on knowing the source of the information about Kim James's drug dealing. In fact, the man eventually put forward as having provided the information was 'celebrity criminal' Dave Courtney, the original behind Vinnie Jones's character in the film *Lock, Stock and Two Smoking Barrels*. Courtney claims to have had a long corrupt relationship with DC Austin Warnes, who, he recalls, liked cocaine and had 'a weakness for the ladies'. He says that the detective regularly put up fake informants for rewards, obtained information from the Police National Computer and helped to sabotage prosecutions. On 25 June, Warnes phoned Courtney and outlined the problem. Courtney agreed to help, arranging to meet the officer later the same day at Plumstead Common. It was to be an extraordinary affair, involving layer upon layer of deceit. In the course of a few minutes, three separate recordings were made of what was happening.

Courtney rode his motorbike to the meeting, with his singer wife, Jennifer Pinto, riding pillion. But the cunning criminal had a surprise for the corrupt detective. Fearing that the exercise was going to end in trouble, and wanting insurance, Courtney insisted that he would only help to extricate the officer if Warnes would explain on tape that he was asking for a big favour from the criminal. He also had to agree to be photographed with him. The desperate officer agreed, and Courtney then produced a small cassette and recorded the following conversation:

Warnes: 'We're sitting on Plumstead Common with Dave Courtney and Jenny. I've asked them to get me out of a bit of bother. I've asked him to have a meeting with my boss telling him information passed about a Kim James is to get me out of a bit of bother.'

Courtney: 'I know nothing about it, though, do I?'

Warnes: 'Dave knows nothing about this, no.'

Courtney: 'What is the information you want me to say?'

Warnes: 'Kim James, who lives at **** in Mitcham, and her friend **** were dealing in cocaine and that the information was passed to me by you.'

Courtney: 'And when do you want me to say I done it?'

Warnes: 'A couple of weeks ago. You can't remember the date. That's it, really.'

Courtney, making sure there is no ambiguity: 'Just in case this tape ever comes to light, this is fuck all to do with me. This is to help my fucking pal. All right. Thank you very much.'

However, unknown to the corrupt officer and the criminal, a CIB surveillance team was secretly videoing their meeting from the other side of the common. The pair were sitting on a park bench with their backs to the camera, too far away for any of their conversation to be picked up. The fact that they were meeting so openly was itself surprising. But the surveillance team were amazed to see Jennifer Pinto taking photographs of the pair together (see the illustrated section). They could not work out what was happening. A little later more deception came into play, when Warnes introduced Courtney to his gov'nor, Detective Inspector Latham, who, unknown to them, had just been briefed on the CIB operation. He was co-operating with it by acting the part of someone very concerned at the prospect of being hauled up in front of a High Court judge. He was carrying a hidden tape recorder and is heard explaining the position to Courtney, a club-owner: 'The situation is, I may be called to court to stand in front of a judge and say that a person is helping us, that an informant has given us this information and it's kosher ... So, what you are saying basically, then, is the names of these girls have been told to you by who?'

Courtney responds by weaving a story to the effect that the girls were named to him as drugs suppliers by people he had caught selling 'gear' in the clubs. He adds that he wants to stop drug dealing in his clubs and passed on the information believing that, if he got rid of the suppliers, the dealers would disappear. Satisfied with the story, Latham then left Courtney and Warnes on the park bench.

Armed with the tape recording, and with further evidence of the conspiracy, the CIB operation continued. Detective Superintendent Quick said in a progress report to the then Deputy Commissioner, Sir John Stevens, that the conspirators had planted drugs on an innocent victim: 'The arrest of the victim was orchestrated by a serving detective and this branch was able to put a number of interventions in place to minimise the risk and distress caused to the victim. However, it is necessary to allow this conspiracy to run for the time being in order to secure evidence against all of the conspirators identified to date. Further maintenance of this facility [the bugs at Southern Investigations] is necessary to monitor the threat level against the victim, and to take any action necessary to prevent her from coming to future harm.' Shortly after the report was sent, Kim James was seen by CIB. They told her that they knew she was not guilty, and gave her details of some aspects of their operation. She received the news with mixed feelings. 'I was very relieved,' she said later. 'But I was angry because I had been left to suffer for weeks, having to look after my child with all that hanging over my head. The police explained why it had been necessary and I was content with the explanation.'

With the arrests of the conspirators pending, and the disclosure of the bugging operation inevitable, CIB tried to get more information about the Danny Morgan axe murder, the case originally used to justify all the surveillance. Although by that stage DC Warnes had found a CIB tracking device attached to his car, and his friend, the suspended DC Tom Kingston, believed that his home telephone was bugged, those at Southern Investigations appeared to be unaware that their conversations were being listened to. It was business as usual, with Rees and Fillery continuing to discuss obtaining confidential police information and selling it on to newspapers. But they had said almost nothing about the Morgan murder. To remedy that, CIB decided to give a newspaper a story about a new lead in the murder investigation, which, it was hoped, would spark a fresh conversation about the killing. The *Daily Telegraph* duly carried a small story about the driver of the Morgan murder 'getaway vehicle' having been identified by police. The CIB plan was only partially successful. The article was indeed discussed, but Rees and Fillery were unimpressed. Fillery took the view that it was 'good news' because no one had ever alleged that Rees was driving the getaway vehicle, and if the driver had been identified, why had he not been charged or interviewed?

On 24 September 1999, CIB moved in on Southern Investigations and those associated with it. Twelve suspects were arrested and twenty-three premises raided. Six people were charged, including the detective constables Austin Warnes and Tom Kingston, and several computers and a mass of sensitive police documents were seized. Early the next month police asked for the necessary authority for the bugging operation to be cancelled. Although no one had been arrested for the Danny Morgan murder, police had largely cleared out a nest of corruption and disrupted the activities of others.

The following year, five people stood trial at the Old Bailey for conspiracy to pervert the course of justice. Warnes pleaded guilty. It had been expected that he would get a sentence of at least six years, but to CIB and Crown Prosecution Service surprise, he received only four years. Jonathon Rees and Simon James were both found guilty, and both were sentenced to six years' imprisonment. Dave Courtney and another defendant were cleared. Kingston did not stand trial with them. He had been found guilty of stealing drugs in another trial, detailed in the previous chapter, and was already serving a three-and-a-half-year sentence. Sid Fillery was never charged over the drugs planting and has always denied any knowledge of that crime or involvement in any other. He is angry with CIB, believing that he was unjustly targetted.

The Crown took the unusual step of appealing for Warnes' sentence to be increased. In early 2002, the Appeal Court decided to add another year, increasing the sentence to five years. At the same hearing, Rees and James lost their appeal against their convictions and sentences, and the court increased their terms of imprisonment from six to seven years.

fifteen

LOOSE ENDS

*He amazed the officers who questioned him by alleging that
he had paid a detective constable at least £200,000 for
favours and information, and he produced detailed account
books to back up his claims . . . 'I made regular cash payments
for advice on how to import drugs and launder money . . . At
the time of my arrest, these payments had reached the level of
£10,000 a week.'*

It was not until 2002 that resolution of two investigations mounted years
before seemed likely. The first had been started by Detective Chief
Superintendent Roger Gaspar and his ghost squad way back in 1994.
This inquiry exemplified a seesaw quality, with evidential swings and
switches, making it frustrating for anti-corruption officers. But
persistence was the one quality consistently displayed by CIB detectives.
They persevered despite setbacks, convinced that they were on the right
track. If one line of investigation ran into difficulties, another would be
pursued. However, this way of operating led to complaints that they were
unfairly harassing or persecuting some of their suspects. This particular
inquiry had caused problems from the outset, and these were to continue
for no fewer than eight years, with questions about it even being asked in
Parliament.

It was in 1994 that criminal businessman Geoffrey Brennan made
two dramatic confessions to the ghost squad's head, Roger Gaspar. He
admitted stealing £400,000 from a Chinese-American and to paying
£50,000 to two officers, DI John Redgrave and DC Michael Charman,
to cover up the theft. But after being charged, he effected a turnabout
and withdrew his allegations. CIB then mounted a separate sting operation against the two officers and their friend, Debbie Cahill, a caseworker
with the Crown Prosecution Service. However, charges of conspiracy to
pervert the course of justice and of breaches of the Official Secrets Act
against them were thrown out by a magistrate, and then by a judge.

Deeply aggrieved at what had happened to them, the three then counter-attacked, making official complaints against CIB officers. Redgrave's MP, Andrew McKinlay, raised the case in a fifteen-minute speech in the House of Commons.

Cahill's complaint was initially made to Essex Police, as it had been that force which had authorised CIB's use of a bug at her home in South Benfleet, where she had been arrested handling confidential CPS documents with Charman and Redgrave. Later, she complained to the Met. She claimed that the smashing open of her front door while they were eating dinner caused her 'extreme shock, terror and distress' from which she was still suffering a year later. She was on medication, and had been unable to use the dining room since the raid because it was too upsetting for her to be in there. Cahill further claimed that the use of the bug had been unlawful, that she had been wrongfully arrested and detained, and that police had leaked information about her to reporters. She made the complaint after a magistrate had decided there was insufficient evidence to continue the criminal case against her. At the time, she was still suspended from her CPS job. She was later dismissed.

Charman and Redgrave's complaints were similar. Charman claimed that his arrest, detention and prosecution were unlawful, malicious, unwarranted and amounted to a conspiracy to pervert the course of justice. He added that the arresting officer, Detective Superintendent John Coles, had known that he was receiving counselling and medication for post-traumatic stress after an accidental police shooting incident, but the CIB officer had still adopted unwarranted and unnecessary tactics, causing him humiliation and distress. DI John Redgrave claimed that the arresting officers had breached various police codes of practice and should face criminal or disciplinary proceedings. He said he had been subjected to vindictive persecution which had left his personal and professional life in ruins. Later, it emerged that two weeks before his arrest he had been rushed by ambulance to hospital, having taken an overdose of about forty antidepressant and sleeping tablets. It happened the day after he had signed over house ownership documents to his wife as part of divorce proceedings.

He told the Police Complaints Authority of the trauma CIB had put him through: 'This had caused the complete destruction of every aspect of my personal and professional life, friends, financial security, family, marriage, career, reputation. The building blocks of life have all gone, with no hope of recovery. The safeguards built into the judicial process to protect all members of our society have been disregarded for reasons of self-interest and political expediency.'

His complaint added a new dimension to the case, suggesting that CIB officers were part of a wider conspiracy or cover-up. Redgrave said that when anti-corruption officers burst into the house he, Charman and Cahill had been discussing alleged corruption by some of the officers who had given evidence to the inquiry into the murder of Stephen Lawrence. He had declared during the dinner party that he was going to tell what he knew to the Lawrence family's lawyers. He also said in his complaint that just before his original suspension he had reported corrupt behaviour on the part of a senior CIB officer, who was then allowed to retire immediately. He said: 'Every time I have tried to bring to the attention of my senior officers malpractice within the police service, I have been subjected to some form of punitive action, whether it be suspension, arrest or charge.' In another letter to Scotland Yard, he complained of double standards: 'Whenever I gain support or am treated in a fair and equitable manner, I am the subject of an unfair and unreasonable reaction by the organisation … This reinforces my view that I will never be treated in a just manner, and that there seems to be a desire by certain members of the organisation to put me in a position where I will never recover.'

Links were drawn to other cases. Prior to being charged, Redgrave and Charman had said they were prepared to give evidence on behalf of a south London detective who was alleging a cover-up of a police shooting incident in January 1998. That detective was facing discipline, as was Charman, for meeting another Met detective who was awaiting trial for corruption. The detective was Sergeant John Bull, attached to the National Crime Squad, of which SERCS, the South East Regional Crime Squad, had become a part. Bull, his brother and others were charged with conspiracy to supply £12 million worth of cannabis. Their trial at Maidstone, Kent, never properly got off the ground, the judge stopping the proceedings at a pre-trial hearing, declaring that there had been wholesale breaches of the law during the police investigation which involved Kent Police, the National Crime Squad and CIB. The breaches included the non-disclosure of significant documents to the defence team and 'pressure' on a key prosecution witness to implicate Bull, with suggestions of a financial inducement.

Other complaints made against the anti-corruption investigators ranged from impropriety with women officers to accusations that they themselves had bent the rules and regulations. CIB officers were among several Met officers named in a complaint by Keith Pedder, a former detective inspector. Pedder had been charged with conspiracy to corrupt a police officer, the evidence against him coming from a sting operation. This was launched after the officer alleged to CIB that Pedder was asking him for information from the PNC, the Police National Computer. Pedder, like Bull, was cleared by a judge at a pre-trial hearing for lack of evidence. The former DI claimed that he was the victim of a hidden agenda, possibly aimed at stopping publication of a book he had written about the Rachel Nickell murder investigation. His complaint was still being investigated in 2003.

Redgrave and Charman and the other complainants wanted what they called a full, independent investigation into their allegations, conducted by a senior officer from an outside force. Frustrated with the Met's refusal to call in another force and its insistence on carrying out its own investigation, they sought help from MPs, among them Andrew McKinlay, Redgrave's own MP. In the early part of 2000, he tabled a series of parliamentary questions about the cases and the cost of CIB investigations. In July he and other MPs who had expressed interest in anti-corruption work received letters from the Met Commissioner, Sir John Stevens, inviting them to intelligence briefings which would last about two hours and include question-and-answer sessions. McKinlay declined what he said was a wholly improper offer, one which, if he had taken it up, he believed would have precluded him from pursuing his constituent's case.

Certainly, in his account of the affair to Parliament in October 2000, McKinlay spent the fifteen minutes allowed him under the adjournment debate slot to attack the Met and, in particular, CIB. Using parliamentary privilege, which meant he could not be sued for defamation, McKinlay said he wanted the debate because he was seeking 'an end to the agony and unfairness of the inordinate suspension of my constituent'.

He continued: 'There has been widespread misfeasance at the highest level in the Metropolitan Police. I again demand a full judicial inquiry into Operation Nightshade [the gunrunning and money-laundering investigation mounted by Redgrave and Charman] and the consequent

231

malevolence and corrupt practice of those who served, and serve, in the CIB against my constituent and other officers.' Referring to Redgrave's claim that CIB were not interested in following up his allegations of a police cover-up over the Stephen Lawrence murder investigation, McKinlay said: 'The CIB is riddled with people who want to stop further light being shed on those relationships.' He described the disciplinary charges against Redgrave as 'a nonsense' and claimed that the CIB commander, Andy Hayman, was 'refusing to take the counter-complaint seriously'.

Replying to the onslaught, the Home Office minister, Charles Clarke, declared he supported the way the Met was dealing with corrupt officers. He said he was unable to comment on Redgrave and Charman's particular case, but on the question of delays in the disciplinary procedures he pointed out that when the pair were suspended they immediately reported sick. A disciplinary board had been arranged for early 2001, but because their lawyers were not available then, the hearing had to be put back to 2002.

The Metropolitan Police always had robust answers to the criticism, but had difficulty responding publicly because of possible prejudice to forthcoming trials or disciplinary hearings. Anxious to win what appeared to be an increasing propaganda war, behind the scenes the Met continued to arranage briefings for, amongst others, politicians and media editors. At these the magnitude of the problems corruption caused were outlined, it being stressed that corrupt officers were cunning, resourceful and so well trained that they could cover their tracks. And if they were ever caught, they knew how far they could go in frustrating or obstructing prosecutions and disciplinary hearings.

CIB officers hoped that Redgrave and Charman would give evidence for Geoffrey Brennan at his trial in 2001. The pair could have used the proceedings as an opportunity to set the record straight, to deny Brennan's original allegations that he had bunged them £50,000 to cover up his theft of the £400,000 from the Chinese-American businessman, Sam Wang. They could also have backed Brennan's later claims that the police operation mounted by the pair into gunrunning and money laundering had been entirely legitimate, and not a smokescreen, as was being suggested by CIB. If the pair had appeared in the witness box, they would have been open to cross-examination by the CIB prosecution team, determined to get at the truth of Brennan's allegations. But it was not to be. Although Redgrave and Charman's names were continually mentioned throughout the trial, the two suspended officers did not appear at the Old Bailey.

However, information about their finances emerged at a pre-trial hearing. This was held because Brennan's lawyers wanted to have the case against him thrown out, and if that move failed, to have some of the evidence against him excluded at the full jury trial. A single judge heard the issues, with the main witness being Roger Gaspar, the ghost squad's original head. He went through all the meetings he had with Brennan. He started with the early ones in which the crooked businessman had described in great detail how he had paid £50,000 to Redgrave and Charman, allegations which he repeated at later meetings with Gaspar, but later withdrew. Even more than a year after their first meeting in June 1994, Gaspar was still sometimes providing expensive armed police protection to Brennan, believing that his life was in danger. One such occasion occurred when Brennan said he wanted to visit his father, who was in hospital after suffering a heart attack. Gaspar contacted the hospital and subsequently went there himself, making arrangements for Brennan to enter and leave by a side entrance. He was given armed protection on the journey to and from the hospital.

At the pre-trial hearing, Gaspar made two new important disclosures of evidence coming from his investigation. He said he had learned that the separate inquiry into Wang's allegations of theft had been taken over by SERCS, which was an unusual move as that élite group of detectives was not normally involved in such investigations. Gaspar also revealed the results of a secret investigation he had ordered into possible irregularities in the two officers' financial affairs. He said this showed that Redgrave had received unexplained income, over and above his Met police salary. In Charman's case, an unusual spending pattern had started in October 1993, coinciding with the time Brennan had claimed to have paid over the £50,000 bribe.

But Gaspar had to admit that he had not cautioned Brennan that any of his confessions could be used against him. That fact alone, according to the defendant's QC, Andrew Trollope, meant that the officer's notes and tape recordings of meetings should not be allowed as evidence at the main trial. But he advanced further arguments which he said made Brennan's accounts to Gaspar unreliable. He said that Brennan had approached the chief superintendent because he was in fear for his life, someone in the Met having leaked information about him to a violent robber. In order to get police protection, Brennan would have been strongly motivated to say anything. He thought it possible, said Trollope, that either Redgrave or Charman, or both of them, had placed him in danger, so he had a motive for implicating them and seeking protection from them. But while there was no hard evidence that they were corrupt, there was strong evidence that Brennan himself had been a participating informant at the time of the theft, and had been acting for the officers as they investigated drugs dealing, money laundering and gunrunning. The QC also argued that the trial should be abandoned because of the length of time since the original offence, and because of irregularities in the investigation.

For the prosecution, Richard Latham, QC, said that Gaspar had been presented with a unique situation when dealing with Brennan. The businessman had been compromised by the leak of documents that should have remained in police hands, and he was potentially a valuable informant on police corruption. On the other hand he was admitting to the Wang fraud. Gaspar had opposing duties. He was protecting a compromised informant involved with fraud, but he was also investigating corruption, trying to stamp it out.

The officer in overall charge of the ghost squad and CIB, Deputy Assistant Commissioner Roy Clark, amplified on the problems to the court. He said the anti-corruption detectives did not know whom they could trust, particularly in the early days. Excessive secrecy had also hindered their effectiveness.

Having heard both sides, the judge, Brian Barker, ruled that the trial should go ahead in front of a jury, but Gaspar's notes and recordings of Brennan's confessions to stealing the £400,000 should not be allowed in evidence.

The full trial opened with Latham outlining to the jury the prosecution case against Brennan. Studiously avoiding any mention of corruption or of the names Redgrave and Charman, he said that although it might appear complicated, the central issue was simple. The Chinese-American businessman, Sam Wang, had paid Brennan £400,000 for mobile phones that he had never received. Brennan had kept the money. Latham then described the dealings between the pair and Wang's increasing desperation as Brennan failed to deliver. While the duplicitous businessman made reassuring noises to Wang, he was also quitting his mobile-phone shop and taking a suitcase full of money to buy a new house, putting it in his son's name.

After waiting in Hong Kong for the phones to arrive, Wang came back to the UK, looking for Brennan without success. Eventually he went to the police, who mounted a fraud investigation. Brennan's vanishing act was repeated a year later when he learned investigators were closing in. His second disappearance, said Latham, was courtesy of Roger Gaspar of the Met, who believed his story that his life was in danger because someone had leaked to criminals that he was an informant. Gaspar provided him with a new identity and help to buy another house. It was not until two years later that he was arrested for the fraud. Choosing his words carefully, Latham explained that the delay in bringing the case to trial was because Brennan had made allegations against a number of police officers which had to be investigated. Whether that murky area was to be opened up during the trial, he said, was a matter for the defence.

Brennan took up the invitation to some extent when he went into the witness box, answering questions from his own QC, Andrew Trollope. He stuck to his story that he had been a police informant, giving information first to Charman on drugs dealing and then, as the police inquiry expanded, to Redgrave. He claimed that he believed all the money sent from the United States was part of a money-laundering and gunrunning operation being monitored by Scotland Yard, and that he had done nothing without the prior approval of the two detectives. Redgrave was running the operation. He agreed that later he had met Chief Superintendent Gaspar to obtain protection, but the jury heard no mention from him of his confessions to stealing Wang's money or of giving £50,000 to Redgrave and Charman (an allegation later withdrawn).

From the start of his cross-examination, Richard Latham tore into Brennan, exposing a series of lies on the part of the businessman, who counter-attacked, protesting that the prosecution was going down the same vindictive road as the police had done, having waged a vendetta against him for the previous seven years. Worked into a fury, Brennan asked for a break so he could calm down, but his request was refused. It was classic knockabout stuff, and Latham's chronological questioning had not even reached the mobile-phone deal. Brennan could take no more – at that stage, anyway. He said he was ill and the court was adjourned for a day. When it reconvened, Latham did not let up. He was on top of every aspect of the case, having been prosecuting counsel in the CIB sting operation that had netted Redgrave and Charman. He knew how far he could go legally over the two detectives, and he knew how far he could go in goading Brennan.

One exchange was particularly fascinating. It came after Brennan had described giving information to Charman.

'That officer was going to come into your pay?' asked Latham.

'No, he was not,' replied Brennan, who then admitted that he had met Charman and Redgrave at South Mimms, the service station where, unknown to the jury, he had originally claimed to have paid money to the two detectives.

'They wanted money,' said Latham, 'and you gave them money.'

Brennan denied the charge and threw the gauntlet back, demanding to know why the prosecution was not calling the pair to give evidence. In replying, Latham chose his words with care. They were damning:

'I am not going to bring in criminals to give evidence.'

Brennan retorted that they were honest officers who had been doing their job:

'Don't accuse people when they are not here to defend themselves. Why not charge them with corruption?'

'There are few people around when officers are involved in corruption,' replied Latham, going on to warn Brennan: 'Be very careful what you say about these two officers.'

In later exchanges, Latham described the two as 'dishonest' and 'corrupt', claiming they wanted £50,000 from Brennan out of the £400,000 and in exchange they would 'mind his back' with a cover story about money laundering and arms dealing. Brennan denied it, but his back was to the wall and he knew it. Under pressure, his facial twitch became more pronounced. At times he was twitching virtually non-stop. The cross-examination was relentless, until by the end Brennan was on the ropes, red faced and blustering. Some members of the jury were even laughing at a number of his responses.

Although Redgrave and Charman were not on trial, for much of the time it was as if they were in the dock with Brennan. In Latham's closing speech to the jury, much play was made of their alleged corruption. He repeated that the prosecution case was that a total of £50,000 had been paid to the two detectives to provide a smokescreen for the theft of Wang's money, and he attacked the defence team for not producing a single document to support their contention that the £400,000 had been handed back in an operation monitored by the police. If honest officers were mounting an official operation with Brennan playing an important part, he said, there should have been no difficulty in putting the record straight when the businessman was arrested. Instead, Brennan had refused to answer police questions. For the defence, Andrew Trollope said that although the prosecution was calling Redgrave and Charman criminals, there was no evidence that they were paid a penny piece or were party to any plan to steal the money.

The jury took only a few hours to reach their verdict. They were unanimous in finding Geoffrey Brennan guilty. It was then disclosed that he had a previous conviction for fraud. Six years before stealing Sam Wang's money, he had been given a three-month prison sentence, suspended for two years, for obtaining cash from American Express by making a false declaration. Speaking in mitigation for him, Trollope said that the defendant might not have been alone in carrying out the theft and the events that followed. Although the jury had rejected Brennan's defence, Trollope continued that it was unquestionably the case that Redgrave and Charman were in contact with him at the time of the offence and were aware of what was taking place. While acknowledging that they were not before the court, and that there was no evidence as to their role, he went on to make an apparent reference to the pre-trial hearing evidence that Brennan had originally alleged paying the pair £50,000. Cryptically, he said the judge knew 'what the prosecution is about'. If it was right that the officers were compliant in what took place, then they bore a heavy responsibility, particularly as Brennan was an informant passing on genuine information.

When passing sentence on what he called an audacious and opportunistic theft, the judge made no mention of the two detectives, who have both always denied corruption. Brennan was sent to prison for three and a half years. Months later, the CPS and police, using confiscation orders, were still trying to recoup the £400,000 Brennan had stolen. Police experts had traced the various property deals he had made using the money from Sam Wang, and were demanding more than £400,000 back, threatening extra time in prison if he did not pay up. Brennan made the task as difficult as possible with delaying tactics, perhaps hoping that he would be out of prison on parole before any confiscation order became legally enforceable. He switched his legal team, which meant that it was necessary for his new solicitor and barrister to read through all the documents again to make any kind of sense of what was a very complicated case. The matter was still unresolved in early 2002.

As for Redgrave and Charman, a Scotland Yard disciplinary hearing was due to proceed against them in December 2001, although not covering any matter involving Brennan. Instead, the proceedings were for alleged 'discreditable conduct' arising out of breaches of police rules. These involved the two officers' meeting with the CPS caseworker, Debbie Cahill, and the alleged proposal to destroy confidential documents, the offence with which they had been charged, which a magistrate and then a judge had thrown out of court. However, the disciplinary hearing was delayed while the two officers and their lawyers went to the High Court to argue that there should be no internal proceedings against them at all. Having lost the argument, they went to the Appeal court, and lost again. A date was finally fixed for February 2003 for what was expected to be a four week Met Police disciplinary hearing. However, on the first day, after procedural arguments from lawyers for the two men, the hearing was adjourned. Another one was arranged for later in the year. At the time of writing, Redgrave and Charman have been suspended for six years, on full pay the whole time.

Another long series of trials in which an officer was branded as corrupt ended late in 2001, with final internal Scotland Yard action occurring in 2002. These cases featured a big drug-dealing criminal turned supergrass called Michael Michael. He had been a police informant for years, and he accused his detective handler 'Larry Hart' (not his real name) of corruption when he was eventually arrested by Customs officers. He amazed the officers who questioned him by alleging that he had paid Hart, a detective constable, at least £200,000 for favours and information, and he produced detailed account books to back up his claims. Hart was accused of corruption by CIB. But later the charge was dropped. Customs then charged him with drugs dealing. Then they, too, dropped the charge.

Constantine Michael Michael, of Greek Cypriot origin, became a police informant in 1989. He was working as an accountant, helping to run a string of massage parlours with his common-law wife, Lynn. But he was 'turned' after being charged with a £3 million mortgage fraud. In exchange for a reduced eight-month prison sentence he became a registered informant, though he was to claim later that it was because he wanted police protection to keep the massage business running smoothly. The pseudonym he was given, Andrew Ridgeley, was linked to his own name. There was a real Andrew Ridgeley, the singing partner of George Michael in Wham!, who shared the informant's surname. Michael's first handler was DC Craig Allum, to whom he passed valuable information about various drugs dealers and criminals, including members of the Adams and Nash families. He also identified the killer of the great train robber Charlie Wilson. He even told Allum that he had been asked to act as middleman to nobble the jury in the case of the Guinness Four, then running at the Old Bailey. After a scare over the leaking of his registered informant's name, it was changed from Ridgley to Chris Stevens. Michael never made allegations of corruption against Allum. But his relationship with DC Larry Hart, who took over the job of handling him in 1992, was different.

I have obtained copies of all of Michael's 'contact sheets', the forms filled out by an informant's police handler. These are supposed to list each meeting or phone call in which information is passed and the action, if any, that the handler then takes. There are nearly five hundred contact sheets, and they make fascinating reading. Michael continued to supply his new handler with high-quality information. There was more on the Adams family, and other big-time criminals, among them Kenny Noye, the Brink's-Mat robbery suspect who killed a police surveillance officer and was later jailed for a road-rage murder. Michael said that Noye had arranged for two 20-ton loads of cannabis to be routed through Cyprus.

Much of the information passed to Hart concerned a robber turned drugs importer, Michael Green. He was nicknamed 'The Pimpernel' by virtue of the fact that he had managed to evade justice for years. Michael had been asked by police to try to get close to Green, and in June 1994 Hart reported his informant's success: 'The informant stated that he had been asked by Mickey Green to assist him further in the movement of his monies around the world. Green has taken the informant into his organisation in a senior role and will expect him to oversee major parts of his supply chain. He has asked him to be responsible for the payment to the people concerned with the transportation, as well as collecting money from the people who buy the drugs from Green.' Three days after that contact sheet report, an extraordinary meeting took place between Michael, Hart and his 'controller', Detective Chief Inspector Brian Moore, who became a key figure in CIB3 a few years later.

Michael brought £90,000 in cash to the meeting, and both Hart and Moore painstakingly counted it out. Michael had been given the money by one of Green's lieutenants, and it was to be used to help pay for a house with a swimming pool in Ireland which Green was buying. The police plan was to trace the money through the banking system and gain information on Green's money-laundering operations. Hart paid the money into a covert account with the National Westminster bank. But he also reported that Michael had expressed concern about a police undercover officer, apparently working with SERCS, the South East Regional Crime Squad. Whether the informant knew that he was really an undercover officer or simply believed him to be a criminal is unclear. It may also be that the undercover man, known as such to Hart, had no idea of Michael's true role as an informant. However, what is clear from Hart's report is that something had gone wrong with Michael's handling:

> The Undercover Officer had requested that the informant contact him directly if he had financial matters to discuss, even if it revolved around our principal target. The UC officer wished to have a meeting with the informant in the absence of myself and/or the controller [Moore]. The UC asked to be introduced directly to the people who were giving the money to the informant to be laundered. The UC asked for commission for this transaction and would contact the informant on the UC's return from leave. The UC explained that if the informant was getting, for example, 1% commission from the criminals, then he [the UC] would show only 0.5% officially, and they would divide the difference between them. I asked whether the informant could substantiate the allegations. He stated that he could not. I asked whether he would repeat the allegations to his controller, and he stated he would, if necessary.

According to Hart's report, Michael wanted firm guidelines on who he should contact if he was asked to launder money. He was told that it must always be his handler, Hart, who would then decide how to proceed after consultation with other officers. Hart said he also explained to Michael that this could entail further meetings or transactions with the undercover officer. Michael responded that he would prefer not to have any further dealings with the man, unless it was unavoidable, as he no longer had confidence in him.

Michael was becoming more deeply involved in Green's smuggling operations. He ended up supervising the UK distribution of massive amounts of cannabis and cocaine, smuggled into the country by a variety of means. Large quantities of cannabis resin were hidden in drums suspended inside liquid tanker vehicles. Cocaine came hidden in cars. Some of the drugs were hidden inside a secret compartment on a tourist coach, nicknamed the 'Fun Bus' or 'Magic Bus', after the song made famous by the Who. Michael was later to claim that during this time his relationship with his police handler became corrupt. He said he gave cash to Hart, sums of up to £10,000 a week. In return, the detective turned a blind eye to Michael's drugs dealing and, according to the informant, provided tip-offs on police and Customs investigations into Green.

But separately, Customs officers were on to the Michael operation. They had discovered his role while monitoring British drugs dealers in Spain. Early in 1998, a surveillance operation was mounted on the two properties with which he was connected. The first was an industrial unit just off the main road between St Albans and Hatfield, Hertfordshire, where drugs from the tanker lorries, tourist coach and cars were unloaded and stored for distribution. Michael's lavish home in nearby Radlett was also kept under observation and his phone calls were tapped. The identity of one of his contacts, Detective Constable Larry Hart, caused surprise to Customs investigators. Hart was then working with Scotland Yard's criminal intelligence unit, SO11, but Customs took the view that relations between him and Michael were too close for it to be a normal informant-handling operation. The Met was told of what had been discovered, and a joint Customs/CIB operation was then started. It culminated in late April with three raids, the first two carried out simultaneously.

Inside the industrial unit, Customs found 3 tons of cannabis resin worth more than £10 million at street prices, along with 13 kilos of cocaine, worth about £1,800,000. When Customs burst into Michael's home in exclusive Loom Place, Radlett, the drugs dealer thought they were rival criminals out to steal his money. He grabbed hold of a pistol to defend himself. But he threw it away after the raiders identified themselves as being from Customs. He and his wife were arrested. In the house was £800,000 in cash, and a money-counting machine. Hanging on the walls were paintings worth several hundred thousand pounds. Outside were three vehicles, a Range Rover, a Porsche 911 turbo and a Wrangler Jeep, all apparently used to transport drugs.

Next day, DC Larry Hart was arrested just before 6 am by CIB officers. He refused to answer questions at first. Michael Michael took the same attitude during initial questioning at Customs Investigations headquarters in Lower Thames Street, London. He responded 'no comment' to hundreds of questions. But he grew increasingly worried as the interview progressed, with Customs revealing the extent of the information and evidence they had against him. Early in the interrogation, they warned him about the gun, which had had its serial number professionally removed. His possession of the weapon was serious enough on its own, but the Customs officers told him that police could obtain the serial number forensically and he could be in very serious trouble if it had been used in any shooting. But that line was just the beginning of a Customs salvo, spread over several hours.

Officers disclosed that they had seen him meeting with known drugs dealers at various pubs in south-east England, and at expensive hotels in London's West End. They knew he laundered drugs money through an exchange bureau in west London, and they knew the identities of the women he used to carry large sums of cash abroad. The officers told him that these couriers, who included some of his relatives, had flown out of Heathrow on more than forty recent occasions with two-week return tickets. But instead of staying abroad for that time, they had returned the following day. When Michael still refused to comment, the Customs officers revealed that they had arrested three of the women couriers, finding two handguns on one of them. Michael was told that a hotel meeting he had attended with one of the women had been secretly tape recorded and he had been heard talking about 5 kilos of 'charlie' (cocaine) having gone missing. He was informed that his brother, Xanthos, had been arrested as he was about to go through the Channel Tunnel. In his car's spare tyre was about £200,000. Customs told Michael: 'You seem to have money coming out of your ears.' The drugs dealer responded with another 'no comment', and his Customs questioner observed: 'It's like confetti. You've got more money in your house than most people will ever see in their lifetime, and that's including Lottery winners.'

Michael also refused to discuss the vast amount of documentation found at his home, detailing various drugs deals and naming individuals, some of whom had been arrested as well. Customs kept their ace to the end. They had not disclosed that DC Larry Hart had been arrested early that morning. But after six hours of questioning they told Michael of the arrest and that they knew he was Hart's registered informant. They suggested that the detective's real role had been to protect him and his drugs organisation. Michael still failed to respond, but the interview then ended, with Michael being given time to think over all that had been said. Later, having pondered his position, he agreed to provide information. He was to become one of the country's biggest supergrasses.

Over the following months, Customs and CIB recorded hundreds of hours of interviews with him in which he named dozens of drugs dealers, going into great detail about his relationship with Hart. He claimed he had given the detective between £200,000 and £250,000, recording many of the payments in his accounting notebooks, found at his home. In them he had referred to Hart by various nicknames. Two of these related to pigs, the slang term for police. He called him 'Porky' and 'Babe', which came from a film of that name about a talking pig. He also referred to him as 'Pizzaman', a name thought up by his children, as Hart would often arrive on a motorbike, like a pizza delivery man.

In a statement, Michael said that the first payment had been made in 1993:

> Following this payment I regularly received information from Larry about investigations mounted by Customs and Police into my associates. In turn, I told Larry full details of the methods of importing drugs and laundering money I was using. Where information from Larry was specific to other people I would pay money on their behalf to Larry. I would either act as an intermediary for these parties and pass payment from them on to Larry, or make a payment direct to him from money I had under my control. I recorded these payments in my records as I later needed to account for the money paid to the third parties. In addition to these payments, I made regular cash payments to Larry for advice on how to import drugs and launder money. I didn't record these payments as they were out of my personal profit from

money laundering and drug smuggling. At the time of my arrest, these payments had reached the level of £10,000 a week.

To sustain a prosecution against Hart, anti-corruption officers needed firm evidence. What Michael had provided in the form of the notebooks was only supporting evidence, and much of that could be torn to bits in court or be strongly challenged. It was puzzling, for instance, why Michael had used several nicknames for the detective rather than just one. Could the payment amounts recorded against each of the nicknames have gone to different people? Michael had said he had shown the notebooks to his criminal associates to account for money he had been paid by them. Could the dealer have been ripping them off by pretending he was having to pay for the information, but then simply pocketing the money himself? Michael said that on one occasion Hart had given him a Customs report in writing. But he went on to say it had been retyped by Hart, and that he had not kept it. When CIB checked with Customs on what Michael had claimed were the report's contents and its supposed author, they drew a blank. This did not necessarily mean Michael had lied. It could have meant that Hart had drawn up a fictitious report to keep his informant happy, so that he would continue to supply information. But speculation of that sort was pointless. There are inevitably layers of deception in police-informant relations. What was needed was hard evidence. So as their questioning continued, CIB concentrated on what Michael could tell them about what had happened to the cash. First, he was asked whether he thought Hart needed the money.

Answer: 'He didn't strike me as being anyone who actually needed the money . . . It wasn't that kind of relationship where you would sit down and he'd say to me, "I'm in trouble, I need the money." It was never like that.'

Question: 'How was he when you paid him?'

A: 'It was embarrassing. It was like I'd pick up the money, put it on the table or on the bench in the kitchen, and say to him: "There it is, Larry, there's ten grand there." He would get up, put it in his pockets, and go "Thanks", and that was it. It was never spoken about.'

Q: 'The point I'm trying to make, so that we're totally clear, is that did you think that he needed the money to sort out a problem, or he wanted the money through greed?'

A: 'I'm not aware that he wanted the money for any problems. I don't know if he wanted the money for greed or not . . . It was like a taboo subject. We didn't really sit down and talk about it.'

Q: 'It was just like business, really?'

A: 'It weren't even that, really. In business you have a laugh and a joke and maybe have more of a celebration. But it was like pretty embarrassing, I think, for both sides.'

CIB then probed whether he knew what Hart was supposed to have done with the money. Michael agreed that the detective knew a lot about money laundering because he was a meticulous and methodical financial investigator. They had a conversation on one occasion in which Hart had talked about opening a safety-deposit box, and Michael said he advised him to do so in a department store such as Harrods or Selfridges, and to send his wife or a relative to open the account. Michael also recalled that Hart had said one of his in-laws worked for a Swiss bank, but he had no idea whether Hart had money invested through him in Switzerland. CIB pursued another tack:

Q: 'Once he started taking money, was there any way out for him?'

A: 'Taking money from me, you mean?'

Q: 'Yeah, once he'd been dirtied, taken his first payment of money, was there any way out for him?'

A: 'Yes, of course he could. He could have turned round and said "no more".'

Q: 'And the organisation would have allowed him to do that?'

A: 'I think the organisation would have been more worried about me than about Larry.'

Q: 'Why?'

A: 'Because I was the one who was the informant. No one knew who Larry was . . . If Larry had turned round at any one time and said to me, "I'm not telling you anything no more, you're going to stop what you're doing, and it all comes to a stop," I would have had to have done it.'

While what Michael was claiming about Hart was fascinating, it did not amount to really solid evidence. A team of up to twelve CIB officers under Detective Inspector Peter Ward trawled through Hart's financial affairs, but could find virtually nothing to suggest that the detective had received up to £250,000 from the drugs dealer. He appeared to be a hard-working detective with a profile that did not match that of a corrupt officer. After consultation with the Crown Prosecution Service, it was decided not to proceed with any corruption charges against him. But it was far from over for Hart. Shortly after the CIB/CPS decision, Customs charged him with conspiracy over various drugs offences. The intention was that he would be tried after all the drugs dealers named by Michael had been dealt with. This series of trials started in 1999, and over the next two years thirty-four men and women were convicted, receiving a total of 170 years' imprisonment. But in the summer of 2001 there were acquittals after Michael's credibility had been challenged. Worried, prosecution lawyers took another look at the strength of the evidence against Hart. They then decided, in the light of the not-guilty verdicts, to drop the drugs trafficking charges against the detective.

In December 2001, Michael Michael appeared for sentencing, having pleaded guilty to conspiracy to import cannabis and cocaine, conspiracy to launder money, and to possessing firearms. Prosecuting counsel Nicholas Loraine-Smith said that Michael had sold cannabis and cocaine worth at least £58 million. Of the Michael-Hart relationship, he said it remained the case that it was corrupt:

> Michael would provide Hart with information, some of which led to arrests. In turn, Hart would provide him with information which was of great use to the enterprise, and some of which was sold on to other criminals. According to Michael, one of those criminals, indeed the most important, was Michael Green, a man who had been involved in importing drugs for many years. In about 1993, Michael obtained from Hart information about Green, which he passed on to him. Hart was paid for the information and so began the corrupt relationship which was mutually to the benefit of each. Michael was provided with the information he needed to carry on and protect his drug smuggling enterprise. Hart was paid large sums of money, up to £10,000 per week, according to Michael, and was also provided with a wealth of information, only some of which he put into the police system.

Judge Michael Carroll said the amounts of money and drugs involved in the case 'beggared belief', adding there was no doubt that Michael had received assistance from a corrupt person to carry out his drugs importing business. The normal prison sentence would have been one of twenty-four years, but the judge said that because of Michael's co-operation he would sentence him to six years. This meant, because of the time he had already spent in custody, that he would be released. But it is recognised that he is now a marked man, with an underworld contract out on him, so he will remain in the protected witness scheme, receiving help to set up a new life, probably abroad.

Michael himself did not appear at a confiscation hearing against him early in 2003 at Woolwich Crown Court. Customs estimated his worth at more than £1 million when he was arrested and his affairs put under the control of receivers. But their costs as well as legal fees, and other costs, including VAT, ate into the amount. He was ordered to pay £69,844. Meanwhile his police handler, 'Hart', had been dealt with by the Metropolitan Police in August of the previous year. A discipline board recorded that he was guilty of breaching police regulations. He resigned.

sixteen

THE CONTINUING STRUGGLE

'I'm really worried that corruption is going to surface again as a major problem.'

Former CIB3 detective superintendent

Probably the best kept secret of the Met's whole anti-corruption campaign is that the ghost squad still exists and continues to operate under its original cover. That will not only surprise the vast majority of the Metropolitan Police force, but also many of those now working with CIB, who are unaware of its operational name, Athona. They, like others, assumed that the ghost squad and its intelligence gathering work ceased to exist separately in 1998 when CIB3 was formed and the CIB intelligence cell, CIBIC, was expanded. But the ghost squad never died. It still functions in exactly the same way as when it was set up in 1994. Its members still carry out surveillance and bugging operations, and run undercover officers, much as MI5 does. Intelligence packages are delivered up to CIBIC, which in effect launders them, handing them on to CIB detectives to develop into proactive operations. If a curious detective asks where the information came from, all he or she will be told is that it came from CIBIC, which operates out of CIB headquarters in Putney, south-west London. CIBIC, although run secretly itself, acts as the front office for the intelligence gatherers. Behind the scenes is the ghost squad. It still works out of the same secret office building, the location of which remains known to only a handful of very senior officers. Plans prepared years ago to move to new secret premises if the present offices were discovered have not been needed, so far. But a new location has been earmarked and is available. The boast is that a switch could be accomplished within 24 hours.

Those who have worked for the ghost squad keep the fact secret. If they accidentally meet a former squad colleague at a police function, they will usually not acknowledge one another, let alone chat about their previous work. The continued secrecy of the unit is recognised as all-important. One senior CIB officer who liaised with the ghost squad told me he took anti-surveillance measures every time he visited the secret location. 'It's not paranoia,' he said. 'The cops we are up against are very clever. They're experienced detectives and they know all the tricks. If they ever found out you worked for or with the ghost squad, they could target you and follow you around until you led them to the premises. They could also try and blackmail you into revealing the location, or, worse still, force you into revealing its secrets. Only some of the CIB superintendents know where the ghost squad is. The others don't need to know, as a lot of the intelligence reaches CIB electronically. I know where it is and how it operates, but I have no idea when it started and who worked for it before. I'm curious, naturally, but I don't ask about these things. It's not so much that suspicions would be raised. It's more the case that I accept that I simply don't need to know.'

While the ghost squad is still functioning and will continue to do so for many years, the Met's attitude to corruption has changed, as has CIB itself. When the ghost squad was set up to investigate the extent of corruption, no one was quite sure what dirt would be uncovered. By 1998, after the creation of CIB3 following the cannabis sting and the first police officers to turn supergrass, the Met realised that it faced whole networks of corrupt detectives and former officers. Although the problem was not as serious as in Sir Robert Mark's time in the 1970s, it had to be tackled, and while being stamped out, or at least severely diminished, a strategy had to be found to stop corruption catching hold again. To achieve that goal required some understanding of what makes an officer become dishonest. But in 1998 there was virtually no valid, up-to-date research to draw on. Much of what there was on the causes of corruption was based on US studies which were not necessarily relevant to the UK. In this country, the theories put forward were anecdotal, or generalisations over particular cases. While these were not necessarily wrong, the Met decided to do its own research based on the cases it was investigating.

Until the police supergrasses told all, the most common theory on why good detectives turned bad involved 'the slippery slope'. This argument held that officers started their journey to taking bribes or stealing money by first of all bending the rules, so-called 'noble cause' corruption. Frustrated at seeing criminals who were 'well at it' walking free from court, officers would fit them up to gain convictions. After that, so the thinking went, it was easy to take the next step, into thieving or accepting bungs. But the important regional crime squad supergrass Neil Putnam never testified to this kind of activity. Of the two Flying Squad supergrasses, Kevin Garner denied fitting up anyone, and while Terry McGuinness admitted 'gilding the lily', the example he gave of his own gun having been planted on someone proved to be incorrect. This does not mean that corrupt officers did not indulge in noble cause corruption. That is far from the case. Fit-ups did, and do, occur. But the evidence coming from the specialist squads was that such wrong-doing did not inevitably lead to cash corruption.

The first conclusion reached by analysis of the cases was the obvious one that corruption stems very largely from simple greed, a desire for more money. This could arise from an officer's sudden change of circumstances such as a clamp-down on the amount of overtime worked. It could arise from marriage breakdown. Many marriages of male detectives in specialist squads end in divorce, with the officer struggling to make ends meet, having to support a former wife, as happened in the cases of Garner and John Donald. McGuinness had a girlfriend. Putnam's marriage was in trouble, and for a time he lived with another woman, but his problems and those of many others like him who moved into debt, stemmed from the detective life-style with its heavy drinking, late nights and unpredictable hours. Police magazines carry adverts for easy loans with every issue. Given debts, or other personal problems, temptations abound, whether it is selling confidential information or stealing money or drugs.

Such opportunistic corruption is rarely carried out by an individual on his own. It needs other detectives to participate, to share in the spoils, to turn a blind eye to what is going on, or even be so trusting that corruption is simply not noticed. One detective who had served at Stoke Newington in the early 1990s told me that he was ashamed at not having recognised corruption. 'I used to sit opposite Lewandowski' (convicted later of stealing money) 'and he used to produce great wads of money and count it in front of me. It just never crossed my mind that he was corrupt. I respected him as a good detective. Either he'd said, or someone else had told me, that his wife was in business and that the money came from that. I just accepted it as fact.'

CIB found that the pockets of corruption they encountered in some of the specialist squads had often started with a single officer turning corrupt, drawing others in to illegal activity – the rotten apple infecting the rest of the barrel. These detectives usually had twin attributes. They were respected as hard-working detectives who got results. They were good thief-takers. But they also had strong or aggressive personalities and were able to impose their will on others in the group. They would break the rules to achieve results and if other officers were complicit, that could be used later to suck them into full corruption. Officers diligently sticking to rules and regulations would be ridiculed, as happened to the SERCS officer branded 'Paranoid Pat' because he kept his documents locked away.

Putnam and Garner were both 'tested'. As soon as they had accepted small amounts of money they were in the loop, becoming part of an inner circle of bent cops. Once in, Putnam remarked, 'there was no way out'. One senior CIB officer recalled how he had been tested when he was a sergeant in charge of a detective constable, later to stand trial for corruption at the Old Bailey. 'We were out together on a drugs job. We had caught a villain with 25 kilos of cannabis and were taking him to his home to search it. On the way there, he said that he had nine grand hidden somewhere and it would be good for bail. When we got there, the DC found the money and I said we'll count it now and count it again when we get back to the nick. The DC then remarked that it couldn't be for bail. The villain said "well, it was worth a try". All the conversation was ambiguous, but the three of us knew what was going on. The villain was offering the money as a bribe and the DC wanted to take it, but it wasn't on, as I was having none of it. I never reported it. Even if the whole thing had been taped, you couldn't prove anything.'

At the heart of the vast majority of corruption over the years, from long before Sir Robert Mark's time, is abuse of the informant system. Detective work depends on informants but it is generally acknowledged throughout the police service that grasses are the most dangerous of people. Clever, and only able to survive in the underworld because they are good actors with the ability to hide their treachery, they are also highly manipulative, often turning the relationship with their police handlers to their own benefit, whether it is being given something of a free hand to engage in serious crime in return for information, or in other forms of corruption such as the sharing of rewards, or passing bungs.

Grasses featured prominently in nearly all of the cases dealt with or handled by CIB since 1993. John Donald of SERCS took bribes from a criminal acting as his informant, who then sold information on to his associates. Geoffrey Brennan was an informant who claimed to have paid money to his handlers, although he later withdrew the allegation. 'Bobby Freeman' was an informant for the Flying Squad, whose officers he alleged stole £250,000. Bob Clark of SERCS had a thoroughly corrupt relationship with his loving informant Eve Fleckney. The list is endless, with one of the most recent examples being the dealings between DC 'Larry Hart' and Michael Michael. CIB believe that relationship became one of Michael controlling the officer.

The Michael-'Hart' case highlighted for Scotland Yard another huge area of concern. What the ghost squad had been looking at in its early days was organised corruption in the specialist squads, involving two or more officers operating as part of a group. But as these networks were smashed by arrests and prosecutions, or disrupted by CIB activity, it was realised there was another type of corruption within the police service, more insidious than the organised kind. This is the individual operating on his or her own. The damage caused by those nicknamed by investigators the 'Lone Rangers', after the 1950s TV series, is immeasurable in terms of cost, volume and damage. They span all the country's police forces, from urban to rural, and include the huge numbers of civilian workers employed behind the scenes, who have access to supposedly secure police systems. The Lone Ranger's main activity is leaking confidential information, and because they operate alone, they are all the more difficult to detect. They represent the biggest threat to a police organisation, and their work can be seen in 'blown' or failed operations and in criminals evading detection.

The leaking of information can start with someone asking for a little favour or help. It may be a next door neighbour, an old school-friend or a member of the same club as the police officer or the civilian worker. Such requests can be one-offs but others are more sinister, with criminals deliberately targeting those they think are vulnerable. Their tactics vary. A young woman civilian worker can give information to a 'boyfriend', she has met while out clubbing. Some officers become known as needing money to feed a habit, such as gambling or cocaine. Forms of blackmail can be used because in most peoples' pasts there are secrets which can be exploited, or favours to be returned. Whatever the reason for passing over confidential information, once it has been done, there is no way back. The determined big-time criminal will ask for more information, going on to sell or share it with other criminals.

Early in 1999, the Home Office produced a paper 'Understanding and preventing police corruption: lessons from the literature.' But this was not very helpful for the UK as virtually all the literature then in existence emanated in the USA. The first useful new research, published later the same year by the Kent force, was much sounder. The county had been plagued by a series of leaks and the force's director of human resources, Dr Bryn Caless, decided to look at the problem, to see if corrupt officers had a particular character profile. He studied the circumstances of 149 cases of both alleged and actual corruption in England and Wales since 1998, and talked to complaints officers in different forces. He came up with five archetypes of those most vulnerable to corruption:

1. The most likely candidate, wrote Caless, is a male detective constable in his 40s, with more than 18 years of service, but no hope of further promotion. He is a highly regarded 'doer' with a long record of successful arrests and he is an experienced informant handler. Thought of as a 'bit flash' he has probably had discipline problems unconnected with corruption, and he has little time for his supervisors. Divorced and with financial problems, his first offence is passing information to criminals.

2. A female officer, usually uniformed, aged 28–34, who has failed twice to win promotion. Through social activities, she meets, is cultivated by and falls in love with a criminal.

3. A male detective inspector, passed over for promotion to chief inspector rank, with at least one failed marriage behind him. He is an active and effective investigator with lots of charm, and is a specialist in an élite, secretive crime group. Well-liked by subordinates and trusted by his seniors, he has serious financial difficulties.

4. A civilian female worker, divorced and with adult children, but living alone. She has a criminal relative, usually a brother. Although in a lowly position, she has access to the Police National Computer and leaks criminal intelligence.

5. A lazy male uniformed constable, passed over for promotion, takes

short-cuts, is a devotee of 'canteen culture' and is a bully. He steals, and has relationships with criminals' wives or prostitutes.

Caless's research pointed up the great variety of corruption and the different types of officers involved. His profiles were passed on to other forces to help guide them through this murky world. But the Met was already introducing a rolling programme of moves to combat corruption. This had started in December 1998 with the launch of the force's 'Corruption and Dishonesty Prevention Strategy', much of the work for which had been done by a former chief superintendent working for CIB, David Martin. Central to this new strategy was an education programme for all officers of all ranks, to instil a greater awareness that corruption represented a major problem requiring tough measures. A twenty-minute video was prepared containing clips of film of corrupt officers taken from surveillance footage. This included scenes from the dramatic cannabis sting which had netted Kevin Garner and Terry McGuinness. The video compilation was shown during courses given to new recruits to the Met, to detectives and their managers, the idea being that they would recognise corrupt activities and be more willing to accept curbs and restraints.

The introduction of integrity tests (outlined in chapter 10) gave rise to some initial concern amongst Met officers. They worried that every member of the public or unknown police officer they encountered could turn out to be an undercover officer testing them for particular reactions. Such concern caused problems for at least one Police Federation official who wants to remain anonymous. He told me he had been driving his car when he was hit from behind by another vehicle. It was clearly the other man's fault. As the officer got out of his car to exchange details, he saw two uniformed officers on the pavement who had apparently witnessed the incident. 'I shouted over to them that they needn't bother because I was in the Job (the police),' he told me. 'But they thought it was some kind of integrity test – that I was pretending to be drunk, and asking them to go away as a favour. I hadn't had a drink at all, but they insisted on going through the proper procedures, because they thought I was testing them. By the time it was all sorted out, believe it or not, the guy who'd shunted me had driven off. I was left with having to pay for the damage to my car. Luckily, it wasn't a great deal of money.'

How many similar incidents there have been is not known, but officers' anxieties largely evaporated after the Met, supported by the Federation, spelled out at a series of meetings that targeted tests would only be used against those suspected of serious corruption, and that random tests would be used very sparingly.

It was also accepted that there was a need for better vetting of officers, particularly for those in the specialist detective squads. The Met's proposals meant that officers would have to declare any personal problems which could affect their work, for example marriage breakdown or financial debts. The idea was that checks could be made on the information revealed and anyone who had lied or failed to reveal the full truth could find themselves in trouble. Those seeking to join the specialist squads were willing to go along with such personal intrusion, as they wanted promotion. But it was a different matter for some officers already in such squads. A few resented some of the questions, and, at the time of writing, at least two were making a stand against the new vetting rules. One officer says he cannot answer questions about his wife's savings or her financial situation because he does not know her position, and she will not tell him, believing that it is a matter for her alone, and nothing to do with the Met. How such a case will be resolved is not known.

Disciplinary procedures were also changed without too much opposition. The standard of proof required to discipline an officer is now on the balance of probabilities, but if it is a serious matter with sacking the ultimate penalty, then the level of proof expected can move up to 'beyond reasonable doubt', with the officer allowed full legal representation. A new category of discipline was also introduced called 'service confidence'. This was to cover those officers in whom the Met said it had lost confidence. It was to apply to some officers found not guilty at courts, and those suspended for alleged wrong-doing, against whom there was insufficient evidence to charge or bring before a misconduct hearing. The idea was that these officers would be moved to positions where they would have little or no contact with the public and where they could cause no harm. In their new postings, the officers would be given the opportunity to regain the Met's confidence and, if they did so, could again be considered for full police work. However, the problem with the system was that very often the accused would not be told what evidence there was against them, because it was what was termed 'source sensitive'. In other words, the evidence could not be revealed because it had come from phone tapping, a credible informant or an undercover officer.

Although 'service confidence' was discussed at the time of the 'Corruption and Dishonesty Prevention Strategy', it was not used until 2001. The first victim is believed to have been a Flying Squad detective, one of a large number suspended early in 1998 after Garner and McGuinness turned supergrass. This particular detective, a sergeant, complained bitterly to myself and others about having been suspended for such a long time, caught up, he claimed, in a witch-hunt. He said it led to great stress with his marriage breaking up and his daughter turning delinquent. Spurning overtures to retire on grounds of ill-health, he wanted his old job back as he felt he was innocent. Eventually he was forced to go through 'service confidence' procedures and was posted to a humiliating and lowly job at a central London police station without contact with the public and without access to a police computer. 'They won't tell me what I am accused of. I have an idea, but it's not true, and I have had no opportunity to defend myself,' he told me. 'This has been hell for me. They wanted me to go out on stress grounds, but I said I ain't going sick. I've never had a day off through sickness. I didn't want them being able to say that we've got rid of him that way. I've done nothing wrong. I love the police. It's been my life, and I want to stay a copper. I'm not going to let them win.'

Other stories of perceived CIB unfairness circulated, and some were taken up by the London Police Federation. Flying Squad officers had two levels of complaint. First, they had been suspended on flimsy grounds, and then, secondly, when evidence was not forthcoming of their wrong-doing, the Met refused to reinstate them. One of these detectives was eventually accused of a minor breach of rules which he believed had only been brought against him to force him into resigning. The stress caused a nervous breakdown. He disappeared from home and there was concern for his safety, with Scotland Yard even putting out an appeal for him. He was found wandering in a distressed condition and taken to hospital.

'We will always support the removal of corrupt officers, but the system has to be fair,' a Federation official told me. 'We always said that the Met should not go down the road of accusing someone of minor infractions of police regulations. To suspend people without strong evidence is wrong. And it's doubly wrong to keep people suspended for years. What's the point? At the end of the day, even if they are disciplined, their pensions can't be taken away. By the time some of them are dealt with, they'll be over retirement age. The trouble is, no one is particularly concerned about them, because they're not having any financial loss. They're on full pay and the Met's so big it can absorb that money. But imagine if it was a county force. There'd be uproar because even having a couple of detectives suspended causes a noticeable difference. Service confidence? That's another problem. It's not right that the officer is not told why the Met's lost confidence in him or her. How can they redeem themselves if they don't know what they've done? Our goodwill can be taken just so far.'

Over and over again, officers who felt 'wronged', as well as others, attacked Sir Paul Condon for estimating that there were up to 250 corrupt officers in the Met. They claimed CIB's operations and tactics had resulted in injustices, because anti-corruption officers had been trying to justify the Commissioner's figures. One of these aggrieved former officers was ex-detective sergeant Alec Leighton. When I met him, long after he was caught up in the John Donald corruption affair, Leighton showed me a letter he had sent to a reporter who had written a piece in *The Times* in 2001 about the Metropolitan Police crackdown on corrupt officers. Leighton wrote in the unpublished letter that the Met had wasted time and money on CIB and that the squad had relied on dubious and tainted sources for information. 'In an attempt to achieve Sir Paul's number crunching exercise, they have infringed peoples' civil and human rights, and abused their powers.'

The same theme was taken up by the suspended DI John Redgrave in a letter to his MP. He wrote that he was the victim of CIB and police persecution, and warned that the same tactics could be used against ordinary people. 'Although the police service may provide a convincing argument that these methods should be used against police officers, the Government must understand that this is merely being used as a Trojan horse, and if it becomes public policy, will be used against all its citizens ... The thread which runs through the Executive, judiciary and agencies of the state must be cut.'

Without announcement, the Met quietly conceded that its intelligence since 1998 had shown that the number of corrupt officers was probably around the 100 mark. But critics argued that even that figure was too high because far fewer had been brought to justice through prosecution or discipline. The Met's unofficial response to that was to blame the Crown Prosecution Service for being over-cautious in authorising charges and to say that clever defence lawyers were still managing to exploit flaws in the disciplinary procedures.

The problem for those detectives and former officers who felt that they had suffered from CIB wrong-doing was that when allegations of malpractice were made in court, trial judges would usually side with anti-corruption officers. This happened when lawyers defending allegedly corrupt officers tried to have the damning witness evidence of police supergrasses excluded because it was claimed it had been obtained through inducements. The judges accepted that although there had been breaches of police and prison regulations, these had been minor and not intentional. The same applied to defence accusations that some of the bugging had been done without proper authority and that the resulting tape recordings should therefore not be allowed in evidence. The judges ruled that although the correct permission had not been obtained, CIB believed it had been acting within the law, and that there had been no deliberate attempt to get round the regulations.

One of the main difficulties facing CIB3 in its early days was that its officers were working in grey areas. No one had experience of working proactively against detectives. No one knew exactly how to handle police supergrasses. They were on what was described in court as 'a learning curve'. But most uncertainties were swept away in changes of law in the late 1990s. In came European human rights legislation, and Parliament passed two new laws to deal with the issues raised – the Police Act, and, most importantly for CIB and detectives everywhere, the Regulation of Investigatory Powers Act. The latter, known as RIPA, came into force in 2000, and covered surveillance and the use of informants. It set out in precise terms exactly when and where covert surveillance and bugging could be used and whose permission had to be obtained beforehand. Although the new system could be cumbersome, once it was complied with, it resulted in fewer arguments in court about the admissibility of tape recordings or surveillance video footage.

A whole new set of rules and regulations were also introduced for the handling of informants, who were to be known officially as 'covert human intelligence sources', or CHIS for short. A review of all existing informants resulted in a large number being ditched. The new controls also meant less opportunity for corruption.

One change lobbied for by CIB officers was over telephone tapping or intercepts. Tapes or transcripts of private telephone calls can still not be used in court and the very existence of such evidence cannot even be referred to. But the same rules apply at internal police disciplinary hearings. One former CIB superintendent told me: 'It's ridiculous that the law prevents us using good intelligence information against criminals in court, but it's doubly ridiculous that we can't use it at discipline boards against bent cops. There are very senior police officers sitting in judgement in these serious cases, and the idea that this material is too sensitive for them to see or hear just doesn't make any sense at all. If we had been able to get such intelligence in at these hearings, then more corrupt officers would have had to go, one way or another.'

Coinciding with the changes, the Met re-organised CIB, with its overall head Roy Clark, leaving to become the head of Crimestoppers. Taking over was a new department called the Professional Standards Directorate under DAC Andy Hayman. Praise for what was being done came from the head of the Home Office policing and reducing crime unit: 'Individual forces, most notably the Met, are putting in place preventive strategies more robust than those previously introduced in the UK.' In a report 'Police Integrity' from Inspectorate of Constabulary all the country's forces were encouraged to follow the Met's lead. The Association of Chief Police Oficers set up an Anti-Corruption Group under Andy Hayman to help spread the Met's measures to other forces. Scotland Yard even went as far as claiming that its anti-corruption strategy and achievements were the best of any of the world's major cities. Certainly, after 2000, anti-corruption detectives were visiting London from cities such as Sydney and New York. This reversed a process of a few years before. These were places which Scotland Yard detectives had been visiting to learn from them how corruption should be tackled.

Although proud of what the Met had achieved, several senior former CIB officers gave me warnings about the future, echoing what had been said about corruption by Sir Paul Condon shortly before leaving the Met: 'It would have been easier to have gone through my commissioner-ship without opening this can of worms. I felt I owed it to the public and to the majority of good men and women in the service to confront the problem. Police chiefs and politicians must continue to face up to the challenge. The battle against corruption needs to be constant and enduring, otherwise it will lose ground again.'

Those concerns were repeated in 2002 by detective chief superintendents who had joined CIB3 four years before. 'We were told then that the Met had taken its eye off the ball. I fear that the same is happening now. We piled the best detectives into fighting corruption, then along came concern about Irish terrorist groups and there was a change of emphasis. Then came September 11 and another change. Now we're all concentrating on street crime, and CIB is being run down. I'm really worried that corruption is going to surface again as a major problem.'

Such pessimism was shared by another very senior officer: 'CIB had the best detectives. We took risks. We were described as "legally audacious". We pushed jobs to the edge of criminality but it didn't stay that way. People moved on, and there were not enough good, trained, experienced detectives to replace them. The Met had not put enough detectives through training school and there was also a reduction in the number of proactive operations, which we had all experienced before joining CIB. These new detectives just don't have that experience, and we have created a management structure where people are rushed from one job to another. People now join CIB to get on in the police, but they don't want to take the risks, the bold steps that are still needed against corruption. Now? The intent might be there, but I don't think the organisation has the stomach for a fight any more.'

These views were received with some sympathy by one of CIB's existing senior officers. He conceded that there were now more financial constraints and investigations were more difficult because the suspect officers were aware of CIB activities. But times had changed. 'In the early days there were corrupt networks in the specialist squads and we had to have organised crime detectives to deal with them. We've now largely dealt with the networks and now different officers are needed because we have different problems. We're looking at corrupt individuals, the Lone Rangers who could be uniformed officers or civilian staff.'

He said the coupling of this detective effort with the various preventative measures meant that the Met's fight was a continuing success. The former CIB officers do not share such confidence. Only time will tell who is right. However, all agree that corruption will never be completely wiped out. Temptation will always be there. It's in the nature of the job. And police are only human; there will always be weak or greedy officers. The best that can be hoped for – and no one can possibly guarantee it – is that the Met and the other forces now seriously tackling corruption, stay on top of the problem, controlling it, keeping it to a much diminished but acceptable level.

INDEX

INDEX